Search Engines for Children

Tatiana Gossen

Search Engines for Children

Search User Interfaces and Information-Seeking Behaviour

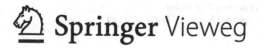
Springer Vieweg

Tatiana Gossen
Magdeburg, Germany

Dissertation at Otto-von-Guericke University Magdeburg, Germany, 2015

ISBN 978-3-658-12068-9   ISBN 978-3-658-12069-6 (eBook)
DOI 10.1007/978-3-658-12069-6

Library of Congress Control Number: 2015954962

Springer Vieweg

Printed on acid-free paper

Springer Vieweg is a brand of Springer Fachmedien Wiesbaden
Springer Fachmedien Wiesbaden is part of Springer Science+Business Media
(www.springer.com)

"The best way to make children
good is to make them happy."

— *Oscar Wilde.*

Acknowledgments

I would like to thank all the people that have supported me during these past years and in particular during the development of this thesis. First at all, I want to thank my supervisor, Andreas Nürnberger, who gave me the opportunity of writing this thesis and supported all my research endeavours. I am especially grateful for the freedom that I had being able to choose the direction of my research for my PhD and to carry out my research activities. I also want to thank Birger Larsen and Ian Ruthven for kindly agreeing to review my thesis. Thank you for taking time to read it and to give feedback.

I furthermore thank my colleagues and the whole staff of the faculty of computer science at the *Otto-von-Guericke-University* for the pleasant working atmosphere. I would further like to give special thanks to all the colleagues and students that – in one way or another – were involved in some parts of this work. In particular, I value Thomas Low and Marcus Nitsche. It was a great pleasure to have Thomas Low as my research assistant and later colleague during the logfile analysis project with the German Youth Institute. Marcus Nitsche shared his expertise in user interface design. He inspired me to conduct research in the area of human computer interaction with regards to the retrieval of information for children. A special thank you goes to Sebastian Stober whose comments, corrections and criticism have made this thesis more understandable. I would also like to thank the following students, which I had the pleasure of supervising and working with, for their contribution to this thesis: Juliane Höbel, Julia Hempel, Rene Müller, Jana Vos and Ina Bosse.

I would also like to thank the many participants of the user studies for their valuable time and effort. I especially want to thank the staff of the primary school in Biederitz and the trilingual international primary school

VIII

in Magdeburg for their kind support in the organisation of the conducted user studies with the children.

Last but not least, I want to thank my family. I thank my husband Gerhard Gossen for all his love, for his emotional and professional support. I owe my thanks to Gerhard for his patience, valuable feedback, proofreading of the manuscript and showing me useful LaTeX hacks.

Abstract

Children are a fast growing user group on the Internet. Among different online activities, children use web search engines in order to gather information related to their personal interests and school activities. Children's knowledge, cognitive abilities and fine motor skills are different from those of adults. Therefore, they may experience difficulties with search engines that are built using standard information retrieval algorithms and search interfaces for adults. Special or targeted search engines for children are essential in order to better support children in their search tasks. Therefore, the goal of this thesis is to design appropriate search engines for children with a focus on the search user interface. However, this is not an easy task to accomplish. Not only are children's abilities different from the abilities of adults, children also undergo relatively fast changes in their abilities.

The specific and dynamically changing characteristics of young users pose a great challenge. In order to address this challenge, first, the specifics of information retrieval for young users are analysed. Second, open issues are identified in user studies with children using logfile analysis and eye-tracking. The conceptual challenges in the design of user interfaces regarding search engines for children are derived based on the findings of one's own and previous user studies as well as theories of human development. Third, user interfaces of search engines that address these conceptual challenges are designed, prototypically implemented and evaluated in user studies with children following a user-centered design. Specifically, the proposed user interfaces of the search engine address the changing characteristics of the users by providing a means of adaptation. Furthermore, a novel type of search result visualisation for children with cartoon style characters is developed which takes the children's preference for visual information into account. Both approaches were very positively received by children during evaluation. Children rated different user interface aspects of the search user interface prototypes as good, e.g. the adaptation of the search user interface towards user wishes and the helpfulness of the cartoon style characters during search. Finally, this thesis provides criteria and guidelines on how to design the user interfaces of the search engine for children.

Zusammenfassung

Kinder sind eine schnell wachsende Nutzergruppe im Internet. Sie führen unterschiedliche Aktivitäten durch, unter anderem verwenden die Kinder Suchmaschinen, um Informationen über ihre Lieblingsthemen oder Schulaufgaben zu sammeln. Der Wissensstand der Kinder, ihre motorischen und kognitiven Fähigkeiten sind anders als bei Erwachsenen. Demzufolge können Kinder Schwierigkeiten bei der Verwendung von Suchmaschinen haben, die vorrangig für Erwachsene mit entsprechenden Retrieval-Algorithmen und Suchschnittstellen entwickelt wurden. Spezielle oder nutzerorientierte Suchmaschinen für Kinder sind wichtig, um eine bessere Unterstützung der Kinder bei ihren Suchaufgaben zu gewährleisten. Deswegen ist das Ziel dieser Arbeit Suchmaschinen zu konzipieren, die auf die speziellen Bedürfnisse von Kindern eingehen. Der Schwerpunkt liegt dabei auf der Entwicklung einer ergonomischen Suchschnittstelle für Kinder. Diese Aufgabe ist herausfordernd, da sich die Fähigkeiten von Kindern nicht nur von denen der erwachsenen Nutzer unterscheiden, sondern auch relativ schnell verändern.

Die spezifischen und sich dynamisch ändernden Eigenschaften der jungen Nutzer stellen eine große Herausforderung dar. Diese Herausforderung wird in dieser Arbeit zuerst adressiert, indem die Besonderheiten der Informationssuche der Kinder analysiert werden. Im zweiten Schritt werden fehlende Informationen über das Suchverhalten in Benutzerstudien mit Logfiles und Eye-Tracking gesammelt. Aus den Erkenntnissen der eigenen und früheren Benutzerstudien sowie Theorien der menschlichen Entwicklung werden in dieser Arbeit die konzeptionellen Anforderungen an die Gestaltung von Benutzerschnittstellen von Suchmaschinen für Kinder abgeleitet. Im dritten Schritt werden die Benutzeroberflächen von Suchmaschinen, die diese konzeptionellen Herausforderungen angehen, in einem nutzerorientierten Gestaltungsprozess konzipiert, prototypisch implementiert und in Benutzerstudien mit Kindern evaluiert. Es wird eine adaptive Suchmaschinen-Benutzerschnittstelle vorgeschlagen, die sich flexibel an die Veränderungen der Nutzerfähigkeiten anpassen lässt. Darüber hinaus wird ein neuer Ansatz zur Visualisierung von Suchergebnissen mit Charakteren im Cartoon-Stil vorgeschlagen. Dieser Ansatz berücksichtigt die Vorliebe von Kindern für visuelle Informationen. Beide Ansätze wurden in Benutzerstudien sehr positiv von den Kindern aufgenommen. Unter anderem wurde die Möglichkeit der Anpassung der Suchoberfläche an die Benutzerwünsche und die Nützlichkeit der Charaktere bei der Suche untersucht. Die Kinder vergaben eine hohe Bewertung für die Benutzerfreundlichkeit der Prototypen. Abschließend stellt diese Arbeit Kriterien und Richtlinien zusammen, wie die Benutzerschnittstellen zur Suche an Kinder angepasst werden können.

Contents

Part IV   Conclusion and Outlook

Part V   APPENDIX

List of Figures

List of Tables

List of Acronyms

API Application Programming Interface
BK Blinde-Kuh.de
ESUI Evolving Search User Interface
GL Google-like
GUI Graphical User Interface
HCIR Human-Computer Interaction in Information Retrieval
ID Document Identifier
IR Information Retrieval
KJ Knowledge Journey
KJE Knowledge Journey Exhibit
OPAC Online Public Access Catalog
SERP Search Engine Result Page
SUI Search User Interface
UI User Interface
URL Uniform Resource Locator

Chapter 1

Introduction

Nowadays, Internet usage knows no age limits. Since an increasing number of households all over the world own a computer and have Internet access, many children have access to the Internet and explore the web from a young age. The German study KIM[1] continuously examines the media usage of children aged between six and thirteen years old. According to this study [15], on average 62 % of German children use the Internet. This number for children increases with age from 21% by six years old to 93% by thirteen years old. 75% of the children use a search engine (e.g. Google) at least once a week.

Children use the Internet not only for entertainment, but it also plays an increasing role in education. On average half of the children use a computer to find information for school at least once per week [15]. They look for facts about historical events, mathematical formulas, the latest news and much more. To do so, children use computers at school or at home. Teachers or parents are not always around to support them: 60% of children search the Internet predominantly alone [15]. In order to better support children at their search tasks, several websites that provide special search services for children have been launched. Meanwhile, their main purpose is helping children to find child-suitable, in particular child-safe, content on the Internet.

However, this is only one important aspect of such search engines for children. Another important aspect is the usability of these search engines. Children should be able to successfully use a search engine without the help of adults. But unfortunately, not all children succeed in information inquiry, and especially the younger children can experience strong difficulties [15]. A possible explanation of failure is the children's difficulty in being able to use the search engines due to their insufficient usability.

The usability of web search engines is of special importance for children since their cognitive abilities and motor skills are not fully formed. Young

---

[1] KIM is a German acronym for Children and Media ("Kinder + Medien, Computer + Internet").

children have difficulties with abstract concepts, can process less information and their performance in pointing movements, e.g. using a mouse, are lower than that of adults [102]. It is not only desirable that children are supported according to their skills during search sessions, so that they are able to find good results, but the success in searching also plays a major role in the development of children. Erikson [62] found that primary school-aged children want to learn and to show what they can produce. They want to achieve the skills that seem to be important to their cultural environment and win the recognition of parents, teachers and peers by doing so [62]. Finding information on the Internet is an important skill that children need to develop and it is important to provide them with the necessary tools to succeed. If children succeed in finding information, they will feel competent and develop their self confidence. In contrast, if they are not able to find good results, children may develop a feeling of incompetence that could even lead to a feeling of inferiority [62]. In order to avoid those consequences, a search engine for children has to support children in finding good results, that is, it has to be adapted to the special needs — the motor skills, cognitive abilities and knowledge — of children in the respective age groups.

Currently, there are many good techniques in Information Retrieval (IR) for adults, but not much insight on how to design search engines for children in terms of both user interfaces and underlying algorithms. Most of the current IR systems are designed for adults. However, previous user studies indicate that there are significant differences between a child's and an adult's search behaviour. For instance, children can get easily frustrated if they do not find relevant results, do not understand the search engine output or if a failure emerges [17]. The fact that children also have difficulties when trying to evaluate the relevance of retrieved documents to their information needs aggravates this [92]. Furthermore, most children have difficulties with typing [25]. They are not able to type commands without looking at the keyboard (touch-typing). Instead they typically hunt-and-peck on the keyboard for correct keys. By looking at the keyboard while typing, children often do not spot spelling mistakes. In addition, some interaction techniques like scrolling or drag-and-drop are difficult for young users [25]. Therefore, young users would benefit from search user interfaces and algorithms that would take the special requirements of children into account.

1.1 Research Questions

Based on the motivation, this thesis addresses the following research questions (*RQ*):

1. What aspects of child development are important for information retrieval tasks?

2. What components of an IR system can be adapted to the targeted user group?

3. To what extent are the existing search engines for children appropriate for their motor and cognitive skills?

4. What are the characteristics of children's information seeking behaviour? Specifically, what are the differences of a child's and an adult's web information seeking behaviour:

    a) with regard to queries and search interactions?
    b) with regard to search performance?
    c) with regard to perception of search engine result pages?
    d) with regard to search strategies?

5. How can the user interface better support search to fulfill a child's information needs:

    a) considering children in a concrete operational development stage (age 7-11)?
    b) designing an IR system that grows with the children?

6. What are alternative ways to visualise search results for children?

    a) What features of web documents do children consider to be important?
    b) How do children visualise a web document as a search result?

These questions aim at achieving the following overall research goal: the development of interactive systems for information search for children as a targeted user group with special focus on the user interface. The goal is furthermore to identify open issues, analyse conceptual challenges when designing web search user interfaces for children, propose feasible solutions and demonstrate their applicability.

This thesis addresses young users between seven and eleven as a target user group. This choice is motivated by the theories of human development that are described later in Section 2.2 (see also Section 2.4). Within this work, we use the terms "children" and "young users" interchangeably. Furthermore, this thesis mainly concentrates on information search in a web document collection. During the search children intend to find information relevant to their information needs. In order to search successfully, children require special search engines that should be designed considering the specific requirements and needs of a child.

1.2 Thesis Outline

This thesis is structured into four main parts and an appendix. Part I provides the reader with fundamental knowledge that is important for the understanding of this thesis: Chapter 2 introduces the fundamental concepts and approaches in Information Retrieval (IR), describes the specifics of young users from the human development perspective (that are important to consider in IR for children), and briefly discusses the basic user research methods that can be applied for information-seeking investigation and evaluation of IR systems. Chapter 3 summarises the main previous finding about the information-seeking behaviour of children and provides an overview of existing algorithms and search user interfaces that are developed for children. This chapter provides information about what components of an IR system should be adapted to the targeted user group children and what methods currently exist.

Part II describes the research that was conducted in this thesis in order to identify open issues concerning targeted search engines for children and children's usage of those search engines. In particular, in Chapter 4 a case study about the usability of existing search engines for young users is conducted. Chapter 5 presents the large-scale study of logfiles of search engines for children. Children's search queries and interactions are analysed in order to identify the differences of a child's and an adult's web information search. In order to compare children's and adults' perception and performance on targeted web search engines, an eyetracking user study was conducted. This study is described in Chapter 6.

Part III focuses on the design of search user interfaces for children in primary school age. In Chapter 7 both, the findings of this thesis and from previous research, were considered in the analysis of conceptual challenges in the design of user interfaces in search engines for children. Chapter 7 also proposes several solutions for the design of children's search user interface (SUI). In order to demonstrate these solutions, a SUI for children called *Knowledge Journey* was developed. *Knowledge Journey* was evaluated in a user study with children against a classical search user interface. This user study motivated the need for an evolving search user interface that adapts to a particular young user. A second pilot study was conducted in order to investigate the potentials of a voice-controlled version of the *Knowledge Journey*. The idea of an evolving search user interface that addresses changing user requirements is elaborated in Chapter 8. An evolving search user interface which enables a flexible adaptation of the SUI to address changing user characteristics was developed and a user study was conducted in order to find a mapping between users of different age groups and SUI elements. Based on the Evolving Knowledge Journey, *Knowledge Journey Exhibit* (KJE) was developed as a robust information terminal. Chapter 9 investigates alternative ways to visualise search results for children and support them in the processing of search results. A novel approach is described that suggests to visualise each search result as a character where a character visually provides clues about the content of the result web page. Following a user-centered design, children were involved in the design of characters and the evaluation of different search result layouts with characters.

Part IV summarises the achieved results in respect to the specified research questions. Furthermore, an overview of open research issues is given. Directions concerning search histories, ranking algorithms, collaborative IR systems and evaluation methods for children are discussed.

Part I
Fundamentals

Chapter 2

Information Retrieval for Young Users

This chapter introduces the fundamental concepts and approaches that are prerequisites for the work described in this thesis. In Section 2.1 an introduction to Information Retrieval (IR) is given by defining the research field and describing IR system architecture. Furthermore, this section provides explanation of relevance ranking and introduction to search user interfaces. An introduction to targeted search engines is given in Section 2.1.4. The main aspects of children's development relevant to IR tasks are described in Section 2.2. In Section 2.3, basic user research methods and user evaluation types are briefly discussed.

2.1 Basics of Information Retrieval

The research field of Information Retrieval was defined by Salton [167, p. v] as:

> **Definition**
>
> *"Information retrieval* is a field concerned with the structure, analysis, organization, storage, searching, and retrieval of information."

Information retrieval is an activity that a user is engaged in. The user has a perceived gap in his or her knowledge, also called *information need*. This information is assumed to be present in a collection. In order to find this information, the user interacts with an IR system. The most common scenario is a search in a collection of text documents. In this thesis, we focus on textual information retrieval that is important in order to make the search in a web document collection work. Multimedia retrieval that deals with visual and sound data, e.g. images, music, videos [10, Chapter 14], is out of the scope of this thesis.

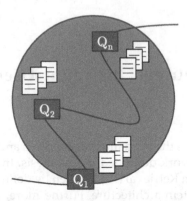

Fig. 2.1: Berrypicking search consists of a series of user interaction with an IR system. User learn bits of information one step at a time. Starting with a query Q_1, the user learns new information from the retrieved documents. This may lead to new queries until the user's information need is satisfied (this figure is modified from [13]).

The human interaction process with an IR system may be complex [13, 128]. Starting with one information need that may be vague in nature, a user submits a query and views the search results. They learn new information from these results, such as new facts or new vocabulary, that might lead to a drift in their information need or the understanding that rephrasing the query will lead to better search results. Therefore, they continue to query the search engine until the information need is satisfied. In other words, not every information need can be resolved with a single query and a single set of search results, but a series of queries and user examining the results might be necessary where a user is learning bits of information one step at a time. This bit-at-a-time retrieval is called berrypicking [13] by the analogy of picking berries from a bush (see Fig. 2.1).

Manning et al. [125, p. 1] defines Information Retrieval pointing out the unstructured nature of documents:

Definition

"Information retrieval (IR) is finding material (usually documents) of an unstructured nature (usually text) that satisfies an information need from within large collections (usually stored on computers)."

This means that in IR we deal with data which does not have a clear semantic structure. This leads to differences between data and information retrieval. The main differences are summarized by van Rijsbergen [164] as in Table 2.1. In data retrieval our goal is to find an exact match that is conformant with our query. An example of data retrieval is searching in a relational database [32]. A database has an underlying schema. Therefore, it is possible to find the exact database entries that match the query. In information retrieval we are interested in best matches, even if these matches are only partial. In some cases the answer to a user's information need is spread across several documents and these two partial matches reveal the desired information (see Berrypicking model above – Fig. 2.1). The query language for data retrieval is usually artificial with a restricted syntax and vocabulary. This language allows a user to give an exact and complete specification of what is wanted. In IR an exact specification is not possible because of the unstructured nature of text documents. To specify their information need, users in IR mainly use the vocabulary of natural languages. The retrieved results in IR indicate the likelihood of their relevance to user's information need and are usually sorted according to the relevance. Relevance is a measure of how closely a given document matches a user's information need. This judgment is done by the user and depends on different factors, e.g. his domain knowledge, the context of the search or previously seen results. As we deal with probabilities, in IR small errors in matching generally are not critical, whereas errors in data retrieval imply a total failure of the system.

2.1.1 Architecture of an IR System

Fig. 2.2 shows the main components of an IR system according to Baeza-Yates and Ribeiro-Neto [10]. An IR system has a frontend, also known as a

	Data Retrieval	Information Retrieval
Matching	Exact match	Partial match, best match
Inference	Deduction	Induction
Model	Deterministic	Probabilistic
Classification	Monothetic	Polythetic
Query language	Artificial	Natural
Query specification	Complete	Incomplete
Items wanted	Matching	Relevant
Error response	Sensitive	Insensitive

Table 2.1: Difference between data and information retrieval [164].

search user interface (SUI). The user has to formulate their information need in a specific form that can be understood by the IR system. Most common search engines allow to input a textual search query. Using the SUI the user submits a search query and also receives the visualised search results for the query.

The backend of an IR system manages the retrieval of relevant results. It requires a document collection which usually consists of text documents. In contrast to a document collection that is already in place, e.g. stored on the hard drive of a computer, web documents are scattered on the Web and located on different servers. Therefore, a web search engine has to gather web pages as a first step. This procedure is done by a crawler. The crawler collects information in a central location to be further analysed.

Web documents are usually in a HTML format that uses markup tags, e.g. indicating the body or font size. Therefore, web documents are parsed to extract the actual content. However, this content is only a sequence of characters and has to be processed in order to detect a well-defined sequence of linguistically-meaningful units [149]. This procedure is called pre-processing and consists of several steps. The main steps are tokenization, stopword elimination and stemming.

The first step is to convert the character sequence into a set of meaningful information terms (tokens), that are words or phrases (in case of names such as San Francisco) [126, p. 124]. Some of these tokens, e.g. articles and prepositions, are extremely common words which are of little value in helping to select documents matching the user's query. These tokens are called stop words and can be omitted [126, Chapter 15]. However, a user query may only contain stop words, e.g. "to be or not to be" (William

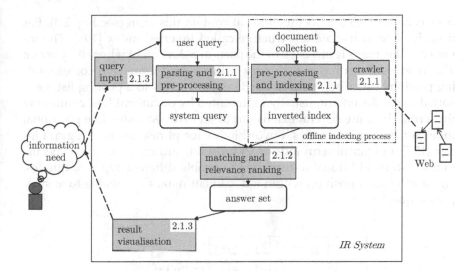

Fig. 2.2: Information flow in the high-level software architecture of an IR system based on [10]. Numbers indicate the section where the process is discussed in more detail.

Shakespeare, Hamlet). Removal of stop words makes it impossible to answer such queries. For this reason, many modern search engines do not remove stop words but rather assign a lower weight during the relevance calculation (see Section 2.1.2).

The next step of pre-processing is stemming where related forms of a word are reduced to a common base form (stem) [126, Chapter 15]. For grammatical reasons, documents contain different forms of a word, such as "process", "processing", "processed". Stemming make it possible, given a search term in one form, to find the documents that also contain a search term in other grammatical forms. Stemming algorithms are language dependent. The widely used stemming algorithm for English language is Porter stemmer that performs rules based suffix removal [158].

The search query has to be parsed and pre-processed as well. Parsing is done in order to detect special query types, e.g. phrase queries (exact occurrence of a series of words) that are defined by quotation marks.

The output of document pre-processing are terms that will be indexed, i.e. stored in the internal data storage. The data storage contains references from each term to the documents that contain this term (see Fig. 2.3). For this, IR systems use a data structure called inverted index [195]. The inverted index maps terms back to the parts of a document where they occur. The inverted index has a dictionary with indexed terms and corresponding postings lists. Each term in the dictionary refers to a posting list, i.e. a sorted list of document, usually represented by document IDs, containing the term. There are several extensions of an inverted index like positional index for proximity queries, biword index for phrase queries, q-gram index [137] and permuterm index [67] for wild-card queries. These specific indexes store additional information to enable different types of queries, e.g. storing term position within a document makes it possible to answer phrase queries.

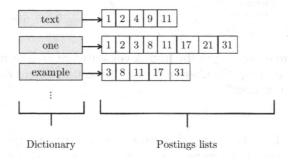

Dictionary   Postings lists

Fig. 2.3: Example of an inverted index based on [125]. The inverted index consists of the dictionary with index terms and the postings lists with document IDs that contain the corresponding terms. According to the presented inverted index, the term "text" can be found in documents $1, 2, 4, 9, 11$.

After query pre-processing, a retrieval model is used to match search query and data collection, and to conduct relevance ranking. There exist different models, e.g. boolean, vector space, probabilistic and language model (see [10, 125]).

The process of crawling, document pre-processing and indexing is performed offline, while a user's interaction with a system and relevance ranking of documents to the user's query are done in real-time. In the following, the most commonly used retrieval approaches, vector space model, and the link-based algorithms for web retrieval, PageRank and HITS, are described.

2.1.2 Relevance Ranking

The goal of relevance ranking is to estimate the relevance of a document to a user query. Documents are then ranked according to the likelihood of relevance to the user. Here we describe several retrieval approaches that are largely used. We start with the vector space model. Then, two link-based models, PageRank and HITS, are introduced.

Vector Space Model: The vector space model [10, 169] considers each document d within the document collection D to be a vector in a vector space. The dimensions of the vector space are the index terms. The index terms may be weighted according to their importance for the corresponding document, or be binary (1 if the term is present in the document and 0 if not). An illustration of the vector space model based on a three-dimensional example is given in Fig. 2.4. In general, each document is a t-dimensional vector:

$$d_j = (w_{1,j}, w_{2,j}, ..., w_{t,j}), \tag{2.1}$$

where $w_{i,j}$ represents the weight of the ith term for this document. A query is represented as a t-dimensional vector as well:

$$q = (w_{1,q}, w_{2,q}, ..., w_{t,q}), \tag{2.2}$$

where $w_{i,q}$ represents the weight of the ith term for this query.

The most popular weighting approach combines the term frequency (TF) and the inverse document frequency (IDF) [170]. TF counts the number of appearances of the term in the document. IDF takes into account the frequency of the term in the collection:

$$IDF_i = log\frac{N}{df_i}, \tag{2.3}$$

where N is the total number of documents in the collection and df_i is the number of documents the term i occurs in. Then the calculation of the weight for term i and document j using TFIDF is as follows:

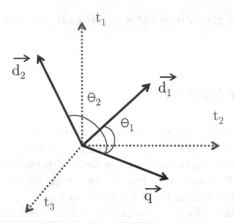

Fig. 2.4: Illustration of the vector space model based on [169]. Three-dimensional example with two documents d_1, d_2 and a query q is shown. The query is treated as a document in the space as well. Given the query, the documents are ranked according to their similarity to the query, for instance, by the cosine of the angle between the document and the query vector. The document ranking is d_1, d_2 as $\theta_1 < \theta_2$.

$$w_{i,j} = TF_{i,j} \times IDF_i \qquad (2.4)$$

Thus a term has a high weight in case this term is frequent in the document but rare in the document collection. Frequent words that occur in all the documents (stop words) receive a term weight equal to zero.

The vector model measures the relevance of a document given a query by the degree of similarity between the corresponding two vectors. A common similarity measure is the cosine similarity that calculates the cosine of the angle between the two vectors:

$$sim(d_j, q) = cos(\theta) = \frac{\mathbf{d_j} \cdot \mathbf{q}}{|\mathbf{d_j}| \times |\mathbf{q}|} = \frac{\sum_{i=1}^{t} w_{i,j} \times w_{i,q}}{\sum_{i=1}^{t} w_{i,j}^2 \times \sum_{i=1}^{t} w_{i,q}^2} \qquad (2.5)$$

The cosine similarity has a built-in document length normalization.

The vector space model has several important advantages, e.g. over the Boolean model[1]. Its ranking scheme improves retrieval quality. It allows matching of documents that may contain only some of the query terms. The vector space model supports the ranking of documents and sorting the results according to their similarity to the query. In theory, the vector space model has some limitations. In the vector space model, documents and queries are represented by their terms, as a bag of terms. The order of terms is ignored. Furthermore, the assumption is made that the terms are all mutually independent. However, it is not true for natural languages. Despite of the limitations, the model is a reliable ranking method for general document collections.

PageRank: The PageRank algorithm [23, 147] is a link-based approach for web retrieval which was part of the ranking algorithm originally used by the Google web search engine. It exploits the link structure of the web. The web can be seen as a directed graph with web pages as nodes and hyperlinks between them as edges (see Figure 2.5). PageRank determines the importance or quality of a particular page using the information obtained from the link structure. Each page has a rank. An intuitive assumption is made that a page has a high rank value if it is linked to by many other pages with high rank values.

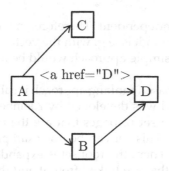

Fig. 2.5: Illustration of a web graph. Four pages A,B,C and D are graph nodes. The graph is directed. For example, hyperlinks of page A result in graph edges to B,C and D. Page D does not contain any hyperlinks.

---

[1] The boolean model only considers, if a query term is contained in a document. The query may contain boolean operators (AND, OR, NOT), which are transformed into set operations (intersection, union, set negation) on the result sets for individual terms [10].

Let u be a web page. Then the PageRank $R(u)$ of u is calculated as follows:

$$R(u) = c \sum_{v \in B_u} \frac{R(v)}{N_v}, \tag{2.6}$$

where B_u is the set of pages that have a link to u. N_v is the number of outgoing links from v. c is normalization factor. Thus, the rank of a page is divided among its outgoing links equally to contribute to the ranks of the pages they point to. This simulates a random web surfer staying on one web page with N_v outgoing links. This surfer can follow one of the links with $\frac{1}{N_v}$ probability.

However, the formula 2.6 does not work in case the web graph has dead ends (pages with no outgoing links) and cycles. To prevent this, an additional parameter, damping factor d, is introduced that simulates the ability of a web surfer to teleport from one page to another using other methods than following links, e.g. given the URL-address directly in the browser.

$$PR(u) = (1 - d) + d \sum_{v \in B_u} \frac{R(v)}{N_v}, \tag{2.7}$$

The PageRank can be calculated using a simple iterative algorithm. It corresponds to the principal eigenvector of the normalised link matrix of the web.

PageRank is query independent. Therefore, in web retrieval PageRank is combined with other models, e.g. with the vector space model [10]. Just to give an idea, a very simple approach would be a linear combination of the two measures.

HITS: Another link-based ranking approach is called Hyperlink-Induced Topic Search (HITS) and was developed by Kleinberg [105]. The HITS algorithm operates with a set of pages that are the most relevant pages to a user query (root set). This set can be, for example, obtained using the vector space approach. Then, the root set is expanded to a base set by including the web pages that are linked from it and the pages that link to it. The pages in the base set and the hyperlinks between them form a focused subgraph where all the calculations are performed.

HITS distinguishes between pages that are an "authoritative" information source on a certain topic and "hub pages" that are link collection pages referring to authoritative pages. Hubs and authorities have a mutually reinforcing relationship, i.e. a good hub points to many good authorities and

a good authority is referred by many good hubs. Therefore, an iterative
algorithm that maintains and updates numerical weights for each page is
applied. Note that a page can be both an authority and a hub. Therefore,
a non-negative authority weight $a(p)$ and a non-negative hub weight $h(p)$
are assigned to each page. The larger authority or hub weight of the page
is, the better authority or hub is the corresponding page. Starting with initial weights equal to 1 for each page, the update operations at each iteration
are the following:

$$a(p) = \sum_{q:(q,p)\in E} h(q), \tag{2.8}$$

$$h(p) = \sum_{q:(p,q)\in E} a(q), \tag{2.9}$$

$(p, q) \in E$ indicates a directed edge from p to q.

Typically about five to ten iterations are applied. At the end of each iteration, both authority and hub weights are normalised so their squares sum
to 1. This is done in order for values to converge (directly and iteratively
applying the updates rules lead to diverging values).

$$\sum_{p}(h(p))^2 = 1 \tag{2.10}$$

$$\sum_{p}(a(p))^2 = 1 \tag{2.11}$$

The obtained weights are used to rank the web pages, e.g. output top
hubs and top authorities first.

2.1.3 Search User Interfaces

An important part of a search engine is the search user interface (SUI). The
SUI is an interface that allows a human user to interact with the IR system
(see [81]). From our point of view, the SUI consists of three main components. The first component is a *query input*, i.e. UI elements which allow
a user to transform their information need into a machine understandable
format [81, Chapter 4]. This component is traditionally represented by an

input field and a search button. Other examples are a catalogue (directory) with different categories or voice input. Textual input is often supported by a query autocomplete function. Search engines also may provide a list with query suggestions for misspelled queries.

The second component is an *output* or results visualisation [81, Chapter 5]. The output consists of UI elements that provide an overview of search results, e.g. as a vertical list. Each element of a result list serves as a document surrogate, i.e. summarises important information about the document for users to be able to judge its relevance without opening the document. A document surrogate (further referred to as "surrogate") traditionally contains the document title, a summary and the URL (for web documents) [81]. To support users at relevance judgment, the search engine takes the user's query terms into account and generates query-specific or keyword-in-context summaries [190]. In contrast to a static summary of a document, whose goal is to summarise its content, query-specific summary shows sentences where the query terms appear within the document. Furthermore, the query terms are highlighted in the surrogate in order to make them more visually salient.

The third component is the *management* of the information seeking process [81, Chapter 7]. Management covers UI elements that support users in information processing and retaining. Management of results is especially important in the case of an evolving search (see berrypicking described in Section 2.1). Examples of management UI elements are bookmark management components or other history mechanisms like breadcrumbs. They record the information-seeking steps of a user, i.e. their queries, search results and relevant contextual information. For example, Google shows if a user has visited a search result in the past and the time of last visit. There is also a research in this direction, mainly for collaborative information retrieval where multiple users are explicitly searching together. One example is a free Internet Explorer plug-in called SearchTogether [133]. It allows each group member to see a group query history and a list of all web pages that have been annotated (rated or commented on) by any group member.

2.1.4 Targeted Search Engines

In general, there are different applications of information retrieval. Some examples of them are digital libraries, desktop search, enterprise search and web search engines. Most common IR systems appear in the form of web search engines with an audience of hundreds of millions of people[2] all over the world. There also exist search engines aimed for a specific user group. In this work we call them *targeted search engines* and provide the following definition:

(**Definition**)

In contrast to common search engines that are optimized for a generic user, a *targeted search engine* is designed and tuned for a specific user group. Users within the group are similar, e.g. concerning their information need, age or level of expertise. These properties influence decisions made in the design process of the search engines.

User characteristics of users that can be targeted by search engines are the following (see Fig. 2.6):

▶ *Age*: The cognitive abilities, fine motor skills, emotional maturity, knowledge and interests of a fifty year old man, a fourteen year old teenager and a seven year old child differ strongly [146]. Therefore, some search engines target users of a specific age range, e.g. children and elderly people (for example the search engine for children *blinde-kuh.de*). In general, it would be more specific to address the development stage of users (see Section 2.2) than the age because the age is a fuzzy indicator of human abilities. However, information about age is easier to obtain.

▶ *Information need*: Users' information needs can be differentiated by type and knowledge domain. Examples of different domains are the educational, medical and legal domains. For example, the *iSEEK Education* search engine targets students (educational domain). It retrieves documents from universities, government sites, and established noncommercial providers. User can have different types of information needs. Some users want to get an answer to a concrete question they have in mind, e.g. about the weather in Berlin for tomorrow. There are also users who are uncertain about their information needs or are unfamiliar with

---

[2] The web search engine Google, for example, has over 170 million unique visitors per month in the U.S. alone: http://www.nielsen.com/us/en/insights/news/2013/january-2013--top-u-s--entertainment-sites-and-web-brands.html

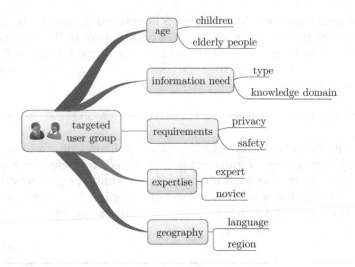

Fig. 2.6: Characteristics of users that might be targeted by search engines. Target user group can be described by a subset of the characteristics, e.g. children who speak Spanish.

the domain. They perform an exploratory search that is characterized as an investigative process rather than a simple lookup for facts [128]. To support exploratory search, there are also special search engines like *eyePlorer*[3].

▶ *Requirements*: Some web search engine users are concerned about their privacy. Cooper [33] lists such privacy risks as accidental or malicious disclosure of sensitive personal information, compelled disclosure to third parties, disclosure to the government and misuse of user profiles. Therefore, search engines like *duckduckgo.com* emerged that do not collect or share personal user information. Safety is another example of possible user requirements. Users concerned about safety want to receive search results that do not contain any material that is harmful, such as pornography, violence or spam.

▶ *Expertise*: We can distinguish between novice users and experts in respect to their information search expertise (see [114]). An example of an information search system for experienced users is an online public ac-

---
[3] http://vionto.com/

cess catalog (OPAC). OPAC is an online database of the resources held in the library, e.g. books. OPACs are difficult to use for novice users because searchers need to translate their question into a precise structure that the system can interpret. Online catalogs require users to specify a query in terms of field tags (e.g. author, year), search terms, and Boolean operators to begin a search [21]. Another example is patent search that also requires users' search expertise. Searching full-text patent data requires exhaustive usage of synonyms, usage of search operators (proximity, truncation, Boolean), iterative modification of previously issued search queries using newly learned terminology etc. [123].

▶ *Geography*: Users can have preferences to search using a specific language and also to receive documents written in a specific language. Furthermore, users might be interested in content that is relevant for a specific region, e.g. the search engine *yandex.ru* targets Russian users.

We also distinguish between targeted search and vertical or domain-specific search. Curran et al. [38] define a vertical search engine as one that only contains documents gathered from a specific segment of online content. In other words, vertical search engines index the documents that only belong to a specific domain using a focused crawler [4]. This makes vertical search engines attractive to certain user groups. Some examples of vertical search engines include blog, job, travel or hotel search engines (e.g. *hotels.com*). In contrast to vertical search engines, targeted ones may also adapt the ranking of results and the search user interface to the targeted user group. Furthermore, targeted search engines can have further restrictions on having the content not only from a specific segment but also content that has some specific properties like language complexity. For example, search engines for children should retrieve search results that are easily read and understood by children.

2.2 Aspects of Child Development Relevant for Information Retrieval Tasks

When designing tools for children, it is important to target very narrow age groups because children of different age have different needs [140]. Studies of cognitive science about human development help to achieve this goal. In this section we briefly describe a human cognitive development model, the main idea of information processing theory and a theory of human psychosocial development, which explain the fact that children's emotional states, cognitive and motor skills are developing and differ from that of adults. Further insights into theories from cognitive science and their impact on digital design for children is provided by Cooper [34]. This section concludes with a discussion of the implications that the specifics of young users in different development stages have on the design of information retrieval systems for children. Within this work we use the term "adults" when referring to grown ups without specific disabilities. We use the term "child" when referring to a human being whose cognitive abilities are not fully formed. The content of this section was published in [pub:7].

2.2.1 Human Cognitive Development

A foundational theory of human intellectual development is given by Piaget et al. [154] and further discussed, for example, by Ormrod and Davis [146] and Cooper [34]. Piaget's theory describes the differences in the human abilities at different ages. It says that human development occurs in a sequential order in which later knowledge, abilities and skills build upon the previous ones. According to Piaget, there are four human developmental stages: *sensorimotor* (age 0-2), *pre-operational* (age 2-7), *concrete operational* (age 7-11) and *formal operational* (from age 11). These are distinct cognitive development stages characterised as follows:

▶ *Sensorimotor stage:* The child begins to recognise cause-and-effect relationships, but is not yet able to think about objects other than those directly in front of it [146].

▶ *Pre-operational stage:* Preschool or primary school children are most likely in the pre-operational stage of development. In this stage they learn to use a language. They often think illogical by adults standards. Most preoperational thinking is self-centred. Children in the pre-operational stage may have difficulties with classification. They can classify objects according to one feature (e.g. "select all yellow bricks") [146]. Children of age four to five gain pre-reading skills, i.e. they can substitute words in rhyming patterns, write some letters, pronounce simple words, develop vocabulary [186].

▶ *Concrete operational stage:* Children are most likely in second or third grade (see Table 2.2) at the beginning of this stage. They use the trial and error approach, and begin to reason logically. However, their understanding is limited to concrete and physical concepts (in contrast to abstract ones), they can classify physical objects according to several features and order them along a single dimension such as size [146]. At the age of six to ten children learn to read. They can read simple books by mid-first grade and know about 100 common words. They learn to write by first grade. They can write stories with a character, action, setting, and a little detail by second grade [186].

▶ *Formal operational stage:* Children in the formal operational stage learn to think logically about abstract concepts. This stage begins around age 11 and is typically achieved by age 15 [146].

At the age of eleven to thirteen adolescents read to learn about their hobbies and other interests. They read to study for school, understand more what they have read, read fiction and nonfiction, including magazines and newspapers. Their writing skills are more developed with the use of correct grammar, punctuation and spelling. They become more fluent writers. The children use a computer for writing and research [186].

Educational stage (grades)	Age	Development stage
first	6-7	pre-operational
second-sixth	7-11	concrete operational
seventh-twelfth	11-18	formal operational

Table 2.2: Correspondence between school grades in the USA, age and Piaget's development stages. Educational stages and corresponding age depend on the country [pub:7].

It is worth to note that recent research does not entirely support Piaget's theory: he overestimated the capabilities of adolescents and even adults (they often show signs of the concrete operational stage, not formal operational) and underestimated infants and young children in the sensorimotor and pre-operational stages [146]. The age boundaries of each development level are approximate, i.e. the exact age may vary from child to child. The development speed differs from human to human (caused by cultural and social environment) and even one person could be placed in different stages at the same time considering his or her understanding of concepts from different domains like social, mathematical, or spatial [146]. Maccoby and Jacklin [124] also discovered gender-based differences in human cognitive abilities: girls are more talented verbally and usually more active in social domains, whereas boys tend to have better mathematical and spatial skills. Furthermore, children's information needs depend on and relate to their developmental stage [109].

2.2.2 *Information Processing Theory*

The so called neo-Piagetian theorists explain cognitive growth along Piaget's development stages from an information processing perspective. Even though there are many variations of the theory, the fundamental idea is that children's information processing differs from the adults' in terms of how they apply information and what memory limits they have, i.e. how much information children can represent and process.

Every act of thinking depends on the sensory memory, the working memory and the long-term memory. External and internal stimuli, e.g. sounds, pictures, hunger, are received and held in the sensory memory. This unanalysed information is stored briefly (for a few seconds) during which subconscious processes determine whether to transfer it to the working memory or discard it. Active thinking, e.g. problem-solving or constructing of new strategies requires the use of information stored in the working memory (also called short-term memory). Active thinking is performed using the information in sensory memory in combination with information from the long-term memory by transforming both into "new" information. The working memory has a limited capacity, i.e. it can only operate on a limited number of symbols at once. Information which is not processed further (e.g. by moving it to the long-term memory) will be lost. The long-term memory has no real limits on the information amount or time period to be stored. Information in long-term memory is rarely forgotten, but can be difficult to access [102, 138]. Table 2.3 summarises the characteristics of short-term and long-term memory.

Young children learn new skills and how to perform new tasks using their working memory. Having less experience than adolescents or adults, children's information processing requires a much larger part of the working memory. After children succeed in performing a task, some informa-

Memory type	Capacity	Information storage
Short-term	Limited (span 7 ± 2 items)	Rapid loss of information
Long-term	Huge	Reliable

Table 2.3: Characteristics of short-term and long-term memory [102, 138, pub:7].

tion of the underlying processes can be transferred to the long-term memory. The working memory gains some free space and the child's learning of new tasks can proceed. Thus, older children have a larger chance and need less time to succeed in performing complex tasks involving many processes, as they can retrieve some of the processes from long-term memory and perform them automatically. Young children have to think about most of the processes, which leads to a huge load on the working memory's capacity. The capacity of the working memory for verbal/visual information increases with age [171]. Younger children need longer time periods than older ones to perform the same processes[4] [102, 138].

As children grow older, they can process information faster [101]. Card et al. [27] and Hourcade et al. [82] found that the information processing rate influences the fine motor skills. Pointing movements that are required to operate input devices, consist of a distance covering phase and a homing phase. Homing phase movements are not continuous. A homing phase movement is a series of micro-movements with micro-corrections [131]. The larger the information processing rate is, the larger is the number of micro-corrections that can be performed in the same amount of time, which translates into smoother motion and better performance. As a consequence, a young child's performance in pointing movements, e.g. using a mouse, is lower than that of an adult and increases with age.

---

[4] Adults know more than children and tend to apply this knowledge when learning new information. But an interesting fact is that for some goals existing knowledge may lead to a decrease in task performance. For example, researchers showed that adults use category-based induction (which is likely to be a product of past learning) whereas young children generalise on the basis of similarities among presented entities in the absence of category information [65]. For some tasks, this similarity-based strategy is more useful.

2.2.3 Psychosocial Development

Another perspective on human development is given by Erikson [62]. He considers changes from a psychosocial point of view. Based on this, a child is immature in the emotional domain, requires emotional support and a feeling of success and increasing confidence, especially in the "industry versus inferiority" stage (age 6 – 12). According to Erikson, children of this stage want to learn and to show what they can produce. They want to achieve the skills which seem to be important to their cultural environment and win the recognition of parents, teachers and peers by doing so. Finding information on the Internet is an important skill that a child needs to develop. If children succeed in finding the information, they will feel competent and develop self-confidence. In contrast, if they are unable to find good results, children may develop a feeling of incompetence. This could even lead to a feeling of inferiority.

Figure 2.7 summarises the findings about child development that were described in Section 2.2.

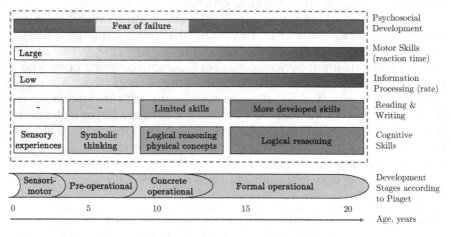

Fig. 2.7: Stages of human development and their characteristics (modified from [pub:7]).

2.3 User Studies and Evaluation

In order to develop user-friendly IR systems, research on how the targeted user group actually use the systems for information inquiry is essential. Research methods exist that enable you to investigate user behaviour (Section 2.3.1). These methods can be also applied to evaluate software products. We are going to describe different types of evaluation in Section 2.3.2. While discussing evaluation in general, we outline the specifics of research that involve children's participation in Section 2.3.3.

2.3.1 Methods in User Studies

In this thesis, we use the term "user study" in a broader sense than evaluation. User studies intend to understand user interactions with systems, while evaluation is more focused on the judgment of the system's value. In the following we briefly summarise the main research instruments such as user surveys, observations and transaction log analysis [162]. Usually a combination of these instruments is used in user studies.

Survey methods involve asking users questions and analysing their answers [129]. Surveys allow us to collect demographic data, data about previous or current behaviours, attitudes, beliefs and level of satisfaction of users [162]. The survey may be conducted in form of an interview or a questionnaire. In interviews people respond verbally, while in questionnaires they have to write the answers down. The questionnaire can be distributed directly or provided online. Survey methods have the advantage that they can reach a greater number of users and retrieve quantitative data. However, survey methods might provide less accurate results: Participants may forget or leave out some pertinent details, e.g. about person-sensitive matters [156].

During *observations* detailed information about a situation or event is gathered [162]. Observations are commonly conducted in a lab setting. During lab experiments researchers can observe users directly. Usually users receive some tasks to complete, e.g. using an IR system to answer some pre-defined questions. There are different techniques that may be applied during the lab experiment. The researcher may observe how the participants behave, what they do and how they use the system to achieve a specific goal. Audio and video recording of the user and his computer monitor during the experiment is possible. Using special software, user interactions with the system can be logged. Furthermore, with the help of special eye-tracking devices, it is possible to record the user's eye gaze to measure the position and duration of eye fixations. One can also use the "think-aloud"-method by asking the participants to express their thoughts loudly while using the system [129]. Lab experiments have the advantage that they allow you to observe the user directly and, at least in regard to the given tasks, to capture the user's real behaviour. The disadvantage of the method is the larger amount of work (more complex to carry out, for example, than questionnaires) and the artificial lab situation [115, Chapter 2.6.1].

A *transaction log* (or *logfile*) is a history of actions executed by users of a system. Logfile data can be collected through special transaction monitoring software that is built into a system, e.g. by a web server that automatically tracks specific interactions [162]. In contrast to lab experiments, where users are observed only over a short period of time, logfiles make it possible to analyse user behaviour over a longer period of time (longitudinal) [115, Chapter 2.6.1]. Transaction log analysis allows to unobtrusively track how users are using the system [162]. Therefore, they reflect a more natural user behaviour in comparison to direct observations. Logfile analysis offers the possibility to analyse a high amount of usage data. A prominent example is the logfile analysis of user interactions with web search engines, digital libraries and web sites [e.g. 97]. The disadvantage of the method is the lack of some important information such as the demographics of the users [183, Chapter 3]. Additional identification and tracking methods are often required in order to determine the demographics of a specific user. This task is not trivial. It is also legally controversial. Therefore, generally researchers do not have the demographic data. Transaction log analysis can be combined with other methods such as surveys and experiments [e.g. 70].

An interesting framework for user studies is *gamification* where game design elements are used in non-gaming contexts [43]. For example, Purvis and Azzopardi [159] use gamification to study children's and adults' performance in search. They designed an Information Retrieval based game called PageFetch. Players of PageFetch are shown a web page and need to enter a query that would retrieve the page. Players have limited time and have to find as many pages as possible. They receive points depending on the ranking position of the page in the returned ranking and how short the query is (in terms of query words). A later version of PageFetch [8] has additional gamification features such as leaderboards, badges and an avatar component in order to motivate the players. Gamification is a promising approach in IR to conduct experiments by making them more fun. However, it is laborious to implement, because gamification requires additional programming of the game environment and customisation for each new experiment type.

2.3.2 Types of Evaluation

In order to design a high quality product, the intended or targeted user group of a product should be at the center of the design process, ideally throughout all design steps. This approach is called the User-Centered Design (UCD) [87, 142]. Users can participate in the design process as co-designers (co-design with children is described in [48]). However, mostly they participate in the role of evaluators (evaluation with children is described in [129]).

In general, evaluation methods can be divided into inquiry methods, observational evaluation methods, and analytical evaluation methods [129] (see Figure 2.8). Analytical evaluation methods or inspections do not involve users, but rely on the opinion of experts. An example of analytical evaluation is heuristic evaluation [143], where a number of usability experts are presented with an interface and discuss usability problems they uncover. An additional example of analytical evaluation is cognitive walkthrough [116], where usability experts work through a series of tasks making decisions based on the analysis of a user's mental processes.

Inquiry and observational evaluation imply the involvement of the targeted user group. These evaluations are conducted in user studies applying methods described in Section 2.3.1. Inquiry methods involve collecting qualitative data from users, e.g. by using questionnaires (see Section 2.3.1) about what users like and dislike. Observational evaluation methods involve collecting data by observing user's experiences with a software product. Observational evaluation can be conducted directly, e.g. in form of a lab experiment, or indirectly, e.g. in form of logfiles[5] (see Section 2.3.1).

---

[5] Users may not be explicitly involved in the evaluation that are conducted in form of logfiles.

An interesting setup for an observational evaluation is a *Wizard-of-Oz-Experiment* [129, Chapter 12]. During this experiment a user interacts with a program that seems to be autonomous, but is remotely controlled through a hidden person (the wizard) instead. This method allows you to study a users' behaviour without any limitations and even appropriately react to unexpected user actions. Afterwards, the missing functionality of the system will be implemented based on the results of the Wizard-of-Oz-Experiment.

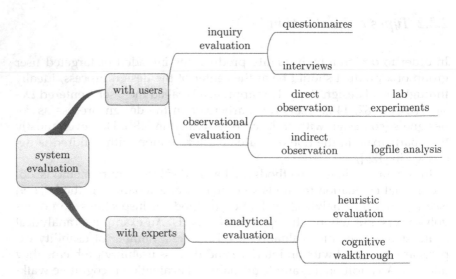

Fig. 2.8: Different types of system evaluation grouped by user involvement.

Furthermore, observational evaluation can have the specific goal to measure the usability of the software. As a result of usability evaluation, quantitative measures like efficiency, effectiveness, and satisfaction are obtained. The term usability is defined by the International Standardization Organization as "the extent to which a product can be used by specified users to achieve specified goals with effectiveness, efficiency, and satisfaction in a specified context of use" ([86], quoted in [1, p. 326]). Effectiveness is measured by the accuracy and completeness with which users achieve specific goals. Efficiency is measured in resources required to complete the task. Satisfaction is a subjective user assessment of his attitude towards the product.

Evaluation can also have the goal to compare the usability of one software product with competitive products. This type of evaluation can have two experimental designs such as a *within-participants* and a *between-participants* design. In the within-participants design each participant is introduced to all the software products. The within-participants design allows for direct comparisons of participants' judgments; however the order of exposure to experimental conditions can bias the results. In order to reduce the bias caused by the order in which participants are introduced to the different products, one can employ a *Latin Square blocking design*. In simple terms, the order is varied among the participants in which they are exposed to different product and tasks. In the between-participants design each participant is introduced only to one software product. Therefore, the direct comparison of products can be done only approximately. Furthermore, the between-participants design requires a larger number of participants in order to get statistically meaningful results [81, Chapter 2].

In the usability evaluation, one can distinguish between *formative* and *summative* evaluation [142, 79]. Formative evaluation accompanies the whole design process and is conducted at the end of each design cycle. In formative evaluation, evaluation is conducted during development, often iteratively. The goal of formative evaluation is an early detection of usability problems. Summative evaluation is conducted after the development with a complete or near-complete design (see Fig. 2.9).

2.3.3 Evaluation with Children

When using the standard research methods in research with children, one should keep in mind that children's abilities are different from those of adults (see Section 2.2). Therefore, standard research tools are not directly applicable to children. For example, it is unwise to use question–answer approaches (questionnaires, diaries, interviews) with very young children that have limited language and thinking processes. Children aged eight to eleven can be surveyed using simple questionnaires written in the language used by the children [129]. The think-aloud method requires high degrees of cognitive aptitude and is not effective with children without a longer training period [129].

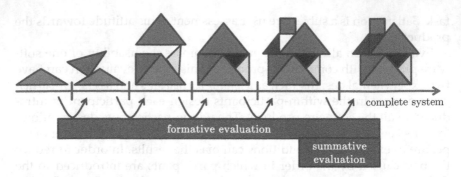

Fig. 2.9: Illustration of formative and summative usability evaluation using an example of house design. Summative evaluation is conducted with a complete or near-complete design. Formative evaluation accompanies the whole design process, evaluation is conducted in each step.

Mohd, Landoni, and Ruthven [132] suggest that *fun* should be measured when evaluating online systems designed for children. They discuss the differences of evaluations where children participate and conducted a user study to test their evaluation methodology. The study with young children aged three to four years old in a nursery and five to six years old in a school was carried out to see if the children have fun playing a game which they could chose from the web site *CBeebies*. The conclusions from the study are that, as children are emotionally driven, evaluation techniques should pay attention to their emotional state: shyness, boredom, joy etc. As a reflection of the emotional state researchers asked the children to draw a figure which they associated with the web site. They used the children's pictures as a fun indicator. They also showed that children have difficulties in answering open-ended questions.

Furthermore, there are legal aspects about user studies with children. In order to legally involve children as participants in user studies, researchers must obtain agreements from the parents, i.e. before the study parents must sign an agreement form to approve children's participation. For studies at schools, the research must be approved by the school director who might request the researchers to get a permit from a local authority, e.g. the state administration office for education and culture in Germany[6]. It can take months to obtain these permits which should be considered during the research planning [25].

Hanna, Risden, and Alexander [76] proposed guidelines for usability testing with children:

▶ Avoid tasks that may be too tiring or demanding for the children. The session should not take longer than an hour and even less (about 30 minutes) for preschool children. Experiments require children to concentrate on the task and after a while children get tired and distracted.

▶ When conducting a series of tasks (e.g. different search tasks or using a set of search engines), switch the order around for different children. It will help to avoid the bias due to order of exposure to experimental conditions.

▶ Motivate children by emphasizing the importance of their role. For example, the researcher can admit that he has forgotten what it is like to be a child and the children's opinion is important to make a really good search engine for children all around the world.

▶ Prepare a script to describe the procedure and emphasize that the goal is not to test the abilities of a child but to get his help to improve the software.

▶ Laboratory equipment should be placed as unobtrusively as possible in order to avoid participants' discomfort and distraction.

However, these guidelines are very general and applicable to other age groups as well.

2.4 Discussion

In this section we will answer the first research question.

---

[6] The documents requested by the administration office are listed in German at http://www.bildung.sachsen-anhalt.de/schulen/schulinhalte-und-qualitaet/ sonstige-inhalte/empirische-untersuchungen/, accessed on 27-11-2014.

┌─ RQ1 ───┐
│   │
│   What aspects of child development are important for information   │
│   retrieval tasks?   │
│   │
└──┘

In Section 2.2 we provided a short overview of the basic theories about child development[7]. We considered aspects such as cognitive skills, reading and writing abilities, information processing rates, motor skills and physiosocial maturity important for information retrieval tasks. Cognitive science explains the specifics of children in different age groups and helps us to derive requirements for the design of IR systems.

▶ *Human Cognitive Development:* Children in the sensorimotor and pre-ope-rational development stages are unlikely to use an (textual) information retrieval system because they have limited reading abilities. They are also more likely to enjoy online games or watch videos and inquire for leisure information. Children in the concrete operational stage are potential users of IR systems, but have their special characteristics and requirements. These children have more difficulty in translating their information needs into a keyword query than adults. Finding the right query requires the ability to think in abstract categories, a large vocabulary and good writing skills, which children of the concrete operational stage lack in. Children in the formal operational stage are also potential users of IR systems, but their characteristics become similar to the ones of adults. They also require supporting at information retrieval tasks but less than children in the concrete operational stage.

▶ *Information Processing Theory:* Information retrieval processes may cause children's working memory to overload. To support children's limited cognitive recall, IR systems should have simple and consistent graphical user interfaces. Due to memory overload, children can forget actions they have already done, like what queries they have already used or which documents contained interesting information.

▶ *Psychosocial Development:* As children are immature in the emotional domain, IR systems should provide emotional support in form of extensive help mechanisms. All actions which can lead to failure in retrieval

---

[7] We concentrated on the common theories in cognitive science. These theories might be not entirely accurate. More information about the human development can be found in Ormrod and Davis [146] and Kail [102].

should be covered by the system and hints should be provided if such an action is undertaken by a child.

This thesis concentrates on children of ages seven to eleven. More specifically, the age range we chose falls into the "industry versus inferiority" period of child's psychosocial development, age 6–12 [62]. In this period it is important that a child succeeds in finding information. In this way, he or she feels competent and develops self-confidence. In contrast, if a child is not able to find good results, he or she may develop a feeling of incompetence [62]. Besides the immaturity in the emotional domain, children's cognitive abilities are also not fully formed [154]. According to Piaget [154] children of age seven to eleven are in the *concrete operational stage* of development with its unique cognitive characteristics. Furthermore, as we are interested in textual information search, our user group should at least be able to read. This is usually the case for children of age nine, as they can read simple texts by this age [186].

Chapter 3

State of the Art

Following up on the general introduction of IR and targeted search engines, this chapter takes a closer look on the specifics of information retrieval for young users based on the existing research in this field. Section 3.1 summarises the findings of various user studies about children's information seeking behaviour. Section 3.2 provides a structured view on the existing algorithms and search user interface concepts applied to the architecture of an IR system. Section 3.3 gives a short overview of existing search engines and digital libraries for children. The content of this chapter was partially published in [pub:7].

3.1 Children's Information-Seeking Behaviour

Information-seeking behaviour is the behaviour of a user during the process of information acquisition; it describes how people search for information. Sociologists have been studying the information-seeking behaviour of children for decades. In this section, we briefly summarise their main findings. We also discuss problems related to the design of user studies with young users. From the current perspective, many of the "older" user studies with children have different conceptual issues, which we discuss in the following.

Research about children's information-seeking behaviour began in the nineties with the appearance of school class rooms with computer equipment. In the beginning, researchers made observations of children performing different tasks using school computers in groups [e.g. 113]. With the increasing availability of computers, children started to operate computers individually. But the fact remained that user studies with children were mainly done in the form of lab experiments within the school setting. Thus, findings of these studies may have bias due to the experimental situation (e.g. the presence of the experimenter).

The research in the area of children's information-seeking behaviour addresses children of different or mixed age groups, e.g. [17] (seventh grade), [113] (sixth grade), [20] (ages 9-12). This inhomogeneity leads to the problem that the findings cannot be accurately applied to any specific age level or to a specific development stage. By only providing information about the school grade or age of the studied children, the researchers did not pay sufficient attention to the level of their computer skills or Internet competence. Nowadays children gain computer experience and skills from an increasingly younger age. In other words, results obtained for a ten-year old a decade ago most probably cannot be transferred to a ten-year old today. Another problem is the information retrieval systems used in these studies. In the "old" studies children were observed using information retrieval systems designed for adults while nowadays the first attempts in the direction of child-friendly search service environments are being made. In addition, the studies were done mostly with keyword based interfaces (library catalogues and web search engines). Some results can not be generalised and are artefacts of the test setup, i.e. may depend on features of a specific interface.

Because of the reasons we mentioned above the results of recent studies can be different from those done a few decades ago [25, 140]. We advise to take the newer findings into consideration when designing IR systems for children. The results of "old" user studies that provide information about children's cognitive and computer skills are partially applicable by taking into account the new developments in software and hardware. We also suggest for user studies to provide information about computer skills and Internet competence as the age itself is only a very fuzzy indicator of children's abilities.

In the following we discuss the results of previous studies about children's information-seeking behaviour, considering the issues mentioned above. We describe such aspects of children's information-seeking behaviour as searching strategies, queries, navigation style, interface preferences and relevance judgement (see Figure 3.1).

3.1.1 Querying Behaviour

IR systems should provide the children with information that corresponds to their *information needs*. Common sociological methods such as user stud-

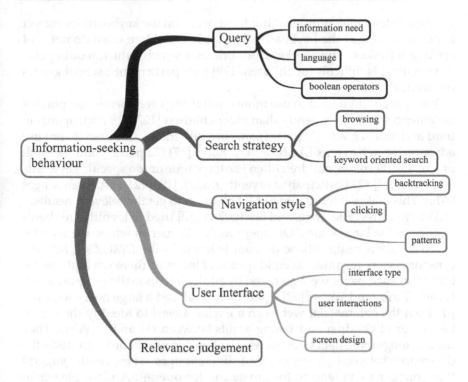

Fig. 3.1: Aspects of information-seeking behaviour [pub:7].

ies in the form of questionnaires and interviews can be used in order to identify children's information needs. However, they are known to give imprecise results and can be challenging for adults, and especially for children [129]. To overcome these difficulties and get more reliable results, researchers have also used log files of search sessions to identify the query intent.

In order to initiate a search, a child has to transform his information need into a form that can be processed by a computer, i.e. a search query. In contrast to adults, children have more problems when trying to formulate (explain) their information need due to their limited vocabulary and cognitive abilities. Furthermore, most children have difficulties with typing [92] (32 participants: ages 8-12), [20] (33 participants: ages 9-12). They are not able to type commands without looking at the keyboard (touch-typing). Instead they typically "hunt and peck" on the keyboard for correct keys. By looking at the keyboard while typing, children often do not spot spelling mistakes. Utilising keyword oriented search, which requires correct spelling, is difficult for children [179] (679 participants: school grades one through six).

Younger children tend to use more natural *language* queries, i.e. phrases or sentences, more frequently than older children [127] (28 participants in third and fourth grade, 24 participants in sixth grade). Children do not use advanced search syntax like *boolean operators* [17] (22 participants: seventh grade). Furthermore, children often use too vague or too specific keywords in queries [17] (22 participants: seventh grade), [104] (21 participants: ages 8–10). This makes it more difficult for children to get the relevant results.

Duarte Torres, Hiemstra, and Serdyukov [50] tried to identify children's queries in the large-scale *AOL* query log[1]. All queries where the user selected a search result whose domain is listed in the *DMOZ's kids&teens* directory[2] were regarded as child queries. However, there is a high probability that such pages were accessed by adults intentionally or by accident. Duarte Torres and Weber [52] extensively analysed a large query log sample from the commercial web search engine *Yahoo!* to identify the search behaviour of children and young adults between six and 18 years. They used demographic data of users who had an account in order to study the differences between young users of different ages. Their results suggest that younger users tend to formulate shorter queries. A plausible explanation of this behaviour is that younger users have difficulties in trying to express their information needs using keywords. Younger children surprisingly tend to undo spelling corrections provided by the search engine to insist on their original spelling. They also tend to click on the results presented first regardless of their actual quality. Therefore, they also click on advertisements more often than older users [52]. Young users under the age of 19 have considerably shorter search sessions than adults which also correlates with a smaller amount of query reformulation [52, 53]. Duarte Torres suggests that this is an indicator of children having a greater level of frustration than adults. While this might be true, there is also a possibility that adults have more complex information needs resulting in a longer sessions. Children also have shorter attention spans (time to be focused

---

[1] www.aol.com is a web search engine. The AOL query log contains data of the AOL search engine from the period March to May 2006.

[2] http://www.dmoz.org/ is an Open Directory Project which has a goal to construct and maintain the most comprehensive human-edited directory of the Web.

on a specific task) than adults [36], get easily distracted and off task [49]. This could lead to shorter search session times in comparison to adults because children simply switch to other tasks sooner. Further analysis of search queries revealed that children up to 12 tend to search for games and recreation more than older users. In addition, the vocabulary size of web queries increases with age [53, Chapter 3].

3.1.2 Search Strategy

There are two interface types for search engines that are currently in use: catalogue and query oriented (or keyword) search engines. In query oriented search engines the user needs to input some keywords, whereas in catalogue oriented search he browses/navigates through pre-defined categories. Search engines that integrate both interface types are also common.

Researchers [20] (33 participants: ages 9-12) found that the *browsing* performance of children is better and that children prefer browsing. One reason for this preference is that browsing imposes less cognitive load (see Section 2.2.1). More knowledge is required to recall concepts from the memory, instead of simply recognizing and reacting to offered terms. Borgman et al. [20, p. 665] explain that browsing fits into a child's "natural tendency to explore". This also fits in better with the motor skills of children. Whereas keyword oriented search engines require correct spelling and typing, browsing is possible with simple point-and-click interactions. Nevertheless there are potential problems in browsing. As children have only little domain knowledge and a smaller vocabulary, they may have problems finding the right category. Thus, it is important to design categories which match the cognitive abilities of children.

Some research was undertaken about the *structure of categories*. Hutchinson et al. [85] (72 participants: ages 6-11) confirm that children are able to use both flat and hierarchical organised categories to browse. They found that young children are comfortable navigating a two-level hierarchy. Bar-Ilan and Belous [12] (48 participants: fourth and fifth grades) investigated the process of information categorization of elementary school children using a card-sorting method. When applying this method, each category is written on a card and people are asked to sort the cards into groups [181]. Bar-Ilan and Belous [12] found that children can create hierarchical structures (with depth between three and five), but only with concrete objects.

The limited domain knowledge of children is also a problem in *keyword oriented search* engines. To formulate a search query, the user needs sufficient domain knowledge to think about useful keywords [83] (72 participants: ages 6-11). Many children do not even know that they have to select single keywords, so they tend to input full natural language queries [127] (28 participants in third and fourth grades, 24 participants in sixth grade). Even if they understand that they have to input keywords, it is difficult for children to select the keywords, because it requires the ability of thinking in abstract categories [85].

Jochmann-Mannak et al. [92] (32 participants: ages 8-12) found that children prefer typing keywords rather than browsing categories. This can be explained with the fact that these children already had experience with Google, which is a keyword oriented interface (children's familiarity and positive perception of Google was also acknowledged by Druin et al. [47]). Also the search interfaces used in the study did not have good browsing capabilities, e.g. categories were hidden within the interface.

Furthermore, researchers studied different *search roles* or search behaviour types of children using keyword search interfaces. Druin et al. [49] (83 participants: ages 7,9,11) conducted a qualitative home study using interviews with both parents and children and observed the children using a web search engine of their choice. Druin et al. described seven search roles of children as information seekers using query oriented search engines at home:

▶ The *developing searcher* is the most common role among children between the ages of seven, nine and eleven. The developing searcher is motivated to search, but does not always succeed. The developing searcher often uses natural language queries as opposed to keywords. He has difficulties with typing, spelling, reading and lack of understanding how to formulate a query.

▶ The *content searcher* searches only to find specific content related to personal interests, usually a small set of websites he returns to.

▶ The *power searcher* understands how to use keywords and can explain his search strategy. He successfully searches for information not only for fun but also related to school assignments.

▶ The *non-motivated searcher* is not really interested in searching. If asked to find some information he can guess the answer. When searching he clicks on the first result or just reads the result surrogates but not the actual result pages.

▶ The *distracted searcher* gets easily off-task. He can be distracted by animation, blinking text, videos or their surroundings.
▶ The *visual searcher* prefers to search for visual information, e.g. using image and video search engines. He experiences difficulties when the desired information is only present in a textual but not in a visual form.
▶ The *rule-bound searcher* is the least common role among children between the ages of seven, nine and eleven. He has a specific set of rules and follows them. However, he has difficulties when trying to adjust the rules depending on the situation.

A child can exhibit several roles. The most frequent combination found by Druin et al. was the developing searcher in combination with other roles such as the rule-bound, content and distracted searcher. Eickhoff, Dekker, and de Vries [59] (29 participants: ages 9-12) conducted a user study with elementary school children. They used the role classification of Druin et al. and proposed an automatic method to distinguish between developing searchers and power searchers. For this they derived three types of features accessible during a search session and trained a classifier using the data they collected during the user study:

▶ *Task-independent features* such as a child's demographic data;
▶ *Task-dependent direct features* are features that are extracted from the interaction log, e.g. the number of issued queries or the number of mouse clicks;
▶ *Task-dependent inferred features* are features that require further processing steps to be taken of the search log and may involve external data, e.g. average number of verbs, nouns and adjectives per query.

Eickhoff, Dekker, and de Vries [59] showed that successful searchers or power searchers have a higher school grade and formulate shorter queries with only a few nouns.

3.1.3 Navigation Style

Compared to adults, children have a different navigational style. Bilal and Kirby [17] (22 participants: seventh grade) found that children tend to backtrack very often. When children start a new search, they often navigate back to the home page first. Children have a *loopy* browsing style, whereas adults' browsing style is *linear* or *systematic*: Children *click*, repeat searches and revisit the same result web page more often than adults. This characteristic agrees with children's lower cognitive recall, i.e. children probably forget about visiting a page previously. Children may also repeat searches/resubmit queries in the expectation that an IR system will provide new search results. Hence, the children's search behaviour can be described by many looping and *backtracking* actions, with fast reading of the retrieved documents and little focus on the search goal. This *chaotic pattern* of information seeking is also called fast surfing [175].

Researchers also explored the influence of children's gender on patterns of searching the Web. Roy and Chi [166] (14 participants: ages 13-14) investigated how boys and girls use the Web to find the answer to a specific question. They found that girls and boys have different pattern of search. Boys use *horizontal search*. They iteratively submit searches and scan the document snippets returned as search results. Girls imploy *vertical search*. They tend to open and browse the result web pages (returned by the search engine) without going through the list and filtering the non relevant results in the first place. The boys' strategy leads them to better search performance in the end. Large, Beheshti, and Rahman [113] (53 participants: sixth grade) studied collaborative search behaviour in same-sex groups of boys and girls. They found that boys make significantly more clicks (in the number of searches executed, the extent of clicking on hits, the next page of search results, etc.) during browsing than girls. Groups of girls tend to use natural language queries more often than boys, whereas boys use fewer words (sometimes even only one) to formulate the query.

3.1.4 User Interface

There is evidence that children can experience difficulties with advanced metaphorical navigation interfaces[3] whose meaning they do not understand [92] (32 participants: ages 8-12). Additionally, researchers suggest that the *interface* should support both educational and entertainment needs of children [112] (23 participants: ages 10-13).

---

[3] A metaphorical interface employs a visual metaphor. It makes the computer screen appear as if users are moving not through a screen but rather through some familiar environment [144]. The purpose of it is to provide users with knowledge about how to interact with the user interface. An example is the shop metaphor, i.e. using a "shopping basket" in an e-commerce shop [110].

There is some research on *children's interactions* with interfaces using a mouse or similar devices. The results are important to consider when designing interfaces for children's IR systems. Certain mouse interactions are very difficult for children. Children have difficulties with drag-and-drop interactions because they can not coordinate dragging and holding at the same time [185] (94 participants: first and second grade). However, better design decisions might help to decrease the errors during drag-and-drop interactions [46] (103 participants: Kindergarten 2 and Grade 1, six years old on average). Furthermore, children often do not use complex interactions like scrolling a page [136] (30 participants: ages 7-11). Interface elements should be large enough because the fine motor skills of children are still developing and are not as good as those of adults. The time for moving a mouse is inversely proportional to the size of the target object. This means that larger target sizes allow children especially to make selections quicker [82] (39 participants: ages 4-5, ages 19-22).

Naidu [136] (30 participants: ages 7-11) found that children in general prefer websites with many pictures. This is consistent with Large, Beheshti, and Rahman [112] (23 participants: ages 10-13) whose user study results suggest to use attractive *screen designs* based especially on effective use of colour, graphics, and animation and allow individual user personalisation in areas such as colour and graphics.

Budiu and Nielsen [25] (35 children, ages 3-12) studied usability issues in designing websites for children. They claim that metaphors, especially spatial navigation, work very well for children. There are only problems if virtual attributes differ from the ones in the physical world. Children like movement, graphics, funny sounds, and colours. However, it should be in reasonable portions in order not to overwhelm them. Children understand icons better when they represent real-world concepts they are familiar with. Uncomplicated text fonts (Size: 14 point for young children and 12 point for older children) and simple text layouts make reading easier. Both adults and children avoid reading long texts on the Web. Budiu and Nielsen also confirm that children use a hunt-and-peck approach to typing and therefore make relatively more typing errors than adults. Thus, spelling correction and query suggestion mechanisms are important. Children in the study also had problems with the mouse and many didn't know how to drag. Budiu and Nielsen [25] suggest to make the clickable targets big and static to overcome these problems. The study also shows that most modern children older than nine are fairly comfortable with scrolling but younger children are not. During the web search children tend to formulate natural queries instead of using keywords for search. Thus, Budiu and Nielsen [25] recommend to use a large search box.

Jochmann-Mannak [94] and Jochmann-Mannak et al. [93] (158 children, ages 10-12) identified three design types of search user interfaces designed for children:

▶ *The Classic design type* is a simplistic and minimalistic search user interface, with classical aesthetics and a classical vertical navigation menu placed on the left side.

▶ *The Classical play design type* uses expressive aesthetics and a classical horizontal navigation menu placed above. The menu categories contain textual labels along with icons.

▶ *The Image map design type* has both expressive aesthetics and a playful navigation menu in the form of an image map. The map incorporates objects or locations that children know from real life or from fiction.

Each interface type can also be manipulated by presenting the navigation menu with or without a keyword input field. Jochmann-Mannak conducted a user study to investigate the influence of the interface type on the children's search performance and on the children's attitudes towards these six interfaces. During the user study the children performed five answer-oriented search tasks using each one of the six search interfaces. As a result, no significant difference in performance was found between the three designs of search interfaces. However, children who used the query oriented search engine achieved significantly better results than children who did not have this option or had chosen to use the navigation menu instead of the keyword search. This was true for all the three design types. Thus, the design type did not influence the search performance, but the type of search user interface or search strategy did. Independent of the search success, the children were most positive about the Classical play interface type and rated the Image map design type less attractive than the other two.

3.1.5 Relevance Judgement

Children also have difficulties when judging the relevance of the retrieved documents to their information need [92] (32 participants: ages 8-12). Children are frustrated by too many results and do not have the ability to determine the most relevant and "best" documents [111] (50 participants: sixth grade). In a task-oriented search, children look for the final "concrete" answer in documents, without trying to read and understand the content [16, 18] (22 participants in seventh grade). Most children visit only the first result page and click on the first item in the result list [47] (12 children: ages 7,9,11).

In the next section 3.2, we discuss existing algorithms and user interface concepts which were proposed to be used in IR systems for children.

3.2 Existing Algorithms and User Interface Concepts for Children

Sociologists started studying the information-seeking behaviour of children several decades ago and marked the beginning of children's information retrieval as a research field. Some years ago computer scientists joined them to apply algorithms and techniques from information retrieval, natural language processing, machine learning and human computer interaction[4].

In this section we analyse related work in the area of children IR, i.e. what methods were proposed by computer scientists to contribute to children IR and adapt IR systems to the children's needs. We start with the architecture of an information system (see Figure 2.2) and analyse how each of the components can be adapted for children. There are various challenges to design IR systems for young users: supporting the children's information needs and making it possible for the children to submit the right query, rank/retrieve documents that are relevant for the children, provide high quality content, visualise the results properly, and carry out an evaluation of a newly designed system. An overview of these aspects and related work about proposed algorithms and user interfaces is given below.

---

[4] A good example of the work in this direction is the PuppyIR project (http://www.puppyir.eu/).

3.2.1 Query

Researchers study children's search queries to provide methods of automatic query reformulation and get better search results. Kalsbeek et al. [103] explored different types of query errors made by children, e.g. typing errors, slang or no vowels, and explored the potential solutions for each of the error types. Synonym expansion (using WordNet) and phonetic expansion showed promising improvements.

Duarte Torres et al. [55] and Duarte Torres [53] explored query recommendation methods using the tags from a social bookmarking system. Given the web results for a search query, keyword candidates are extracted from the snippets and titles. Using the information about the tags, keyword candidates that are used as tags for websites for children more frequently than for websites for adult users are boosted and get a higher rank in the suggestion list. Duarte Torres evaluated the method and showed that it performs best for the youngest groups of users (eight to nine years old). An advantage of this approach is that this method does not require having a query log and is a useful approach for a privacy preserving search engine (that does not store user's search history).

Alternative input methods for specifying a query that can replace the keyword query input using a keyboard were studied. For instance, Jansen et al. [90] proposed a tangible interface called *TeddIR*. The system helps children to retrieve books they are looking for. Instead of typing in keywords, children search by putting tangible figurines or books in the boxes to indicate that they like or dislike them. Thus, difficulties in spelling and finding query terms are overcome. A user study with seventeen children (third or fourth grade pupils) showed that children playing with *TeddIR* were successful in retrieving the books using several figurines for connecting the search concepts (AND operator). However, this tangible solution only works for a small number of search concepts. *Junior Search (JuSe)* [157] is an interface that enables searching through adaptable picture dictionaries. Children can construct queries using the pictures. *JuSe* uses categories derived from children's vocabulary lists. Parents can adjust the list, e.g. add new words. *EmSe* [60] is a search service for children in a hospital environment. It was designed for children of ages 8–12. In order to overcome terminology difficulties a novel visual querying interface *Body Browser* is offered which lets children explore medical information. Furthermore, *EmSe* provides children with relevant documents where medical terms are annotated with explanations.

3.2.2 Content

Search systems for young users should provide a child with *child-suitable* results which are on the one hand *child-safe* (child-safe content should not contain any material that is harmful to child's development, such as pornography or violence) and on the other hand not too complex for a child, i.e. *child-appropriate*. Thus, the construction of a document collection is an issue. There are several possibilities to create a child-suitable collection:

▶ *Manually:* Educators filter suitable documents/content before it is added to the index of the IR system[5]. This requires a lot of effort and the number of checked documents is limited, but it guaranties that the documents are child-suitable.

▶ *Automatically:* One can use machine learning techniques, e.g. classification, to identify suitable content. Machine approaches allow checking a great number of documents, but missclassifications are possible.

The two methods can be combined to maximise both precision and recall: first automatically identify potential documents and then manually verify them.

Eickhoff, Serdyukov, and de Vries [58] and Eickhoff and de Vries [57] studied document classification for child suitability. They propose features for automatic web page classification with two classes, suitable for children or not: child-friendliness to identify child-appropriate results (textual complexity, presentation and navigation) and focus towards child audiences (language models, reference analysis and URL features). They also use classification to identify suitable YouTube videos for children. The features for classification they propose are video tags and description, author information, meta information and community-created information.

Text or web documents can be written using varying language complexity. Therefore, providing a safe content only is not enough: children should also be able to understand its meaning. There are several ways to over-

---

[5] An example is the German search engine Blinde-Kuh.de

come this problem. First, texts written in a complex language can be simplified. De Belder, Deschacht, and Moens [40] and De Belder and Moens [41] proposed lexical and syntactic methods of text simplification. In the lexical case they simplify the text by replacing each individual word with a synonym that should be easier to understand. These synonyms are found using language models from a large, unlabeled training corpus or WordNet. In the syntactic case they split complex sentences into several simple sentences. The researchers did not succeed in reducing the reading difficulty enough for children, at least not without removing information from the text.

Another way to provide an understandable content is to influence the document ranking so that documents written in a simple language are ranked higher and are shown first to children. Approaches that follow this idea are discussed in the following.

3.2.3 Ranking

As already mentioned in Section 3.1, children visit only the first result page and click on the first item in the result list [47]. Therefore, the search results ordering, i.e. ranking, is of importance. The standard method for document ranking in common IR systems is to calculate the similarity between the query and the documents and rank the documents according to the achieved similarity score (see Section 2.1.2). For web documents we can also calculate the popularity of the document given the link structure of the web, i.e. hyperlinks are also used for ranking web search results. *PageRank* (Section 2.1.2) is a popular algorithms which uses the link structure. *PageRank* is based on the assumption that a good document is linked to by many other good documents. The overall ranking of web documents is calculated by combining the similarity score and the popularity of the page.

Gyllstrom and Moens [74] adapted *PageRank* to a link-based ranking algorithm for children. The proposed ranking algorithm *AgeRank* ranks web pages according to their age appropriateness. AgeRank is a modification of PageRank, which considers that pages for kids are more likely to link to and be linked from other kids pages. Each page receives positive and negative scores from incoming and outgoing links ($p_{out}, p_{in}, n_{out}, n_{in}$). These scores indicate the degree of a page being for children (positive) or for adults (negative) based on the link structure. The AgeRank value of a page, called *Tot*, is based on these four components and is calculated as the ratio of the positive scores (p_{out}, p_{in}) to the negative scores (n_{out}, n_{in}). The authors evaluated the algorithm using Mechanical Turk[6] (adult) participants. They found that AgeRank scores had a significant positive relationship with human ratings.

An important factor for children is the complexity of the language in a document. Researchers suggest to use the complexity to additionally influence the ranking. Where two topical articles are available, the simpler one should be preferred [174]. Sluis, Dijk, and Broek [176] and Sluis and Dijk [175] discuss three components that should be considered by children IR: *complexity*, *interestingness*, and *affective value*. The complexity can be measured, for example, through text readability and coherence. The interestingness of information can increase motivation. The interestingness can be measured, for example, through novelty. The website interactivity can influence the affective state. Text, interactivity of a website and multimedia can influence the emotions like enjoyment and are indicators of the affective state.

3.2.4 Search Result Visualisation

In addition to ranking, the visualisation and presentation of results is important as it affects the searcher's judgement of the documents' relevance [81, Chapter 5]. Elliot et al. [61] and Glassey et al. [68] propose a result presentation interface where the amount of space allocated to the document title indicates the relevance of a document. Akkersdijk et al. [3] suggest an alternative presentation of the search results for a touch interface, called *ImagePile*. *ImagePile* displays the results as a pile of images where the user navigates horizontally instead of the commonly used vertical scrolling. The results of their user study show that five out of eight children aged eight to eleven preferred the ImagePile over the common vertical result list.

Besides visualisation methods, there is also work on the construction of search results for children. *CollAge*, a system which combines search results for children's web queries with child-oriented multimedia results, such as colouring pages and music sheets, was proposed by Gyllstrom and Moens [73]. Given a query, researchers create new queries for each media

---

[6] https://www.mturk.com/mturk/welcome

type like paintings, maps, puzzles, etc. They verify if the new queries make sense using the Google Suggest database. For each media query, they run a Google image search and return images as results in addition to the existing search results. Combination of textual and child-oriented multimedia results makes them more attractive for children.

Duarte Torres, Hiemstra, and Huibers [54] and Duarte Torres [53] propose to aggregate search results from different sources, also called *verticals*, in order to increase the quality of search results for children from 8 to 12 years old. The vision is that parents or teachers add verticals to the collection, e.g. to search for colouring pages or for videos. Duarte Torres et al. also propose a method to retrieve the most relevant verticals from the collection given a search query. Each vertical is represented as a bag of tags associated with the URLs. The information about the tags is obtained using a social bookmarking system (Delicious). The query is also represented as a bag of words that are extracted from the top ten results of an index based on the *Dmoz kids and teens* directory. Duarte Torres et al. used a language model on these tags to rank the relevancy of the verticals given a query.

3.3 Existing Information Retrieval Systems for Children

While we have discussed research prototypes above, there exist several IR systems for children that are publicly available. Those are mainly web search engines whose target group are children. However, there are also digital book libraries for children. where children can search in a collection of digitized books or books that can be later borrowed from the library. Some UI aspects of digital libraries can be also applied to search engines. In the following we describe their main characteristics.

3.3.1 Digital Book Libraries

Pejtersen [151] developed a Danish system for information retrieval in a fiction book collection aimed both for children (seven to sixteen) and adults. The system called *The Book House* has a graphical user interface and uses a spatial metaphor for both database content and structure as well as support for information retrieval. The users are offered to choose a database to search in and to select a strategy they would like to employ. Several strategies are available, i.e. analytical search (selecting features, e.g. genre, plot, place, readability), search by analogy (finding similar books), browsing through pictures or through descriptions of books. In order to find features that would describe fiction books, Pejtersen investigated user needs and requests. She found out that the readability (related to school grade or age group) of books is very important for children. Furthermore, in contrast to adults, children often requested pictures as a form of query formulation. Children also judged the book content by the information found on the book cover. In addition to the textual description of books, The Book House uses icons to represent the book content. The findings of Pejtersen show that icons are successful when used in combination with text.

Hutchinson, Bederson, and Druin [84] developed a searching and browsing tool for the *International Children's Digital Library* suitable for children[7] (see Figure 3.2). They considered the children's differences in motor skills when designing the system and provided large icons and simple *Point and Click* actions to interact with the system. Besides searching, the system supports browsing where child appropriate categories are used. These categories are represented by icons to support children with weak reading abilities. Search results can be filtered by different parameters using the category buttons. Sequential clicking on the categories leads to Boolean conjunctive operations which is also indicated in the user interface.

3.3.2 Web Search Engines

There are a number of web search engines for children. They primarily provide child-safe content. Examples of English and German search engines are *quinturakids.com, kidrex.org, onekey.com, askkids.com, kidsclick.org, blinde-kuh.de, helles-koepfchen.de, fragfinn.de, dipty.com* etc. The majority of these engines have a colourful design of the start page to attract children's attention, e.g. *quinturakids.com* (see Figure 3.3).

Existing web search engines for children have a design similar to common search engines. They have a keyword-based interface. Thus, a child enters a textual query to an input field to initiate the search. A few web

---

[7] http://www.childrenslibrary.org/icdl/SimpleSearchCategory?ilang=English, accessed on 10-12-2014.

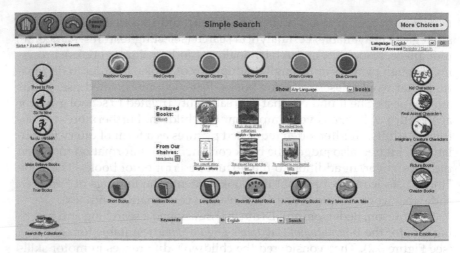

Fig. 3.2: Simple Search mode in the *International Children's Digital Library*. The search results in the form of book covers are shown in the middle. Along the edges, category buttons are placed to specify the search [pub:7].

This screenshot was taken from the International Children's Digital Library on 2012-03-09.

search engines also have (flat) categories. For example, *quinturakids.com* has five categories (music, history, animal, computer games, sport and recreation) which are shown using images of moving kites. In contrast to other search engines, *Quinturakids* also offers a dynamic tag cloud based on the user's current query and suggesting what the user can search next.

The visualisation of search results is also very similar to standard search engines, i.e. a vertical results list of text snippets. Some search engines also provide pictures along with text summaries to support the relevance filtering process of children (e.g. *helles-koepfchen.de*). Usually, there are ten results per page. However, for example, the search engine *kidsclick.org* places all the results on one page. Thus, they can be 40 to 50 results on the page. The query input field is placed after the search results and moves to the bottom of the page. This makes scrolling unavoidable which may be difficult for children. Some search engines for children, e.g. *Kidrex*, also provide advertisements along with organic search results.

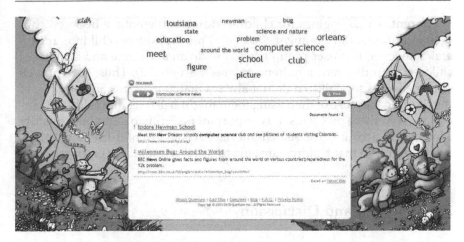

Fig. 3.3: Colourful design of the *Quinturakids.com*. The search engine has a dynamic tag cloud, placed above the input field, and a menu with five categories shown as moving kites [pub:7].

This screenshot was taken from the Quinturakids.com on 2012-03-09.

Most of these web search engines (e.g. *blinde-kuh.de, askkids.com, kidsclick.org*) also account for text complexity and provide only those web pages as search results that are easy to read for children. *kidsclick.org* also provides information about the reading level of the retrieved web pages. In the Advanced Search mode users can limit the search results using three grade ranges. *blinde-kuh.de* provides additional information about the search results such as the result's category, language and the target age group in categories "S", "M", "L", "XL" for children from six to thirteen. There is also an option to sort the results such that the results for younger children appear first.

One drawback of many search engines for children is the absence of spellchecking and query suggestion mechanisms. For example, *askkids.com* only shows an error message for misspelled queries. Many search engines for children, e.g. *kidsclick.org*, do not use any keyword highlighting in the search results. This makes it harder for children to estimate how relevant each search result is. Another drawback are the small text fonts which make it hard to read for children.

Current search engines for children do not differentiate between children in different development stages and mostly address children in general. However, this user group has too wide an age range and consists of children with different requirements (see Section 2.2). Thus, current web search engines for children do not always match the skills and abilities of the children. Because of that, using them might frustrate the children. In order to avoid these problems, it is important not only to take child-friendly content into account. The search interface has to be child-friendly (usable for children), so that children are able to use it without any problems.

3.4 Summary and Discussion

This chapter provided an overview of existing achievements in the field of IR for children. Information retrieval for young users is a complex topic. It is strongly related to the cognitive science on human development and sociological studies on the information-seeking behaviour of children. Much knowledge has already been gained in those two fields that can be transferred to information retrieval for young users.

Results of user studies about information-seeking behaviour are just as important as the knowledge from cognitive science because they provide empirical proof for the latter, complement and enrich the knowledge needed to derive the implications for the design of IR systems for children. We summarised the main findings about children's queries, search strategy, navigation style, preferred user interfaces and relevance judgement. We also discussed several conceptual issues of these studies. When describing children's information retrieval systems and information-seeking behaviour in this thesis, we mainly concentrated on information search in a web document collection.

Furthermore, we gave an overview of existing algorithms and user interface concepts in the field of information retrieval for young users. We also described existing information retrieval systems, web search engines and a digital library for children that are publicly available. Nevertheless, many research questions are still open. There are no solid and proven solutions for a child-specific IR system. In our opinion, the current problem in the research on information retrieval for young users is that researchers view children as a homogenous user group. They often do not consider that children of different ages may require different solutions that influence the design of information retrieval systems. Theories of human development confirm that children in different development stages do differ in cognitive abilities (and motor skills). This is why there is a need to target very narrow age groups when designing UI concepts and algorithms for children.

Children are seldom involved in the design process of user interfaces. To our knowledge, only the International Children's Digital Library [84] was co-designed with children. Current research also requires more evaluation of recently proposed algorithms and user interface concepts. Many promising interface concepts and algorithms, e.g. CollAge [73] or AgeRank [74], should be evaluated in user studies with children. Children's information-seeking behaviour was studied mostly on keyword oriented IR systems. "New" user interface concepts, e.g., *JuSe* [157], still need to be examined in comparative user studies to evaluate them against existing alternative interface concepts. Children's perception of user interface elements, e.g., different forms of results visualisation, should be compared in the future. Furthermore, some usability questions still require an answer [25], e.g. what children consider to be clickable. It would be beneficial to apply modern evaluation methods like *eye tracking* [56] to study the children's usage of IR systems. Furthermore, it is still unclear how to deal with the children's *loopy* browsing style. In fact, no solution was proposed to solve this problem. This type of browsing behaviour can be a sign of children's cognitive overload. There is also no study of mechanisms for emotional support of children during the search, which is also a potential future direction.

There is also much potential in the development of new ranking algorithms for children. Until now, only one algorithm, AgeRank [74], was proposed. There are some conceptual suggestions as to what features should effect the ranking for children, e.g. complexity, interestingness, and affective value. Ranking algorithms based on these suggestions should be implemented in the future. An open research question here is how much influence each of the mentioned components has on the target ranking value.

The content of this chapter provides answers to the following research question of the thesis:

Component	Possible adaptation
Query input	tangible interface, searching through adaptable picture dictionaries, visual querying interface, voice input, query-by-drawing
Query parsing and pre-processing	child-oriented query recommendations
Document pre-processing and indexing	filtering of child-suitable documents, methods of text simplification
Crawler	focused crawler
Matching and relevance ranking	incorporation of complexity, interestingness and affective value
Search results visualisation	incorporation of child-oriented multimedia results, visual relevance cues

Table 3.1: IR system components that can be adapted to the targeted user group and possible adaptation for children: All processing steps can be adapted to the targeted user group (cf. Fig. 2.2).

RQ2

What components of an IR system can be adapted to the targeted user group?

In order to design a targeted search engine for children several components both from the frontend and the backend of an IR system can be adapted to better match and support this specific user group. Section 3.2 gave an overview of existing algorithms and user interface concepts in this area of research. IR system components that can be adapted to the targeted user group and possible adaptation for children are summarised in Table 3.1. Important adaptation directions are the design of alternative input methods for specifying a query, algorithms for query correction and query suggestion for children. Furthermore, methods are required to insure that the underlying collection only contains documents that are not harmful in content and can be understood by children. It is possible to employ a child-oriented ranking algorithm, i.e. to position the documents, that are easier

Aspect	Findings
Query	use natural language queries, make spelling mistakes
Search strategy	use query oriented search engines
Navigation style	have a loopy browsing style
User Interface	prefer attractive design, usage of colour, graphics, and animation (in reasonable portions), simple interactions, large objects, UI personalisation
Relevance judgement	have difficulties to determine the most relevant result

Table 3.2: Main finding of user studies on children's information seeking behaviour.

to understand for children, higher in the ranking. The results can be also visualised in a more child-friendly way, e.g. to support interaction or to add multimedia results for visual searchers.

This thesis has a focus on the frontend design of a targeted search engine for children. The results of studies about children's information-seeking behaviour and theories of human development help us to understand the challenges and later derive guidelines on how to design search systems that would support the children at their search tasks.

> **RQ4**
>
> What are the characteristics of children's information seeking behaviour?

A summary of the main findings of the studies on children's information seeking behaviour is shown in Table 3.2. Children tend to formulate natural language queries, probably due to the lack of abstract thinking. Furthermore, children often do not spot spelling mistakes because they concentrate on typing. In contrast to adults, children have a limited domain knowledge, which causes difficulties when trying to formulate a query in the case of an keyword oriented search. It is more natural for children to use catalogue oriented search engines, however children tend to use query oriented search engines most likely because they are exposed to search engines like Google from an early age. Compared to adults, children have a different navigational style, called a *loopy* browsing. Children click, repeat searches and revisit the same result web page more often than adults. It is more difficult for children to determine the most relevant result than for adults. Children like attractive designs. However, the search user interface should not be too crowded. Children have difficulties to use complex interactions, e.g. drag-and-drop. Large fonts and large clickable elements are more comfortable for children.

However, the existing studies provide only a partial answer to the research question about the characteristics of children's information seeking behaviour (cf. *RQ4*). There are still some open issues: Previous findings were mainly based on small user studies with lab experiments and may not show real life behaviour. There is no large-scale study of search behaviour on children's web search engines. In addition, previous user studies do not provide details about the children's perception of the search engines' interface elements during information-seeking. There is also no direct comparison of children's and adults' web information seeking behaviour. Furthermore, it is unknown if the existing targeted search engines are appropriate for the motor and cognitive skills of children. We are going to study these open issues in Part II.

Part II
Studying Open Issues

Chapter 4

Usability of Existing Search Engines for Young Users

In this Chapter, a study about the usability assessment of existing search engines for young users is described. There are several IR systems for children that are publicly available (see Section 3.3). In June 2011, we conducted a study to analyse the usability of search engines for children. The goal was to verify whether current search engines are appropriate for the motor and cognitive skills of children. To this end, we analysed twelve search engines whose main target group are children. We first choose formal criteria based on the results of previous studies and recommendations in this field (see Section 2.2 and 3.1). Afterwards, we analysed the search engines and evaluated the results. Here we applied an analytical evaluation method (see Section 2.3.2). In the following, we describe the selected search engines, our criteria and present the method we used to analyse the data. The work presented in this chapter has been published in [pub:6].

In order to obtain a better overview of the currently available search engines for children on the Internet, we selected seven English search engines and five German search engines:

▶ onekey.com	▶ blinde-kuh.de
▶ kids.yahoo.com	▶ fragfinn.de
▶ askkids.com	▶ helles-koepfchen.de
▶ dibdabdoo.com	▶ loopilino.com
▶ factmonster.com	▶ dipty.com
▶ kids.aol.com	
▶ kidsclick.org	

This list includes the English search engines that we found on the Internet and all the known German search engines for children. We used the browser developer tool *inspector* to determine the websites' parameters. Therefore, we did not consider search engines that used *Adobe Flash* (e.g. quinturakids.com). Adobe Flash makes it hard to measure some characteristics of the website like the font size. We also analysed the popular search engine Google to compare between child-focused and more mainstream search engines. Indeed, the user study of Jochmann-Mannak et al. [92] indicates that children are likely to use Google and even perform better using Google than on special search engines designed for them, in particular children need less time and are most successful when conducting the search task with Google.

4.1 Assessment Criteria

Our goal was to analyse the degree of adaptation of search engines for children to the children's motor and cognitive skills. For this purpose, we defined criteria for measuring the degree of this conformance.

4.1.1 Criteria for Matching the Motor Skills

Size of the buttons: As target objects get smaller, the time needed to accurately move the cursor towards them increases [85]. This means that larger target sizes allow children to make their selections quicker. As the fine motor skills of young children are not as good as the ones of adults, big target sizes are even more important for child-friendly user interfaces. Therefore, we chose the button size as an evaluation criterion.

We examined the size of the "Search" button on the home page and the size of the main navigation links/buttons. We assessed the buttons using the results of a study by Hourcade et al. [82]. They found that the accuracy of clicking on targets with a diameter of 32 pixel was significantly better than on 16 pixel targets for both children and adults. The level of accuracy of the young children got even higher, when the target size was 64 pixels[1]. To compare the button sizes, we calculated the area of the buttons with the help of its width and height in pixel[2]. We grouped the results into three

---

[1] The targets used in the study were circles. The (21") monitor resolution used in the study was 1,024x768 pixels.

[2] All measurements were in pixel, but it would be more accurate to refer to the absolute surface size which depends on a particular monitor that is used. Furthermore, the performance in point-and-click tasks correlates not only with the target size but also with

Category	Surface areas of the "Search" and a main navigation button
0 (not good)	At least one area is < 32x32 pixels
1 (fair)	Both areas are $\geq$ 32x32 pixels; but at least one area is < 64x64 pixels
2 (good)	Both areas are $\geq$ 64x64 pixels

Table 4.1: Categorisation according to the type of search tool [pub:6].

categories as presented in Table 4.1. The overall result combines both the size of the search button and the size of a main navigation button.

Length of the home page: Scrolling a page is a difficult task for children because they need to use drag-and-drop or the scroll wheel of the mouse. Both alternatives do not match the motor skills of young children [85]. Therefore, the page length of a child-friendly search engine should be short to avoid too much scrolling [25]. We measured this characteristic in the number of screens required to see the whole page. Note that we used a 11.6" monitor with a resolution of 1,366x768 pixels[3] and the normal view settings of the browser during the whole analysis. We simply counted the number of screens that are necessary to see the whole home page. After that, we grouped the results into three categories (see Table 4.2).

4.1.2 Criteria for Matching the Cognitive Skills

Type of the search tool: Currently, there are two types of search tools in use: browsing- and keyword-oriented search tools. As discussed above, many researchers agree that browsing better matches the cognitive skills of children [92]. Nevertheless, it is good to offer both interface types, because it

---

the distance to the monitor and computer mouse sensitivity. Therefore, it is possible to make only rough estimations about an appropriate button size for other settings than used in the study of Hourcade et al. [82].

[3] The monitor that we used in this study influenced only the results about the length of the home page. All other measurements were independent of the hardware that we used.

Category	Number of screens required
0 (not good)	More than 3 screens
1 (fair)	2 or 3 screens
2 (good)	One screen

Table 4.2: Categorization according to the length of the home page [pub:6].

Category	Type of the search tool
0 (not good)	Only keyword oriented
1 (fair)	Only browsing oriented
2 (good)	Browsing and keyword oriented

Table 4.3: Categorization according to the type of search tool [pub:6].

enables children to search more flexibly and to learn and improve both techniques. In order to analyse this criterion, we checked which type was offered by the respective search engine. We grouped the results into three categories as presented in Table 4.3.

Support of backtracking: Children very often backtrack to pages that they have already visited [17, 92]. Additionally, many children first go back to the home page if they want to start a new query [92]. As a result, children use the "Back" and "Home" buttons of the browser very often. Therefore, a clear "Home" button is important for the child friendliness of a search interface. Moreover, new websites should not be opened in a new tab or window as this inhibits backtracking (see Section 3.1). In order to analyse these characteristics, we checked whether the search engine has a home button and whether result websites were opened in a new browser tab or window. The overall result of each search engine was calculated as presented in Table 4.4.

Presentation of search results: As discussed in Section 3.1, children often face difficulties when trying to find the relevant results in a search result list [92], and most children examine only the first three results [pub:15]. If

Category	"Home" button	Link opened in the same window or tab
0 (not good)	No	No
1 (fair)	Yes	No
2 (fair)	No	Yes
3 (good)	Yes	Yes

Table 4.4: Method to calculate the overall result for the criterion "Support of backtracking" [pub:6].

combining this with the fact that children avoid scrolling [25], it seems to be reasonable to place no more than ten results on a page. Furthermore, many elementary-age children are not yet experienced readers. Hence, the result surrogate should contain a short textual summary. Large font sizes help the children to read the texts [140], and highlighted keywords provide clues about the relevance of the retrieved result [81]. Also, it is very useful to illustrate the summary with pictures or other media, because images better match the cognitive skills of children than written words [75]. Children learn to think in images from the ages between two and seven [75]. We searched for the word "rabbit" in the English search engines or accordingly "Hase" in the German search engines[4]. We counted the number of results presented on the first result page. We also checked whether multimedia was used to present the search results and whether the word "rabbit" or "Hase" was highlighted in the summary. The font size of the summary text was extracted with the help of the development tool of the Safari browser and converted to point (pt).

As discussed before, most children have problems when trying to find the right keys on the keyboard and therefore make many spelling mistakes. This often results in "no hit" results, which frustrate the children [20]. In order to avoid frustration, spell checking is very important. We input "encycloedia" instead of "encyclopedia" in the English search engines and "Enzykloädie" instead of "Enzyklopädie" in the German search engines to check whether search engines offer spelling suggestion and/or do spelling

---

[4] According to the user study [14], children are interested in such topics as animals. Therefore, we considered the search query "rabbit" to be realistic and representative for children.

Points	Number of results	Font size	Usage of multimedia	Accentuation of keywords	Spelling correction and/or suggestion
0	> 10	< 14 point	No	No	No
1 (fair)	≤ 10	≥ 14 point	Yes	Yes	Yes

Table 4.5: Subcriteria for "Presentation of search results" [pub:6].

correction and return some results. Based on these characteristics, we chose five criteria to analyse the search engines. A search engine can get 0 points (not good) or 1 point (good) for each of the criteria as shown in Table 4.5. In order to assess the overall search result presentation, we summed up the points of five categories and mapped the result to the interval from 0 (not good) to 2 (good) for simplicity.

4.2 Results

In the following, we discuss the results of our usability study with respect to the motor and cognitive skills of children.

4.2.1 Conformance with Motor Skills

Figures 4.1 and 4.2 illustrate the results of our usability evaluation, in particular the degree of matching to the children's motor skills, for each search engine individually and overall results accordingly. In general, the results are not satisfying. None of the search engines have a good result in all criteria. Problems with handling a mouse are seldom taken into consideration. Furthermore, the home pages of many search engines are very long, which requires scrolling. Three of them even need more than four screens to be shown completely, and thus, scrolling is necessary and might frustrate children, just as small buttons might lead to frustration. Only the search engine

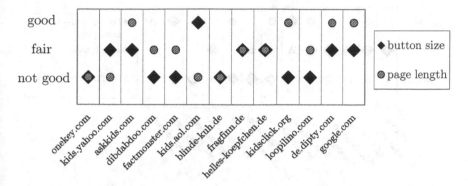

Fig. 4.1: Assessment of conformance for each search engine with the motor skills of children [pub:6].

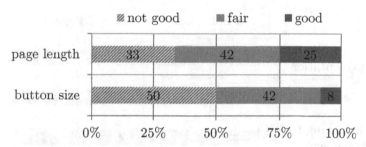

Fig. 4.2: Assessment of overall children's search engines' conformance with the motor skills of children [pub:6].

"kids.aol.com" offers a large search button and large main navigation buttons. All the others are not well adapted to the children's need for big target sizes. Altogether, most search engines for children are not well adapted to the motor skills of their users. They also do not offer observable advantages over the commonly used search engine Google.

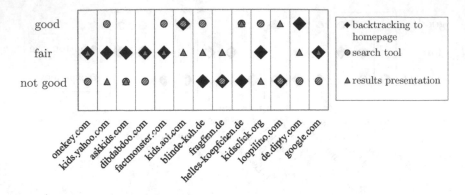

Fig. 4.3: Assessment of conformance of each search engine with the cognitive skills of children [pub:6].

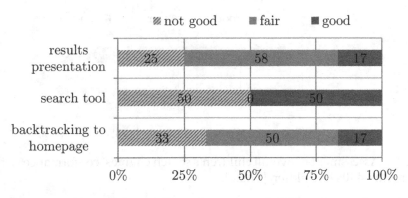

Fig. 4.4: Assessment of overall conformance of children's search engines with the cognitive skills of children [pub:6].

4.2.2 Conformance with the Cognitive Skills

Altogether, only a small number of the evaluated search engines conform to the cognitive skills of children (see Figs. 4.3 and 4.4). This could cause usability problems for children and lead to frustration. In the following, we describe the results for each of the criteria in detail.

4.2.3 Presentation of Search Results

Table 4.6 illustrates the results of our usability evaluation for each search engine individually. The best results are achieved by the German search engines "helles-koepfchen.de" and "loopilino.com". Half of the search engines that are developed specifically for children got worse results than "Google". These search engines do not present the results in a child-friendly way. The English search engines "kids.yahoo.com" and "kidsclick.org" even got zero points.

Number of results: Two search engines show more than 30 results per page: the search engine "kidsclick.org" always presents all search results on one page, and the search engine "kids.yahoo.com" always provides ten additional web search results below the results found in the "Yahoo! Kids" directory, which is too overwhelming for children. About 75% of the children's search engines place around ten results on one page. The search engine "dipty.de" is a good example for a presentation that does not use a long list (see Fig. 4.5). It always fits the results on one screen and has navigation links to further result pages below the result list. Thus, the number of hits might be more intuitively accessible for children.

Font size: Search engines should help children to find the relevant results out of the list of retrieved results. In order to do so, they should pay attention to the lower reading competence of the children by offering short summaries with large font sizes. Nielsen [140] found that 14 point is most comfortable for children. Nevertheless, none of the search engines offers such a big font size. Only "factmonster.com" uses a font size of 12 point. In contrast, text summaries of nine sites for children are even smaller than 10 point. This makes it very difficult for children to read and process the given information.

Usage of multimedia: Icons and pictures can compensate for the cognitive skills of elementary-age children. Nevertheless, only 33.3% of the evaluated search engines for children use pictures to illustrate the search results. An example is the German search engine "helles-koepfchen.de" that offers a picture together with every retrieved result. This helps children to find the relevant result quicker. Other kinds of multimedia could also be used, but no search engine adds audio or video to the search results.

Highlighting of keywords: In order to support the judgement of relevance, it is useful to highlight the words of the search query because it gives the children a clue how relevant the result is [81]. This characteristic is

Search engine	Number of results	Font size	Usage of multimedia	Highlighting of keywords	Spelling correction and/or suggestion
onekey.com	✓	✗	✗	✓	✓
kids.yahoo.com	✗	✗	✗	✗	✗
askkids.com	✓	✗	✗	✗	✗
dibdabdoo.com	✓	✗	✗	✓	✓
factmonster.com	✓	✗	✗	✗	✓
kids.aol.com	✓	✗	✗	✓	✓
blinde-kuh.de	✓	✗	✓	✗	✗
fragfinn.de	✓	✗	✓	✓	✗
helles-koepfchen.de	✓	✗	✓	✓	✓
kidsclick.org	✗	✗	✗	✗	✗
loopilino.com	✓	✗	✓	✓	✓
de.dipty.com	✓	✗	✗	✓	✗
google.com	✓	✗	✗	✓	✓

Table 4.6: Assessment of results presentation of each search engine [pub:6].

taken into consideration by seven out of twelve search engines for children. Google also uses highlighting.

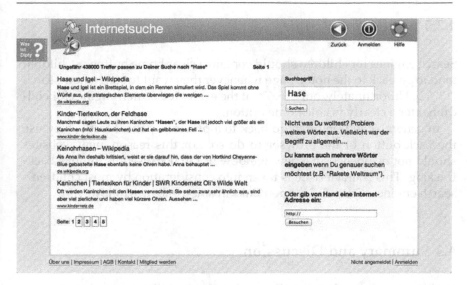

Fig. 4.5: Presentation of the search results in the search engine dipty.com [pub:6].

Spell checking: The best results are obtained in this category. Problems of spelling and typing are taken into account by half of the children's search engines, where three search engines implement their own spell checking tool and three use the Google spell-checking API.

4.2.4 Browsing versus Searching

As discussed above, many researchers agree that selecting pre-defined categories (browsing) better matches the cognitive skills of children than the input of keywords. Half of the evaluated search engines offer this possibility in addition to the keyword search. All other search engines offer only a keyword-oriented interface just like in Google.

4.2.5 Navigational Style

Search engines for children should contain a clear home button as children tend to go back to the home page whenever they want to start a new search [18, 92]. Unfortunately, only 16.6% of the evaluated search engines for children offer a clearly visible home button.

In general, children often go back to a previous page. Mostly, they use the back button of the browser to do so. For this reason, new websites should not be opened in a new window or tab because this inhibits backtracking. This characteristic is taken into consideration by most children's search engines. Only 33.3% open links in a new tab or window.

4.3 Summary and Discussion

In this chapter we describe the results of a usability evaluation we conducted in order to assess how well existing search engines for young users are adapted to their needs. In order to derive the criteria for assessment, we used the findings of previous research. Our work can serve as a starting point to develop a methodology for the usability assessment of web search engines for young users. We suggest using the size of buttons and length of the home page as criteria for assessment as to how well a web search engine matches the motor skills of children. In order to evaluate to what extent current search engines for children support the cognitive skills of children, we advise using such criteria as the type of search tool, support for backtracking and the presentation of search results. A good presentation of search results, in turn, depends on the number of results, font size, multimedia usage, highlighting of keywords and spell checking.

Whereas some criteria are independent of each other, some of them have an inverse relation. There is a tradeoff between the font size, the number of results and scrolling. It is good to have a large font size, not to present too many results on one page and to avoid scrolling. But the larger the font size is, the more space is required to present the results and fewer results can be presented on one page without scrolling. In our opinion, a large font size and an observable number of results are more important than scrolling. Nowadays, children start operating computers and mice very early, and elementary school children most likely can handle the mouse. Unfortunately, we did not find recent research papers that would confirm or reject this hypothesis. Further studies with children are required to establish which of the criteria are more important for children.

The aim of the case study we conducted was to answer the following research question:

RQ3

To what extent are the existing search engines for children appropriate for their motor and cognitive skills?

Our results show that current search engines for children do not always match the skills and abilities of children. We also found that most search engines for children do not offer observable advantages over the common search engine Google. This lack of adaption can lead to the children's frustration during the search. In order to avoid these problems, it is important not only to take child-friendly content into account, but also the search interface itself has to be child friendly, so that children are able to use it without problems.

In addition to good search engines that are designed for children, an underlying web document collection for children is also an essential component in order for children to succeed in their search. However, in this thesis we do not discuss the current usability, quality or amount of websites meant for children. In the time our usability study was conducted, Jochmann-Mannak et al. [95] conducted an investigation in order to estimate to what extent websites for children follow the design conventions. The main difference to our study is that we focused on search engines for children and Jochmann-Mannak et al. studied websites for children which could also contain a search functionality. Their findings indicate that designers of children's websites basically follow general design guidelines, which may be not sufficient for children. Jochmann-Mannak et al. also identified three types of websites for children, i.e. a Classic (with classical aesthetics), a Playful (with expressive aesthetics), and an Image map (expressive aesthetics and navigation based on image maps) type.

In order to design such child-friendly interfaces, more research is needed. Our study offers an overview of the quality of current search engines based on a quantitative analysis. Some questions still require an answer, for example, whether there are real differences between children's and adults' search behaviours. In the following, we are going to verify, enrich and supplement the results of our work through user studies together with children.

Chapter 5

Large-scale Analysis of Children's Queries and Search Interactions

Previous research shows differences between children and adults in their search behaviour [17]. However, these findings were based on small user studies with lab experiments and may not show real life behaviour. Only one research group previously attempted to identify children's queries in a large-scale query log [51]. Here, all queries where the user selected a search result whose domain is listed in the *DMOZ's kids&teens* directory were regarded as child queries. However, there is a significant chance that such pages were clicked by adults by accident. They also define a children's session as one that contains at least one children's query entry, which we do not consider as a good threshold. Additionally, AOL is a broadly used search engine. To our knowledge, this is the first large-scale log study of search behaviour on children's web search engines. The results of the study described in this chapter have been published in [pub:15]. This research is based on data collected by the German Youth Institute[1].

5.1 Dataset

For our analysis we used logfiles of the three major german search engines whose main target group are children from 6 to 13: *Blinde-Kuh.de*, *FragFinn.de, Helles-Koepfchen.de*. The strength of these search engines lies in the retrieval of web documents containing only *child-suitable* content, which means the children are able to understand the content and have no access to "adult" web sites. According to the KIM user study [15], 53% of

---

[1] http://www.dji.de/index.php?id=1276, accessed on 2014-09-17.

the surveyed children know *Blinde-Kuh.de*, 51% know *FragFinn.de* and 31% know *Helles-Koepfchen.de*[2].

The dataset is composed of 2.5 million requests gathered over one week in January 2011. The exact statistics about the sizes of the datasets of each search engine are considered to be a business sensitive information and are not reported here. For the same reason, we aggregated the data from the three search engines in our analysis. The logs contain both *search interaction* and *click-through* records [89]. We specify a query log as the set:

$$Log = \langle\langle u_i, s_i, t_i, q_i, c_i\rangle \mid 1 \leq i \leq n\rangle \qquad (5.1)$$

where u_i, s_i, t_i, q_i, c_i refer to the user information (user agent, geographic information), session ID, time of interaction, submitted query and its details (correction suggestions, total number of hits, list of result URLs with ranking), click-throughs (URL, referrer). Thus, the logs provide insight into interactions with the search engines' user interface: queries, navigation, pages visited before and/or after entering the query and viewings of result pages. Although the logs already contained session data, the session definition was not consistent among all three search engines. We refined the sessions by splitting those which had gaps of more than 15 minutes between session log entries. This is the common approach in logfile analysis, except for some variation of the chosen temporal cutoff parameter (5 to 120 minutes) [88]. The collected data contains a total of 608,162 sessions. Furthermore, for data preparation we parsed the logs from the three search engines and imported the data into a relational database.

5.2 Results

Search engine queries provide an insight into children's information needs. We analysed a total of 725,846 (226,387 unique) queries. Using the *Google Insights for Search* service[3], we compared the most frequent children's queries to the most frequent queries by adults. We retrieved the latter for the same time period and the same location. The most frequent queries of children and adults (translated from German) are shown in Table 5.1.

---

[2] Google is the most well-known search engine among the children from six to thirteen. 97% of the children know Google and 63% know Yahoo [15].

[3] http://www.google.com/insights/search/

rank	children	adults
1	games	facebook
2	sex	youtube
3	electricity	google
4	animals in winter	ebay
5	squirrel	you
6	whale	weather
7	dogs	amazon
8	animals	web.de
9	egypt	gmx

Table 5.1: Most frequent queries from our logs (children) and from Google Insights (adults) during the same period [pub:15].

The results indicate that the information need (in terms of the *Broder taxonomy* [24]) of children differs from that of adults. The children's queries have a more informational intention. The purpose of *informational queries* is to find information about a topic assumed to be available on the web, in order to read about it [24]. Meanwhile, the adults most frequent queries are *navigational* or *transactional*, with the immediate intent to reach a particular website that the user has in mind, or even further carry out some transactions, e.g. purchasing a product [24]. Since children may also use the search engines for homework, queries like "egypt" could reflect the curriculum of their schools.

Figure 5.1(a) presents the distribution of the query length measured in number of words or tokens separated by white-space. Note that the three search engines do not provide query string auto-completion. Queries contain on average 1.8 terms (2.4 for unique queries), whereas queries by adults have between 2.4 and 2.7 terms [66, 182]. Thus, our results contradict previous findings [17, 51] that children would use longer queries on average.

The three search engines combine textual links to search results with images, which also lead to the result web page. This is mainly done due to the belief that pictures attract children's attention more than text. However, our results indicate that the children click on a picture only slightly more often (52%) than on text (48%).

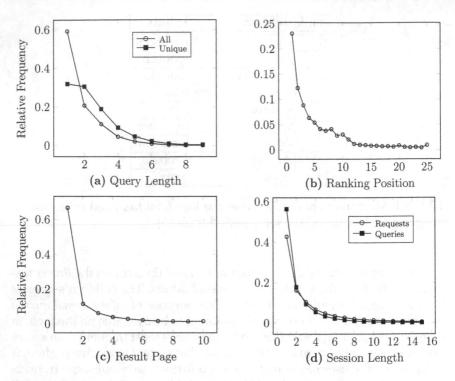

Fig. 5.1: Distributions of relative frequencies of (a) the length of queries in number of words, (b) the ranking position of a clicked result, (c) the number of viewed results' page, and (d) the length of session in both number of all page requests (including queries) and queries only [pub:15].

Figures 5.1(b) and 5.1(c) illustrate how often a query result with rank n is clicked and how often the m_{th} results' page (SERP) is viewed. The search engines provide 10 results per page. Only a few results (2–4) can be seen without scrolling. We found, that most children visited only the first results' page and looked at the first three results. These findings indicate similarity with adult click-through behaviour. More than 70% of the time, adults only view the top ten results [182].

The average session, ignoring identical queries, included about 1.8 queries (Figure 5.1(d)). Most sessions of children consist of one search query. This search behaviour is similar to the web search behaviour of adults: Adult studies found that most web search engine users searched one query per session and an average session included about 1.6 queries [182].

Earlier children studies discovered that children have a *loopy* browsing style, whereas adults' browsing style is *linear* or *systematic* [17] (see Section 3.1). Children are likely to click, repeat searches and revisit the same result web page more often than adults. We found evidence for this behaviour in the percentage of repeated URL clicks within a session given the same query (16.6%) and the percentage of repeated queries within a session (20.5%). Adults repeat roughly 12.4% of queries [30].

Another well known fact is that children have difficulties with spelling [20]. In order to identify spelling errors we used dictionaries such as *Lingua-DE-Wortschatz*[4] and *GNU aspell* dictionary, and checked the occurrence of the query terms. We also did a manual checking based on small random sampling. About 25% (*Lingua-DE-Wortschatz*), 21% (manual checking), 40% (*GNU aspell* dictionary) of all queries contained at least one spelling error. Adults make around 10-15% of spelling errors [37]. This number is significantly less compared to children.

5.3 Summary and Discussion

In order to answer the research questions

> **RQ4a**
>
> What are the differences of a child's and an adult's web information search behaviour with regard to queries and search interactions?

we conducted a large-scale logfile analysis of children's behaviour on targeted web search engines. We compared our findings with previous results about adults' behaviour on common search engines. We did not see any differences in click-through behaviour between children and adults. They both tend to click on the prominent search results. However, we found ev-

---

[4] http://wortschatz.uni-leipzig.de/Webservices/

idence for the "loopy" browsing style of children and spelling errors in queries.

We found that children tend to formulate informational queries while the most frequent queries by adults' are navigational. In contrast to earlier findings, our results show that on average children formulate shorter queries than adults. Short queries indicate that young users may have difficulties with query formulation and finding the right terms. Short queries can be the result of children's problems with typing, i.e. short queries require less typing. Shorter queries also indicate less specific and more ambiguous information needs of children [153]. This makes it harder for children to find the right results. Note that previous research, based primarily on user studies with lab experiments, showed that children tend to use more natural language queries (see Section 3.1) and natural queries are long. However, our logfile analysis shows that on average children produce short queries. In the lab experiments, children were mostly asked to conduct an answer-oriented search for a pre-defined question setting. Thus, children may have simply used the questions for their search without much abstraction.

Our logfile study was conducted in 2011. Later, Duarte Torres and Weber [52] conducted a query log analysis of the commercial web search engine *Yahoo!* to identify the search behaviour of children and young adults between six and 18 years. They used the account information of logged-in users in order to differentiate between users of different ages. Their findings confirm that children use shorter queries (measured in tokens) than adults. Their findings also confirm that younger users and adults tend to click on higher ranked results. Duarte Torres and Weber found that young users have considerably shorter search sessions than adults, which also correlates with a smaller amount of query reformulation. Their results for children's session length measured in number of requests and query refinements are consistent with ours. However, as we only had access to the logfiles for children's search engines, we had no information about adults' search session length for direct comparison. Shorter search sessions of children can be a sign of children becoming frustrated and giving up faster than adults in the case that they do not find the desirable search results. This would confirm the findings of Bilal and Kirby [17]. However, there is also a chance that longer sessions of adults also indicate a more complex information needs resulting in longer sessions. Another, more plausible, explanation might be the fact that children cannot concentrate on a task as long as adults and simply start doing something else earlier than adults [36, 49].

As already mentioned in Section 2.3, logfile analysis has several advantages over other methods in user studies. It offers the chance to analyse a high amount of user data over a longer period of time and presents a collection of evidence about user search behaviour in a natural environment. However, logfile analysis also has some limitations. Logfiles do not contain information about the demographics of the users. We assumed that the users of search engines for children are mostly children. However, concerned parents and teachers may have accessed the search engines as well. Note that even if a small fraction of them accessed the search engines, this is less problematic for general trends, though the actual absolute numbers will be affected.

Chapter 6

Differences in Usability and Perception of Targeted Web Search Engines between Children and Adults

Previous research shows differences between children and adults in their search behaviour. However, these findings were mainly based on observational studies, [e.g. 17], or log file analysis, [e.g. pub:15, 52], and do not provide details about user perception of the search engines' interface elements during information seeking. To complement existing findings eye-tracking devices can be used.

Eye-tracking provides information about users' line of sight at any given time. In the context of a web search, this means that information can be gathered on what web interface elements caught users' attention (*fixations*), for how long (*fixation duration*) and in which order (*scanpaths*) (Figure 6.1). According to Granka et al. [71, p. 348] "a fixation is generally defined as a spatially stable gaze lasting for approximately 200-300 milliseconds, during which visual attention is directed to a specific area of the visual display". The so-called *Strong eye-mind Hypothesis* [98] states that a displayed item that is fixated is also being thought about. The hypothesis holds only if the user's current task requires information from the visual display to be encoded and processed [99], as in the case of an information seeking task. Nevertheless, duration of the gaze provides only an upper bound for the duration of cognitive processes [99]. To summarise, eye-tracker data is very important in order to study the usability of search user interfaces (SUIs) and to design novel search engines for children. It provides information about UI elements that are the most eye-catching, that cause confusion or are ignored altogether.

In this chapter we describe the design and results of an eye-tracking user study with children of primary school age and adults. We study their seeking behaviour and search engine perception during informational and navigational search (in terms of Broder's taxonomy [24]). The purpose of *informational search* is to find information about a topic assumed to be available on the web. Children tend to employ informational search. Adults most frequently employ *navigational* search with the immediate intent to

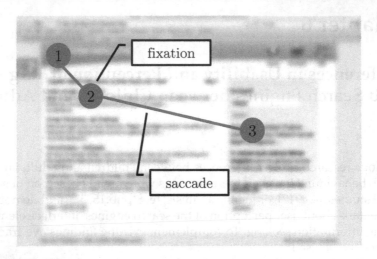

Fig. 6.1: Fixations occur when the eyes focus on a point. Eye movements be-tween the fixations are called saccades. A scanpath ("1-2-3") is a sequence of fixations and saccades. Fixation duration is the length of the stop, when the eyes fixate.

reach a particular website that the user has in mind [pub:15] (see Section 5). Therefore, we study both search variants. We also study the information seeking behaviour not only on a standard search engine (*Google*), but also on a web search engine for children (*Blinde-Kuh.de*).

Our participants are children in third and fourth school grade. At this age, children already have sufficient reading and writing skills to perform the web search, but they are only superficially familiar with web search engines [14]. Therefore, they are an appropriate user group to study how intuitive search engines are. Druin et al. [49] also call these children "de-veloping searchers" who have challenges with spelling, typing, query for-mulation and results interpretation (see Section 3.1).

In summary, the contributions of this user study are threefold:

▶ Using an eye-tracking user study, we analyse the differences in infor-mation seeking behaviour between children and adults during informa-tional and navigational search.

▶ Furthermore, for these two user groups, we compare the information seeking behaviour on two different search engines, i.e. *Google* and a web search engine for children.

▶ Our results provide a deeper understanding of children's search behaviour and perception of search interface elements, so that better search user interfaces for children can be designed in the future.

To our knowledge, this is the first comparative study between children and adults, during both informational and navigational search, on both standard and children's search engine. The results of this study have been published in [pub:2, pub:3].

6.1 Related Work

In this section, we summarise existing eye-tracking user studies about user information seeking behaviour on web search engines. A more general introduction to the usage of eye-tracking in online search is provided by Granka, Feusner, and Lorigo [71].

Granka et al. [72] studied the search behaviour of 36 adults when using *Google* during a task-oriented search given both navigational and informational tasks. The results show that the users spend about equal time to review the first and the second result. After the second result, the fixation time decreases for each following search result. Results ranked 6 to 10 receive approximately equal attention, which can be explained by the fact that these results are placed under the scrolling line. Therefore, Granka et al. consider the rank of a search result to be less relevant when the user starts to scroll. Furthermore, they note that users seldomly click on the seventh result which lies directly below the page break and the scroll border. Users who select the search results with a low rank also tend to read more textual snippets of the search results. The scanning behaviour of users is rather linear as users tend to explore the search results list from top to bottom.

Rele and Duchowski [163] studied the search behaviour of 15 adults during a task-oriented search given both navigational and informational tasks. In particular, they compared a list interface where the results were listed vertically to a tabular interface where each element in the list interface had a corresponding column. The study results show no significant difference in performance or average fixation duration between the two interfaces. The number of fixations in the text descriptions of the search results differs significantly for different types of search tasks: There are more fixations present in the textual snippets given a navigational search task than there are in informational ones. Rele and Duchowski explain this fact as an extensive reading of the snippet content because the navigation tasks are more difficult to solve. An interesting result of the study is that users rather tend to scan within columns and are less likely to shift gaze between the columns. The probability of gaze shift between the same category of result snippets, e.g. from the URL of the first result to the URL of the third one, is larger on the tabular interface.

These two studies provide a detailed quantitative analysis of the distribution of visual attention on search engine results pages (SERPs). There are also studies about visual attention on other aspects of web searches, such as reading. According to Nielsens and Pernice [141], users' reading behaviour across many different web sites and search tasks is almost consistent. It follows a reading pattern in the shape of an "F": in the upper section of the website, users tend to read in the horizontal direction first. This generates the upper bar of "F" shape. After that, the eyes move a little in the direction of the web site bottom followed by eye movement in a second horizontal direction that, however, covers a smaller area than in the first one (people read from left to right and tend to read less of the second area). In this way, the lower horizontal bar of the "F" shape is formed. Finally, the user scans the left web page side in the vertical direction. This scanning can be done slowly and methodically, which appears as a continuous strip on the heat map. On the other hand, the eye movements can also be fast, which leads to a spotty heat map. Nielsen and Pernice [141] also found some variance in visual strategies, e.g. the lower horizontal bar of "F" can be longer than the upper one. This deviation occurs in case the title of the second search result is longer than the title of the first one [45, 141].

Previous user studies with adults also explored different aspects of web search behaviour. For example, Cutrell and Guan [39] studied the influence of the snippet length on users' search behaviour. Adding extra information in the snippets improves the performance significantly in informational search tasks, while the performance in navigational search tasks is best if the snippets are short. Lorigo et al. [122] analysed the influence of gender and task type on Google web searches. The users in the study spent more time solving an informational task than a navigational one. The men explored more search results than the women. Lorigo et al. [121]

surveyed the use of eye tracking to study online search, in particular how users view the ranked results on SERPs and their click-through behaviour. They also conducted a study to compare viewing patterns on the search engines Google and Yahoo!. No differences in terms of search performance and eye movement behaviour were observed between the two search engines. Pan et al. [150] studied the influence of search results' relevance and its ranking position. Users expect the first result to be the most relevant and click on it even when the ranking order in the result list is reversed. Aula et al. [7] studied user's style to evaluate search results. Two types of evaluators were found, economic and exhaustive evaluators. Evaluators with an economic style decide faster about the next move and based on less information than exhaustive ones, therefore being more efficient in search. Buscher et al. [26] studied contemporary search engine elements such as ads and "related" searches. They found that users' attention to ads depends on both task type and ads quality. Joachims et al. [91] evaluated the reliability of implicit feedback generated from click-through data and suggested that clicks are influenced by the relevance of the results, but are biased by the users' trust in the quality of the retrieval function and the result set.

There are several user studies about children's information seeking behaviour, e.g. [17] (seventh grade), [20] (ages 9-12), [92] (ages 8-12), [104] (ages 8-10), [111] (sixth grade). An overview of these studies is given in Section 3.1. To our knowledge there is only one eye-tracking study about children's perception of SERPs. Dinet et al. [45] conducted a user study with young users in the age from 10 to 17 and observed user behaviour on Google SERPs. They suggest that keyword-highlighting and user domain knowledge both influence the users' visual strategies. The results of this study show that the visual exploration of younger children is influenced by highlighting, regardless of prior knowledge of the child and the location of the highlighted terms. The search strategies of older children are affected by highlighting only when the subject of the Web search is unknown. Dinet et al. describe four different search strategies of children:

▶ F-shaped strategy,
▶ Exhaustive strategy, where users read all the information in the result document representative (*surrogate*) before clicking a search result,
▶ Cued visual jumps, where users read one highlighted keyword and then jump to the next one,
▶ F-inverse strategy, where users examine the bottom of the SERP first.

These four strategies are present in all age groups of the users of this study. However, younger children tend to use the "cued visual jumps"-strategy, whereas older children often extensively read the search result's title, snippet and URL. Older kids sometimes also use the "cued visual jumps"-strategy, especially in the case they are not familiar with the search topic or have little knowledge about it.

6.2 User Study

In our study we used *Google* (Fig. 6.2(a)) and the German search engine for children *Blinde-Kuh.de* (Fig. 6.2(b)). Blinde-Kuh.de is often used in German primary schools. Additionally, the search user interface of Blinde-Kuh.de differs from Google's. This makes it an appropriate search engine for children to study. As shown in Figure 6.2(b), Blinde-Kuh.de (BK) offers a keyword search (A) along with navigation in different categories provided on the left side (B). These categories lead to informational pages about the corresponding topic. The search engine presents at most ten results per page as a vertical list. Search results are separated through boxes in contrast to Google where separation is done by whitespace. Each BK surrogate contains a picture (C), textual summary (D), rank (E), information about the result's category (F), the target age group in categories "S", "M", "L", "XL" for children from six to thirteen (G) and does not use any keyword highlighting. To see the BK search result's page, one can click on the title (H), picture or a link below (I).

The main research questions of this study are:

▶ *Are children more successful with Blinde-Kuh than with Google?*
▶ *Do children prefer Blinde-Kuh over Google?*
▶ *Do children and adults have different perception of web search interfaces?*
▶ *Do children and adults employ different search strategies?*

The *Within Participants Design* was used in our study. In particular, we used a two-stage experimental design with two factors: the type of web search engine (standard web search engine and children's web search engine) and the search task type (informational and navigational). We also applied a latin square design, where each participant interacted with both search engines, but in a different order to avoid biases due to usage order, tiredness, etc. We used two informational (Info) and two navigational

(a) Google.de

(b) Blinde-Kuh.de

Fig. 6.2: Screenshot of the studied search engines, taken on 2012-12-18 [pub:2, pub:3]. Letters indicate different user interface elements of Blinde-Kuh.

(Nav) search tasks. Each participant was given one navigational and one informational task. However, due to differences in the provided results between the two search engines and to construct appropriate search scenarios, different search tasks with similar complexity were used for different search engines. The organization of the groups is shown in Table 6.1.

User group	SUI (Task)	SUI (Task)
1	Google (Info-1)	BK (Nav-2)
2	Google (Nav-1)	BK (Info-2)
3	BK (Info-2)	Google (Nav-1)
4	BK (Nav-2)	Google (Info-1)

Table 6.1: *Latin Squares Design* used in the study [pub:3].

Procedure: We tested one participant at a time. Using a structured pre-interview, we gathered the user's demographic data and Internet experience. Users were told that first they would receive search results for a query provided by the study supervisor. Thus, participants began on the same SERP, but were allowed to proceed in any way they chose. Initial SERPs were necessary for the eye-tracking experiment to be able to compare and aggregate users' gaze data. After that, the eye-tracker Tobii Eyetracker T60[1] was calibrated that is integrated in a 17" monitor. Then, each subject received a search task to solve within 10 minutes for each search engine. After each search task, we also asked the participants about their own assessment of search task difficulty and how they liked the search engine's results pages (SERPs). At the end, a structured post-interview about user preferences in the search engines was performed. The questionnaire for children is provided in Appendix A.1.

The search tasks and corresponding initial queries used in the study are presented in Table 6.2. The scope of a task is designed so that it can be solved in a reasonable amount of time, but the solution is not trivial. Initial queries were selected such that they had at least two SERPs, and that the correct answer could be found in one of the first 20 results. For navigational tasks there was only one correct result web page. The initial SERPs contained all important SUI elements. We ensured the search consistency in or-

---

[1] http://www.tobii.com/en/eye-tracking-research/global/products/hardware/tobii-t60t120-eye-tracker/

der for the search conditions to be the same among all participants. In particular, the same SERPs were presented to the users using initial queries. As SUIs could be altered by the search engine owners, we fixed the first two SERPs for the pre-specified queries we used in our study[2]. For this, we used *KImageMapEditor*[3] to set hyperlinks for the search engines' screenshots. The resulting HTML documents had the same characteristics as dynamically generated Google SERPs. After each session, the browser history was automatically deleted to avoid highlighting of previously clicked search results. All browser cookies were automatically deleted to disable the personalisation of search results.

ID	Search task *(Initial Query)*
Info-1	How many animals does the zoo in Magdeburg have? *(Zoo Magdeburg)*
Info-2	What is the name of the largest Saturn moon? *(Saturn Monde)*
Nav-1	Find the homepage of the photographer Michael Jordan. *(Michael Jordan)*
Nav-2	Find the online-game page of ZDF Tivi portal. *(ZDF Tivi)*

Table 6.2: Search tasks and corresponding initial queries used in the study [pub:3].

The user study was conducted in February 2013. We collaborated with a primary school in Biederitz, Germany. 14 children participated in the study. They were between the age of eight and eleven (9.29 on average, $\sigma = 0.73$), 64% were boys. 43% were from third and 57% from fourth grade. 43% of the children use the Internet about once per week. 64% of the pupils use the Internet without any supervision, whereas the rest of the participants are accompanied by their parents or older siblings. 57% of the young participants use the Internet mostly to play online games and to watch videos. 36% also use the Internet to search for information. 7% use the Internet *only* to search for information, for example, to do their homework. More than

---

[2] This procedure was done for Google. The interface of the search engine for children was not modified during the time of the experiment.

[3] http://www.nongnu.org/kimagemap/

80% are familiar with Google and 46% also know BK. Children like both Google and BK because they can provide "a lot of information." Tables B.1, B.3 and B.4 provide more detailed information about the children.

Adults were recruited from an academic and school context. In total, 17 adults participated in the study. They were between 22 and 59 (29.81 on average, $\sigma = 8.93$). 65% were male. 70% of the adults are students in computer science or working in the IT sector. This introduces one side effect. These adults can be considered as search experts, while the children are novices in web search. All the adults use the Internet every day without any supervision. 18% use the Internet only to search for information. The rest also use the Internet for other activities such as chatting etc. All the adult participants usually use Google to search for information. 29% of the adults use other search engines such as Yahoo, Bing or DuckDuckGo along with Google. Adults told us that Google is "concise and user-friendly." It offers "a good balance between speed and quality of search results." Tables B.2, B.3 and B.4 provide more detailed information about the adults.

6.3 Study Results

Search effectiveness: The effectiveness of a user's search describes the degree of success in finding the relevant information or the requested website. We consider not only the fact of finding the result, but also whether a participant required help from the study supervisor telling him what is possible to do next (e.g. formulate a new query, go to the next SERP, view the search results). Table 6.3 shows the calculation of success scores based on two variables, finding the right solution and required help. The best result (4) is achieved when the task is solved without any hints.

Calculation of success scores:	4	3	2	1
Finding the right solution	+	+	-	-
Required help	-	+	-	+

Table 6.3: Calculation of success scores: 4 "very successful", 3 "successful", 2 "less successful" and 1 "not successful" [pub:3].

Fig. 6.3 provides details about participants' success scores. The participants are on average equally successful on both Google and BK, during both informational and navigational search. The data for the children is more dispersed than for the adults. 50% of the children are "successful" in search or have a lower score. This shows that children on average can solve a search task, but not without hints to continue the search. The adults are "very successful" in search and do not require any help. There was only one failure while using BK: This adult did not solve a search task within 10 min, probably due to the unaccustomed search interface (novelty effect). The child who achieved score 1 is a third grade pupil. He uses the Internet rarely and not for search. The child who achieved score 2 is a fourth grade pupil. He uses the Internet under parents supervision and also not for search. Thus, their failures can be due to little search experience. There is a significant difference between children's and adults' success scores (Mann-Whitney-U-test, $p < 0.001$). There is no significant difference between children's search with Google and BK, between children's search during navigational and informational task (Wilcoxon signed-rank test). No significant differences were found for adults.

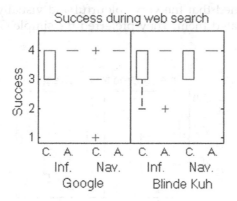

Fig. 6.3: Search effectiveness: boxplots show participants success during the search. Children (C.) are on average "successful" in search and adults (A.) are "very successful" on a scale from 4 - "very successful" to 1 - "not successful" [pub:3].

Search efficiency: We measured the time required by participants to solve the search tasks. As mentioned above, the time for each task was limited to

10 minutes. The results are given in Fig. 6.4. The children needed on average four times longer to solve a search task (298 seconds versus 76 on average). There is a significant difference between children's and adults' search times (t-test, $p < 0.001$). This can be explained by the fact that children read slower than adults [25]. Children also have more difficulties when trying to determine the relevance of results [17, 92], which also results in longer times for children.

The data for the children is more dispersed than for the adults. On average, the children required more time to solve informational search tasks. This is consistent with the fact that more reading within web documents is required to solve an informational task. Navigational tasks are faster to solve because the hints in the title or URL are usually sufficient to successfully navigate to the required web page. The data for children is more dispersed for the search with BK than with Google and for informational search than for navigational one. There is also a significant difference between adult's search times with BK and with Google ($p < 0.05$; on average 114 seconds with BK and 45 with Google), however no significant differences were found for children. The difference for adults can be due to the lack of familiarity with the children's search engine. In addition, the adult participants claimed that the very colourful and visually overloaded design of BK frustrated them. They preferred the simple Google user interface.

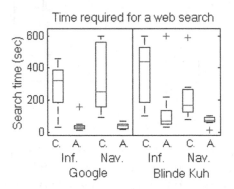

Fig. 6.4: Search efficiency: boxplots show the search time to solve a given search task. Children (C.) require on average four times longer than adults (A.) to solve a search task [pub:3].

Difficulty estimation: After each search task the participants were asked to provide information about how difficult the task was using a five-point Likert scale. We used a five-point smiley scale for children called smiley-ometer [161]. The children estimated their searches as easy on average, while adults found the searches even easier, especially when using Google. There is no difference in children's difficulty estimation between BK and Google.

Search engine preference: According to the post-interview, all the adults and 58% of the children prefer to use Google. The children's preference of Google search engine is consistent with Druin et al. [47] who found that children's perception of Google was quite positive. The children like the SERPs of both search engine equally well. The adults rate the SERPs of BK as moderate and Google's as good on average. The children liked that BK is "lovely and colourful", has "not only text, but also pictures" and offers "a lot of information for children." One child positively mentioned that one "can not only search but also use many other features" of BK (e.g. many categories). Two children found the query suggestions of Google to be helpful. One child had difficulties to find the search box on Google. Children also found it "great that the (Google) SERP has videos." The adults told us that Google's SERPs are "well-structured" and "clearly arranged." They liked the query completion function of Google. However, especially for navigational search, the textual summaries were too short. Adults told us that the SERPs of BK are "very unclear and contain many elements that distract from the actual search", "chaotic" and have a "cluttered layout." Furthermore, according to the adults opinion BK SERP "images contain unclear information." The adults positively mentioned that the SERPs of BK offer meta information about search results such as preview, categories etc.

Visual perception: In order to analyse the participants' perception of SERPs we created *heat maps*. Unfortunately, not all the eye-tracking data is useable as children are very agile and some of them moved too close to the monitor during the session for the eye-tracker to capture their eye movements. Our analysis is based on 11 young users and 17 adults. Fig. 6.5, 6.6, 6.7 and 6.8 show several aggregated heat maps both for children and adults, i.e. accumulated number of fixations from all the selected test persons. Regions in red indicate a high number of fixations, whereas green regions indicate very few fixations, with varying levels in between. The heat maps show a difference between the children's and the adults' search behaviour.

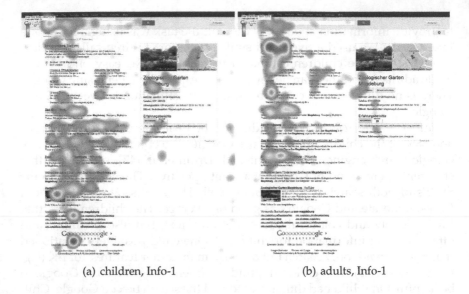

    (a) children, Info-1   (b) adults, Info-1

Fig. 6.5: Aggregated heat maps for Google with informational search [pub:3]. Children's heat maps contain a large cluster of fixations in the middle of SERPs, whereas adults' heat maps show a high number of fixations at the top of SERPs.

On both search engines, the heat maps for children contain relatively closely spaced circular colour-highlighted areas that are spread across all titles of the search results list. This scan pattern indicates a partial reading of the search results' titles. Furthermore, there are visual jumps from a highlighted word in the title to the next one available. Due to this reading style, relevant information can be overlooked, so that children often navigate to the second SERP. Our findings are consistent with Dinet, Bastien, and Kitajima [45] who found a tendency towards a cued visual jump strategy of younger children. However, we also found that children tend to scan the whole result list using jumps between highlighted words, especially in titles.

During navigational search the children paid more attention to snippets than during informational search for both Google and BK. This can be explained by the fact that navigation tasks require an extensive reading of the snippet content [163]. The adults only fixated on the first search results.

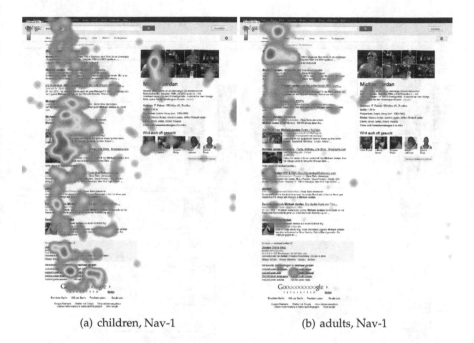

(a) children, Nav-1   (b) adults, Nav-1

Fig. 6.6: Aggregated heat maps for Google with navigational search [pub:3]. Children paid more attention to media elements such as pictures and video elements embedded in a search result than adults.

The fixation areas get smaller for results ranked lower in the list. This pattern is consistent with the F-shaped strategy [141]. In case the answer is not found within the first search results, the adults reformulated the query. This behaviour is similar to the depth-first strategy of processing search result lists described by Klöckner, Wirschum, and Jameson [106].

Children's strategy of processing search result lists is more like the breadth-first strategy [106]. Young users exhaustively explored all the results in the first SERP and used the navigation buttons between results pages to continue further examination. We assume that navigation is easier for children than query modification since children's low capacity for abstraction [154] makes it difficult for children to create their own queries. Children reformulated the query mostly on the second SERP. Overall, there

(a) children, Info-2   (b) adults, Info-2

Fig. 6.7: Aggregated heat maps for Blinde-kuh with informational search [pub:3]. Children explored the results on the first SERP and used the navigation buttons between results pages to continue further examination. In case the answer is not found within the first search results, the adults reformulated the query.

(a) children, Nav-2   (b) adults, Nav-2

Fig. 6.8: Aggregated heat maps for Blinde-kuh with navigational search [pub:3]. Children looked at the navigational menu with categories on the surface of the Blinde-kuh, but adults did not.

is no significant difference in the number of query reformulations (children: 1.69 on average, $\sigma = 1.702$; adults: 1.18 on average, $\sigma = 1.629$).

On both search engines, children paid more attention to media elements such as pictures and video elements embedded in a search result than adults. On Google, children's heat maps contain a large cluster of fixations in the middle of SERPs, whereas adults' heat maps show a high number of fixations in the top of SERPs. Google provides query suggestions placed on the bottom of the page. However, only children paid attention to query suggestions.

In contrast to Google, the BK search engine also provides thumbnails for nearly every search result and uses no highlighting of keywords. The heat map of BK shows a Γ-shaped scanning strategy of children within a search surrogate as children tend to scan the title and look at the web page picture. Adults did not fixate thumbnails as much as children do. Spotty and closely spaced coloured areas in the titles of search results indicate a partial reading by children, the same as for Google. Children fixated informative words, e.g. "television broadcasting" or "tivi online" in the title, but also in the snippet and the link of a search result. The links in the search results, for example the link with the words "Next to Space Agents", were barely perceived by children.

In contrast to adults children looked at the navigational menu with categories on BK. Some children even clicked on the category "Games" that is related to their navigational task to find the online-game page of the ZDF Tivi portal. Both children and adults had difficulties to determine what parts of BK result surrogates are clickable. Probably the box around a surrogate led them to believe that the whole area is clickable.

Relative fixation duration: Fig. 6.9 shows the distribution of the fixation duration depending on the rank of a search result[4]. The adults looked longest at the first result. There is a trend that the higher the results' rank number the less time the adults spent to review it. Overall, children's fixation time did not correlate with the search results' rank, but rather with search results' relevance clues such as highlighted words in the snippet (see the 4th result for informational search in Google), informative words in the title (see the 9th and 10th result for information search in Blinde-Kuh) or embedded media such as Youtube videos (see the 7th result for informational search in Google). No significant differences were

---

[4] The SERP for Google's informational search had only seven results. The first result contained shortcuts into the result website. Therefore, the fixation time for this result is twice as long as for the first results of other SERPs.

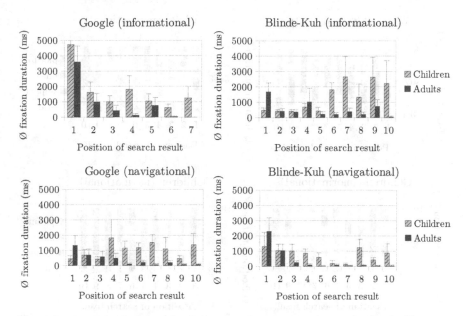

Fig. 6.9: Average fixation duration for the ten search results [pub:3].

found for children and adults in the distribution of time (two-sample Kolmogorov–Smirnov test).

Fig. 6.10 shows average fixation duration for different surrogate elements of Blinde-Kuh such as link, title, snippet and picture (BK surrogates do not contain the URL). The children spent more time looking at pictures than the adults, especially in navigational search. This difference between children and adults in navigational search is significant (t-test, p < 0.01). The children fixated on the title longer during an informational search and the picture during a navigational one. The adults fixated on the title, the snippet and the picture equally long during informational search, while the title was fixated on longer during navigational search. However, this difference is not significant.

Scanning strategy: In order to analyse the participants' scanning strategy of SERPs we created gaze plots. A gaze plot is a map which shows the eye movement sequence, i.e. the gaze fixations on a webpage and in which order they occur. According to Lorigo et al. [122] there are three types of scanning sequences or scanpaths: nonlinear scanning, linear scanning, and

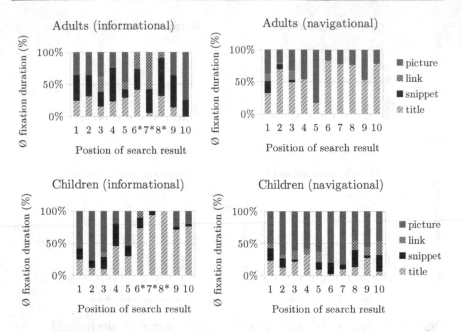

Fig. 6.10: Proportion of average fixation duration for different surrogate elements of Blinde-Kuh such as link, title, snippet and picture. Surrogates that contain no picture are marked with * [pub:3].

strictly linear scanning (see also [71]). Nonlinear scanning implies that the search results are viewed not in a rank induced sequence order, but randomly. Linear scanning means that the search results are viewed sequentially, i.e. a result of rank n is not viewed until all results of a smaller rank have also been seen. However regressions to previously visited results are possible. Strictly linear scanning obeys the rank order and has no regressions to earlier surrogates.

We manually reviewed the individual gaze plots obtained in the study. Scanpath sequences of the adults are relatively short (they only review the first results), while children's scanpath sequences are long and appear chaotic (see Fig. 6.11). During the search with Google, all young users in our study employ the nonlinear scanning strategy, reviewing the results in a random order, but sometimes returning to results which they already viewed. The adults' reading is more linear (40% of adult searches with

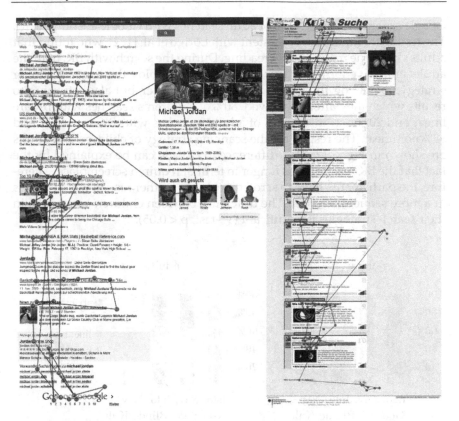

Fig. 6.11: Example of a child's gaze plot during navigational search with Google (left). The scanpath sequence mapped to rank values is "6 − 7 − 6 − 5 − 4 − 2 − 4 − 2 − 3 − 4 − 2 − 1 − 2 − 1 − 4 − 5 − 6 − 7 − 8 − 9 − 10 − 11 − 6 − 7" [pub:3]. Embedded videos of the 6th and 7th search result are fixated first. Example of the same child's gaze plot during informational search with Blinde-Kuh (right). The scanpath sequence mapped to rank values is "1 − 2 − 1 − 2 − 3 − 1 − 2 − 3 − 4 − 5 − 6 − 5 − 6 − 7 − 8 − 7 − 8 − 9 − 10". The picture of the first search result is primarily fixated.

Google are strictly linear, 60% of adult searches with Google are nonlinear). The results for adults are consistent with Lorigo et al. [122], who found that adults skip some results while reading. During the search with BK, both the adults and the children in our study tend to employ the linear scanning strategy: reviewing the results in a sequential order, but also returning to results which they already viewed. 80% of children's searches with BK are linear and 20% nonlinear. 67% of adults' searches with BK are linear and 33% nonlinear. The results for the scanning strategy of children and adults are shown in Fig. 6.12. This difference to Google can be explained by the fact that the BK results list is longer in term of required screen place. Therefore, the participants have to scroll more to see further results which results in a more sequential order. The difference between children and adults in their search strategies is significant (χ^2-test, $p < 0.05$).

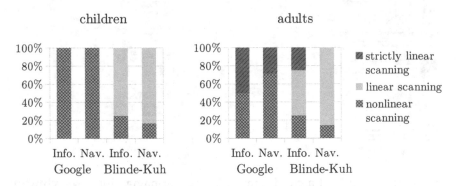

Fig. 6.12: Scanning strategy of the children (left) and of the adults (right) using the classification of Lorigo et al. [122].

6.4 Summary and Discussion

We conducted an eye-tracking user study with children of primary school age and adults to study their seeking behaviour and search engine perception during informational and navigational search, on two different search engines.

> **RQ4b**
>
> What are the differences of a child's and an adult's web information search behaviour with regard to search performance?

Based on the findings of this study we can answer this research question as follows: We found that children require four times longer to solve a search task than adults, are less successful in their searches and need assistance. The large search times of children in comparison to adults indicate the need to mitigate children's difficulties in reading which can be done by text simplification.

We also found that the very colourful and visually cluttered design of BK frustrated the adult participants and the frustration even led to a decrease in search efficiency. The difference between Google and BK for adults can be also due to the lack of familiarity with the children's search engine. For children, we found no difference in search effectiveness and efficiency between Google and BK, both in informational and navigational searches. Our results are consistent with Jochmann-Mannak et al. [92] who found that the children did not perform better on interfaces designed for them than on Google.

Children tend to prefer BK a little less than Google. The children's preference of Google is consistent with Druin et al. [47] who found that children's perception of Google was quite positive. The adults in our study strongly prefer Google.

> **RQ4c**
>
> What are the differences of a child's and an adult's web information search behaviour with regard to perception of search engine result pages?

We found differences in the perception of search engines SERPs between children and adults. User interface elements such as thumbnails and embedded media attracted the children's attention much more than adults. Thus, the children in our study relate to the *visual searcher* role using the classification of Druin et al. [49]. Visual searchers prefer to search using visual information. Though BK provides pictures, they are apparently not well selected as they do not lead to an improvement in children's performance. Therefore, we suggest that those elements be only used in SERPs if they provide better relevance cues so as to improve children's information processing flow.

Furthermore, there is a difference in the distribution of fixation durations between adults and children. There is a negative correlation between the rank of a search result and the fixation duration of adults. However, children's fixation time rather correlates with search results' relevance clues or embedded media. This also confirms the need to provide better relevance cues in media and texts for children. The children only partially read the results' snippets. Therefore, it may be unnecessary to present a long text in each snippet of a search result. Instead, snippets should be short and provide relevant typographical cues to avoid frustration when reading long texts and to help children in finding relevant information. The children also used navigational elements and at least looked at (some also used) the menu with categories, while adults did not. Therefore, these elements should be part of a search engine as they support children who have difficulties when trying to formulate a new query.

RQ4d

What are the differences of a child's and an adult's web information search behaviour with regard to search strategies?

Adults and children employed different search strategies. The children's strategy for processing of search result lists is similar to the breadth-first strategy: They exhaustively explored all the results in the first SERP. Adults only viewed the first results and then reformulated the query. There is also a difference between adults and children in their result scanning style on Google: children viewed the results in a random order, while adults scanned the results in rank order.

The study has some limitations in the sampling nature and sampling size. The young participants of the study were from a more generic population (a school class) than the adults (related to IT). Despite the fact that our results for adults are consistent with other research conducted with larger and more heterogeneous user groups, e.g. the F-shaped strategy of adults [141], complimentary user studies with both larger sample and more general adult population could lead to additional findings.

Part III
Tackling the Challenges

Chapter 7

Search User Interface Design for Children

Based on the user studies previously conducted by other researchers (Section 3.1), theories of human development (Section 2.2), and the findings from our user studies (Part II), in this chapter we derive conceptual challenges when designing web SUIs for children. We also discuss the possible solutions for these challenges and demonstrate some of them in a novel user interface called *Knowledge Journey* (Section 7.2). The evaluation of the *Knowledge Journey* interface is described in Section 7.3. We also conduct a user study in order to investigate the potential of voice controlled interactions. The results are presented in Section 7.4.

7.1 Conceptual Challenges and Possible Solutions

In the following we underline seven challenges in the design of web search user interfaces for children and propose feasible solutions. A part of this analysis has been published previously [pub:8, pub:13, pub:14]. In our analysis of previous studies and of our own research, the following challenges have emerged:

▶ *Emotional Support:* Based on Erickson's theory of psychosocial development [62] children require emotional support and a feeling of success (see Section 2.2.3). Children are frustrated by too many search results [92] and give up faster than adults in case they do not find the desired search results or if a failure emerges [17]. Children's search sessions are shorter than of adults with a smaller number of query reformulation (Chapter 5, [52]). This behaviour of children is a possible indicator of a greater level of frustration of young users.

So far, the problem of emotional support was not covered in Human-Compu-ter Interaction in Information Retrieval (HCIR) for young users. In case of an ideal search engine children would always be satisfied with the search results and would not get frustrated. Until this ideal search engine is developed we suggest supporting children during their search. This can be achieved for example through proper guidance. The idea here is to provide children with enough help during their search process to avoid frustration. We propose building a guidance figure that captures children's failures, e.g. getting no results or spelling mistakes, and explain how to do better. In contrast to adults, less experienced young users, and thus those who especially require support, are willing to read instructions and would pay attention to well-designed help instructions [140]. Furthermore, spoken instructions would be appreciated by children whose reading skills are not well developed.

In order to automatically detect children's emotional states, we can also analyse user's facial expressions and speech. Emotion recognition during the search makes it possible to react not only in cases of obvious failure. Emotion detection is a promising approach especially in the case of young users as they do not have a fully developed ability to control their facial expressions [28]. However, facial recognition would require a camera and good lighting conditions. Children also use impoliteness and insult more frequently than adults when interacting with spoken dialog system [194], thus making it easier to identify emotional states.

▶ *Language Support:* Children, especially in the primary school age, read slowly and are still learning to write [186]. Additionally, children have a limited domain knowledge [85] and have difficulties with typing using a keyboard [179]. This results in problems with query formulation and spelling errors (Chapter 5, [17]). Children use too generic or too specific (natural language) queries [17]. On average, children formulate shorter queries than adults (Chapter 5, [52]). Short queries indicate that young users may have difficulties with query formulation and finding the right terms. This makes it harder for children to find the right results. Thus, spelling correction and query suggestion mechanisms in keyword based search tools are important. Furthermore, a search UI for children should provide different possibilities for children to formulate their information need. Previous research addresses this problem by suggesting alternative ways for query formulation like using a predefined term dictionary in *JuSe* [157] or a set of tangible objects which represent the search terms in *TeddIR* [90] (see Section 3.2).

As children pay attention to a category menu (see Chapter 6), we can combine catalogue and query oriented search. We suggest using a menu with various categories that correspond to children's typical information needs. This menu should be image based and audio supported to support dual information coding [148], thus allowing ergonomic and fast navigation. Besides navigating using the menu, we also suggest to provide the opportunity of keyword-oriented search supported by spelling correction mechanisms. In this way, children can choose how they want to start searching. With an increasing domain knowledge (possibly gained through navigation in categories) children can employ keyword-oriented search more effectively.

Our user study (Chapter 6) shows that children require much more search time in comparison to adults. This might be an indicator for children's difficulties in reading. This problem can be mitigated by text simplification. Additionally, the presentation form of search results should be understandable with respect to the cognitive capabilities of children. Our study (Chapter 6) also shows that children are more visual searchers. Therefore, visual clues in search results are important. For example, each result item may contain a thumbnail (website image). A novel approach to visualise search results for children that supports visual searchers is elaborated in Chapter 9.

▶ *Cognitive Support:* According to theories of human cognitive development, human development occurs in a sequential order in which new knowledge, abilities and skills build upon the previously acquired ones [146]. Piaget [154] describes four development stages (see Section 2.2.1). Children in primary school age are in the concrete operational stage of development. They just learn to reason logically and have difficulties with thinking abstractly. Their understanding is limited to concrete and physical concepts. The children's low capacity for abstraction [154] is a possible explanation for the fact that children do not use advanced search syntax like *boolean operators* (which require logical thinking) and use natural language queries if the search question is given to them, e.g. in a school setting [17].

In order to help children understand the functionality of a search user interface, metaphors can be employed. Metaphors used in the user interface should be familiar to children and have a connection to the physical world which is also advised in [25]. When designing a catalogue oriented search engine, it is important to create categories which match the cognitive abilities of children. The categories should not be abstract and the category menu should have a shallow hierarchical structure [12, 85].

▶ *Memory Support:* According to the information processing theory [102], the information processing of children differs from the adults' in terms of how they apply information and what memory limits they have. Children can hold and process less information (see Section 2.2.2). Information retrieval is a mentally intensive task and may cause children's memory overload. Due to memory overload, children can forget previous actions, like the queries they already used or which documents contained relevant information. This explains children's "looping" behaviour during the information seeking process. Children click, repeat searches and revisit the same result web page more often than adults (Chapter 5, [17]). It is important to show a clear back-button or just present the search result in the same window (e.g. using frames) to prevent children from getting lost. In our opinion, the aspect of memory support is not covered by the current research and researchers should pay more attention to it. Research would benefit from new approaches in *personal information management* for children. To support children's memory recall we suggest providing a built-in history and a result storage functionality. Besides the memory support, these mechanisms are important for children as part of an educational process. Children can learn to plan their searches and better understand the workings of a search system by revisiting their own search history.

Children's mostly non-linear scanning strategy of search results in contrast to the more linear scanning strategy by adults might be also a sign of memory overload (Chapter 6). Therefore, other visualisation types for search results may be more beneficial for children. Akkersdijk et al. [3] suggest displaying the results using a *Coverflow*. Coverflow is an animated graphical user interface that allows a user to browse the search results horizontally by flipping through snapshots of documents. Coverflow allows users to concentrate on one item at a time, thus, reducing the cognitive load. Its central element is clearly separated from the rest. It also does not require complex interactions.

▶ *Interaction Support:* Children's performance in pointing movements, e.g. using a mouse, is lower than that of adults [27, 82]. Children's motor skills should be supported by graphical user interfaces, e.g. with large elements/buttons and simple interactions. The search user interface should prefer simple point-and-click interactions and clickable interface elements should be large enough to be hit easily [25]. Furthermore, touch interaction can be more natural for children than the use of a mouse. An alternative to a tactile input would be voice-control. It is possible to design a voice-controlled search interface that allows a voice interaction in both directions, voice input and output. In case of a voice-controlled search, the system would also be able to analyse the emotional state of the user and guide the user more accurately. We are going to explore the potential of a voice-controlled SUI for young users in Section 7.4.

▶ *Relevance Judgment Support:* Children also have difficulties to judge the relevance of the retrieved documents to their information need [92]. Children do not have the ability to determine the most relevant and "best" documents [111]. Therefore, children should be supported in the judgment of results' relevance, e.g. using a child-suitable form of result presentation. Each result item should at least have a representative image and a title as children pay attention especially to those elements (Chapter 6). In our study, Chapter 6, we found that children require more search time and are less successful than adults. Though the search engine for children provided pictures, these pictures were apparently not well selected as they did not lead to an improvement in children's performance. Therefore, as multimedia attracts children's attention (Chapter 6), those elements should be only used in SERPs if they provide better relevance cues so as to improve the children's information processing flow. In order to support children in estimating the relevance of search results, it is important to understand the children's view on web pages, what features of a web page are important for children and how they would visualise them. We are going to conduct an investigation in order to answer these questions in Chapter 9.

▶ *Diversity Support:* Children undergo relatively fast changes in cognitive skills, fine motor skills and other abilities in comparison to adults [102]. Their abilities are developing. Furthermore, the abilities of a particular child may be different from those of another child even of the same age. As already mentioned in Section 2.2, the age boundaries of human development stages are approximate and the exact age may vary from child to child. This imposes a further requirement on the search user interface: The search user interface has to cover the needs of individual young users. Since user characteristics change rapidly, design requirements change rapidly as well and a flexible modification of the SUI is needed. In order to tackle this issue, we propose to adapt the search user interface to the needs of each individual user. The solution, which we named an *evolving search user interface*, is described in detail in Chapter 8.

7.2 Knowledge Journey Design

We considered the challenges for user interface design and developed a search user interface for children called *Knowledge Journey (KJ)*[1] [pub:13] in order to demonstrate intuitive and relatively simple solutions (see Table 7.1). In Knowledge Journey, we use multimedia elements in the UI design to make the appearance attractive for children. We also take into account that all clickable items are of appropriate size. We use font sizes larger or equal to 14 pt. KJ uses the metaphor of a treasure hunt where a user takes a journey to gather relevant search results. The interface of KJ is shown in Fig. 7.1. It consists of five groups of elements: a guidance figure (here a penguin pirate), a treasure chest, a coverflow visualisation of results, elements for keyword search and a pie-menu for navigation. In the following we describe each element group.

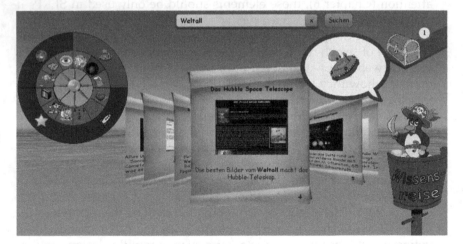

Fig. 7.1: Screenshot of the *Knowledge Journey* user interface: a guidance figure and a treasure chest on the right hand side, query input elements on the top, a navigation menu on the left hand side and a coverflow with search results in the middle [pub:13, pub:14].

---

[1] Ina Bosse [stud:1] helped to design and implement an early version of *Knowledge Journey*.

Guidance Figure: In order to start a "Knowledge Journey" a child selects a guidance figure. The guidance figure concept is familiar to children from computer games where avatars are common. It allows individual user personalisation by providing different figures for different user preferences. The guidance figure supports the children's search process in order to avoid frustration: in the current version it provides a spelling correction after a misspelled query is submitted and enlarges images of menu categories providing animations (Fig. 7.1). A further possible function of the guidance figure is an explanation of how to search and what to do in case of finding no results.

Navigation Menu: In order to support children who have difficulties in query formulation, a category menu is offered. There are different types of menus. We used a pie menu as it can be operated with simple point-and-click interactions and presents a good overview of available categories. The pie menu is placed on a steering wheel. We use the metaphor that a steering wheel is used to define the search coordinates in order to provide a search direction. Initially the top categories of the menu are shown (see Fig. 7.2b). We chose menu categories like entertainment, sports and hobbies, history, universe, geography, nature, persons etc., as they meet the information needs of children [120]. Each category has a number of subcategories. Hutchinson et al. [85] confirm that children can comfortably use a two-level hierarchical organised menu for browsing. Corresponding subcategories are opened when a child clicks on a top-level category. Mousing over the category triggers an action of the guidance figure, i.e. it shows a large animation to explain the category. Icons are used to indicate categories because images better match the cognitive skills of children than written words [75]. They also make the user interface more attractive as children prefer colourful designs with multimedia content [136, 112, 25]. In addition, we provide tooltip text and audio support. When placing the mouse long enough on a pie menu item, a voice explanation is played telling what category is selected. Users can also hide the menu by clicking in the middle of it. Then, only the wheel is shown (see Fig. 7.2a). The menu can be opened again by clicking on the wheel. If a child clicks a category it receives results visualised as a coverflow. The category name is also placed as a text in the search input field.

Result Presentation: The result presentation is shown in Fig. 7.1. We use a coverflow where each item is presented on a papyrus roll that contains the webpage title on top, its thumbnail (preview) in the middle, a textual summary and a result rank according to the relevance at the bottom. A

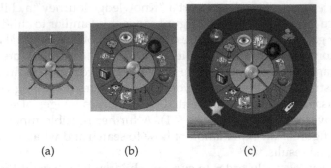

(a)   (b)   (c)

Fig. 7.2: Screenshot of the user interface: navigation menu on a steering wheel in three different levels ((a) closed, (b) opened, (c) opened with 2nd hierarchy level) [pub:13, pub:14].

Conceptual challenges	Design solutions
Emotional Support	guidance figure, personalisation
Language Support	navigation menu, spelling suggestion, audio tooltip
Cognitive Support	metaphor of a treasure hunt, menu categories, shallow menu structure
Memory Support	results storage, coverflow
Interaction Support	simple point-and-click interactions, appropriate font size, appropriate size of clickable UI elements
Relevance Support	thumbnails
Diversity Support	—

Table 7.1: Correspondence table between design solutions in *Knowledge Journey* and conceptual challenges.

child can interact with our coverflow using simple point-and-click operations. It can open a webpage by clicking on the result item that is in focus or switch to the next or previous page by clicking on an item that is not in focus. Children consider larger areas of the UI to be clickable [pub:2]. Therefore, the whole papyrus roll area is clickable and thus easy to hit. We decided to open a webpage in the same window using a frame as results opened in a new window or tab inhibit backtracking with the browser's back button (see Fig. 7.3). In order to return to the search a child clicks on the "X"-Button. They can also store a webpage using a "+"-Button.

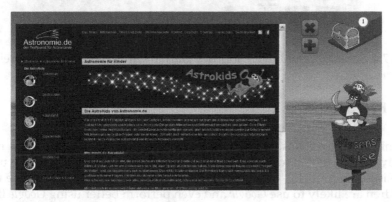

Fig. 7.3: Screenshot of the UI: website (here astronomie.de) opens in a frame.

Result Storage: A child can store relevant results in the "treasure chest". This form of storage aims to support children's memory to prevent cognitive overload. The number of stored results is shown near the chest. Furthermore, we use physical concepts like the size of the chest to show the amount of "treasure", i.e. a chest icon becomes larger with each additional stored result (compare Fig. 7.1 and 7.4). By clicking on the chest, a journey journal opens (Fig. 7.4). We use a book metaphor, where each page spread of the book contain information about a stored webpage: its thumbnail, a textual summary and a title. A child can add notes to each website. He or she can also open the website again by clicking on its picture in the book. If a child does not like a website anymore, he or she can remove it by clicking on the "-"-Button. Tiles in the form of small website thumbnails (below the journal) are used to navigate within the book.

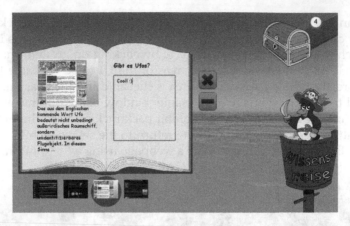

Fig. 7.4: Screenshot of the UI: journey journal with favourite web pages.

7.3 Evaluation

In this section we describe the design and results of a comparative user study we conducted to evaluate the usability of *KJ*. The results have been published in [pub:13]. The results of a recent user study [92] indicate that children are likely to use *Google* and even perform better using *Google* than on search engines designed for them. This is why we compared the *SUI* of *KJ* in our evaluation with a classic keyword-oriented *SUI* we called *Google-like (GL)*. Thus, we used the *GL* search user interface as a baseline. We fixed the underlying search engine, i.e. used the same backend for both SUIs. In this way, the results of comparison are not biased by the underlying index or ranking algorithms, which can happen if the SUIs of two different search engines are compared. In this first user study our goal was to evaluate one of the usability aspects, namely user satisfaction. The following research questions were investigated in the user study:

▶ What search user interface do young children prefer and why?
▶ What are children's attitudes towards new interface elements like the guidance figure, audio support, pie menu and treasure chest?
▶ How can both user interfaces be improved?

7.3.1 Study Design

We build a classic keyword-oriented SUI which is shown in Fig. 7.5. It offers a keyword-oriented search and presents search results as a vertical list of snippets. Each snippet has a title, a URL of the website and a textual summary. For the backend we used $Solr^2$ together with $Nutch^3$ to create a search index and provide keyword-oriented search. Our index contained 60 web documents[4] crawled from web portals for children. In addition, for each menu category we manually selected the corresponding web pages which we added to the results list. Users received the same results whether they clicked on a menu item or typed the category's name in the input field. We also implemented the spelling correction feature using $Solr$ in both SUIs.

Our user study was designed as follows: we used a pre-interview to gather users' demographic information and their Internet experience. Then a lab experiment was performed using the *KJ* and *GL* SUIs. Finally, we asked the participants what user search interface they preferred. We used a *latin square design* in our lab experiment part, i.e. half of the participants were asked to use the Google-like interface first and then to use KJ, whereas another half did this in reverse sequence. The latin square design [81] is used to reduce the bias due to the order in which the participants use the UI. In addition, we took notes about participants UI usage. The participants from the first half were first introduced to the Google-like interface, were ask to perform a task-oriented search and to show the web pages where they found the answers. After that, they were interviewed about UI features that they liked or disliked the most and what could be done to improve the UI. Then, these participants were introduced to the KJ interface. We also presented a short tutorial video about KJ and gave children the opportunity to explore KJ themselves. The participants were asked to perform a task-oriented search using KJ and show the web pages where they found the answers. The same questions as for the Google-like UI were asked about KJ. Another half of the participants started with the KJ UI whereas the procedure remained the same. The questionnaire for the structured interview with children is provided in Appendix A.2.

---

[2] http://lucene.apache.org/solr/

[3] http://nutch.apache.org/

[4] These were also documents relevant to our search tasks.

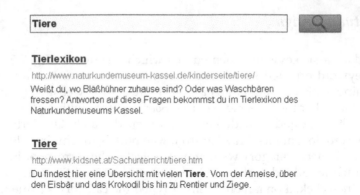

Fig. 7.5: Classic keyword-oriented search user interface [pub:13].

We used search tasks during the lab experiment as we believe a specified task helps the participants to better explore the system including its UI. Nevertheless, we provided participants with help as the focus of the study was the evaluation of the users' attitude towards the UIs and the time per participant was limited to 20 minutes[5]. As we were limited in time, a good balance between time and the right level of complexity was crucial. It was also important that the task was interesting for children and they did not know the answer in advance. Based on those requirements, we used two search tasks of the same degree of complexity, one task per UI:

▶ *Task 1:* Is it colder in the Arctic Circle on the Earth or on the planet Jupiter?

▶ *Task 2:* Is it hotter on the planet Venus or in deserts on the Earth?

A user could answer the question by performing two separate searches: to find the temperature on the planet and on Earth and compare both values. It was possible to find an answer by using the navigation menu of KJ or by employing the keyword-oriented search which was available in both UIs. We also varied the task-UI from participant to participant.

---

[5] This time limit is conformant with the guidelines for usability testing with children (see Section 2.3.3). Additionally, the time limit was necessary due to the user study environment. This evaluation was conducted during a public event.

7.3.2 Study Results

Fig. 7.6: Young girl participating in the user study. [Photo by Hans-Knud Arndt.]

The user study was conducted in June 2012 during the seventh *Long Night of Sciences* event in Magdeburg, Germany. Our 28 participants were of age seven to twelve (average 9.6 years), 14 female and 14 male. They were mostly third (nine children), fourth (eight children) and fifth (seven children) grade pupils (see Fig. 7.6). All the participants had Internet experience. The distribution according to the frequency of the Internet usage is following: everyday (two pupils), two-four times a week (twelve pupils), once a week (nine pupils), once a month (five pupils). We noticed no significant correlation between the frequency of use and age or school grade. 18 participants use the Internet without supervision, seven participants use it with relatives and three participants do both from time to time. All the fifth and sixth grade participants use the Internet without supervision. The children use the Internet mostly to play online games and watch videos on Youtube, but also to search information for school. These activities were mentioned by almost all participants. Some of them also chat. In order to search for information 26 participants use *Google*. Only five participants use also search engines for children. Tables B.5, B.6 and B.7 provide more detailed information about the children.

We noticed that the children had difficulties operating the keyboard and used hunt-and-peck. The participants had no big problems with scrolling operations. Many children's search queries consisted of a group of keywords like "cold planet Jupiter". However, six children (21%) put the whole question as a search query which is known as a type of natural language query. We also noticed the signs of backtracking problems and confusion (see Section 3.1) when users used the Google-like UI where the results where opened in a new tab. When scanning a web page for results many children had difficulties when trying to locate the relevant information on the page. Children were impatient and often skipped the page without trying to read it carefully. Note that our search tasks were to compare temperatures and accordingly figures representing it were expected to be found more easily than textual information.

Comparison of UIs: Overall, 17 participants preferred KJ UI and five liked both UIs. This is statistically significant with $p=0.05$ using the one sample t-test between percents. In the following we discuss the results regarding the different UI elements of both interfaces.

Overall Design: The participants disliked the large amount of white space in the Google-like UI and wished the UI to be more colourful. One participant also suggested putting the result list in the middle of the web page instead of the left side in order to avoid *"too much free space"*. They liked that KJ contains many pictures and is colourful, except for one child who did not like the KJ UI because he found the graphics to be *"babyish"*. Furthermore, the young users wished to select a background in some other colour themselves. This is consistent with suggestions from previous research (see Section 3.1) to allow individual user personalisation in areas such as colour and graphics. Three participants suggested that the background should adapt to their search query, i.e. when searching information about Venus a picture of the planet should be shown in the background. Thus, the results of our user study support the UI concept of *CollAge* [73] (see Section 3.2).

Result Presentation: Overall, the preferences of the users varied: half of them preferred the result presentation using a vertical list whereas the other half liked the result presentation with coverflow. The participants liked that the Google-like UI provides multiple search results and that they could review several result snippets at once. The Google-like UI is also *"simple"*. Three participants mentioned a drawback of the Google-like results presentation, namely that it is not clear that the list contains multiple results because they are not explicitly separated through UI elements from each other (only through whitespaces). The KJ UI, on the other hand, presents each result on a separate papyrus roll, thus the connection of each snippet to a website is made clear. This was mentioned by two participants. In addition, three participants found the textual summaries of the result web pages to be too short and wished for more information. All the participants liked that KJ offers a picture of each website in the results. Even those who had not yet seen KJ remarked that they missed a picture. One participant also wished to make the different elements of the result snippets more colourful.

New Interface Elements: In order to start a *Knowledge Journey* a child needs to select a guidance figure. 18 participants chose the penguin pirate to join them on the knowledge journey. The older pirate was selected by five older children (mostly fifth grade). Three female participants chose the female pirate. The participants liked the possibility of selecting a guidance figure. In this way, a guidance figure creates an emotional bond with an SUI which may increase the children's willingness to accept its help during the search.

About 90% of participants tried the menu while exploring the KJ without any specific task. They liked that the menu contained so many categories: *"you can find everything there"* and *"the menu is lovely"*. We also did not notice any difficulties of users operating the menu. But, when receiving a search task, the participants mainly used the search input field. Only one participant used a menu to solve the entire task. Two participants solved a part of the task using the menu. Four children tried to use the menu to solve the task but then switched to the input field. These children were not successful with the menu as they only explored the categories of the 1st hierarchy level but the relevant pages could only be reached from the second level (it was our design decision to make the solution not too trivial). Therefore, the menu is more likely useful for exploration tasks whereas in our user study we had a well-defined (answer-oriented) search task.

The participants had different opinions regarding the audio support. Two children found it *"useful"* whereas three participants commented that it was *"irritating"*. The remaining participants had a neutral opinion, i.e. *"okay"*. One child told us that *"audio support is for children who cannot read"*. Another child suggested for the voice to speak more slowly. One participant wished also to select the gender of the speaker. Overall, we believe that audio support is useful in order to support navigation in the menu as pictures alone can be misinterpreted by users and it may take some time to read the tooltip text. However, the possibility of turning the sound off should be given.

The idea of saving interesting results in the treasure chest received a highly positive user feedback, i.e. all the participants mentioned the treasure chest as a most liked feature of the SUI: *"Treasure chest is handy"*; *"One does not have to remember"*. One participant said that he could store the links to his online games there. Less than a half of the participants stored the relevant pages when performing the actual task. In our opinion, the treasure chest has no big influence on the success in a task-oriented search as this type of search does not require much memory load. However, children can benefit from the result storage in the case of complex search tasks like research for a child's homework.

UI improvements: Based on the findings of the user study we summarise the possible improvements of the UIs as follows. The background of a result output page should be adaptable and present pictures relevant to the search query. This form of result visualisation would support children who prefer visual information (see Chapter 6). Different kinds of GUI personalisation, including even the colour of different elements of the result snippets, should be provided by the UI. Personalisation of the SUI will increase the satisfaction of children interacting with it. A textual summary of a web page should be long enough (probably more than one sentence). Otherwise, it is hard to judge the relevance of a search result based only on a short textual summary. SUI should also support children in locating the relevant information on the web page, i.e. by highlighting the query words in the target web page to provide better relevance clues.

Classic Keyword-oriented Search User Interface: Each result element should be clearly separated from the rest and have a thumbnail of the corresponding web page. As stated before, all the participants mentioned the importance of websites' pictures. The SUI should show a clear back-button or present the search result in the same window (e.g. using frames) to prevent children from getting lost. New GUI elements like the guidance figure, the wheeled menu and the treasure chest can enhance user experience.

Knowledge Journey: A vertical results list offers a better (and faster) overview of results. Given a proper indicator for items separation we believe that this type of result presentation would lead to a more efficient search over the coverflow. However, this is only true in case of desktop computers which have a relatively large screen. Coverflow visualisation would be appropriate for a SUI designed for touch-based hardware like smartphones. Although some participants did not appreciate the voice support, we would keep this feature to support dual information coding in a menu. However, it is useful to offer the possibility of speaker gender personalisation. In addition, children should be able to turn the sound off. The SUI for KJ was primarily designed and evaluated using desktop computers. However, we believe that the offered solutions and interface itself is applicable for touch hardware. One challenge here is mapping the mousing over gesture from the desktop based solution to touch based devices. This can be realised by setting time constraints that activate a specific system reaction after the user keeps on touching a certain area for a predefined amount of time.

7.4 Voice-Controlled Search: Initial Study

Young users would benefit from support mechanisms to formulate their information need and interact with a search user interface (see Section 7.1). In order to tackle these problems, a voice-controlled search interface can be used that allows a voice interaction in both directions, i.e., voice input and output. By using speech recognition, the user does not need to be good at typing. Additionally, the interaction with a voice-controlled system can be more intuitive and hence more motivating for children as they do not have to learn the cumbersome interaction with mouse and keyboard. These advantages motivate us to investigate voice-controlled search user interfaces (SUI) for young users.

Voice control offers further advantages. There are methods to extract emotions from the users speech (e.g. [108]). Hence a speech interaction can provide us with the necessary information about the emotional and dispositional state of the user. Thus, if a child feels unhappy, e.g. because of a search failure, his or her emotional condition can be recognised using the voice information and the system can initiate countermeasures. User emotions and dispositions were considered in information retrieval before, however mostly for relevance assessment [6] or as additional features, e.g., in collaborative filtering [134, 135]. Our long term goal is to take the emotional states of young users into account in order to provide a better support from the SUI side. To our knowledge, voice control has not been studied before in the context of search engines for children.

In order to develop a well-functioning voice-controlled search engine for young users, it is necessary to analyse users' acceptance towards a system of this kind and how they would use it. One essential part of this is the user behaviour. Therefore, we decided to investigate children's speech patterns and interaction tactics that are used for operating a voice-controlled search engine. For this, a user study was conducted in form of a *Wizard-of-Oz-Experiment* [129, Chapter 12]. During this experiment a user interacts

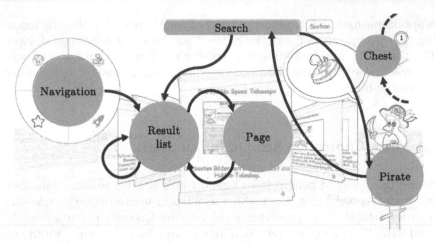

Fig. 7.7: Interaction graph of the *Knowledge Journey*. A user can search for results, navigate using the pie menu, interact with the coverflow, interact with a result page, interact with a guidance figure and operate the treasure chest (modified from [pub:10]).

with a program that seems to be autonomous, but is remotely controlled through a hidden person (the wizard) instead (see Section 2.3.2).

For this study, we used the child-centered search engine *Knowledge Journey* described in the previous section. However for the backend, here we used *Bing Search API*[6] with the safe search option turned on. The *Bing Search API* offers a greater coverage of search results (that was important for the study design where children could execute a free, exploratory search), however it does guarantee that the search results are child-appropriate. Figure 7.7 depicts the possible user interactions with *Knowledge Journey*. In the following, we present our user study which was conducted in order to study children's speech patterns and interaction tactics during a web search using the Knowledge Journey via voice interaction. The content of this section was published in [pub:9, pub:10].

---

[6] https://datamarket.azure.com/dataset/bing/search, accessed on 2013-06-12

7.4.1 User Study

The goal of the user study was to examine how children would interact with a voice-controlled version of the search engine *Knowledge Journey* and what voice commands and interaction patterns they would use. Therefore, a study in form of a so-called "Wizard-of-Oz-Experiment" was designed. In general, two investigators were involved in the study. One was the "wizard", whereas another one conducted the user study with participants by interviewing them, giving instructions etc. The study procedure consisted of the following four steps:

▶ *Pre-interview:* We used a pre-interview to gather the user's demographic information and their experience with computer systems and the Internet. We also asked the participants about their experience with different input methods, i.e., keyboard, mouse, touch and voice control.

▶ *Introduction:* In the next step, we gave the participants an introduction to Knowledge Journey and how to use it. We briefly explained what the different elements are and what purpose they have. We intentionally gave no information about how to use the interface per voice.

▶ *Search Experiment:* In this step, the actual search was done. Children could execute a free, exploratory search where they were able to look for everything they liked and use the elements how they want, but only using voice commands. If a young user had no idea for what or how he or she should use the system, an investigator gave some assistance, e.g., "Currently its Christmas time and there are a lot of things one can do during this time. Maybe you can search for these things?". If a child used an ambiguous command or the system (the Wizard) could not understand the command, a prepared audio message "I cannot understand you." was triggered.

▶ *Post-interview:* The last step was a post-interview to evaluate the users' attitude towards the system and if they would use voice-controlled SUI in the future. We also asked for recommendations to improve our search engine.

Each session with these four steps took about 30 minutes. The questionnaire for the structured interview with children is provided in Appendix

A.3. The user study was conducted in December 2012 at the trilingual international elementary school in Magdeburg, Germany[7].

Participants: Our ten participants were of age eight to ten (average 8.8 years), seven female and three male. They were mostly third (8 children) and fourth (2 children) grade pupils. All children had experience with computer systems and the Internet. Eight children could easily handle mouse and keyboard, one child had some difficulties, one child mainly used touch devices. The frequency distribution of the Internet usage is: everyday (1 pupil), two-four times a week (3 pupils), once a week (1 pupil), once a month (4 pupils), less than once a month (1 pupil). We noticed no significant correlation between the frequency of usage and age or school grade. Four participants use the Internet without any supervision, three participants together with relatives and three participants do both from time to time. The children use the Internet mostly to play online games and watch videos on Youtube, but also to search information for school. These activities were mentioned by almost all participants. Some of them also write messages or look at Amazon or Ebay. In order to search for information, eight participants use Google and five of them also use web search engines for children. Tables B.8, B.9 and B.10 provide more detailed information about the children.

Patterns and Strategies: In the following we describe the command patterns, strategies and the response of the young users to the interaction per voice control. Furthermore, we address the emerging difficulties. All children enjoyed to interact by voice control. This is a good sign as their motivation to use the search engine increases. They perceived as beneficial that queries do not need to be written using a keyboard. However, voice control was perceived as unusual by 90% of the children. Especially at the beginning of the study, the young users were overwhelmed a little bit because they did not know what they can actually say to the system. The researcher had to emphasise that a child could say anything and that there are no restrictions.

Nearly half of the children interacted with the system in a very polite way, e.g., "Please enlarge" or "Could you open the treasure chest please?". But with time they changed the interaction strategy and used only pragmatic, relatively short voice-commands. Eight children used almost exclusively *elliptical constructions* for commands where a word or phrase implied

---

[7] All the relevant agreements from the parents had been obtained. The parents agreed in advance that their children can participate in the study.

by context is omitted from a sentence, e.g., "close", "next page" or "go back".

If an explicit keyword input by voice was done or if a category in the navigation menu was selected by voice, then half of the children also continuously used the descriptive terms for the UI element, e.g., "I'm searching for ..." or "Select calculations on the steering wheel." However, the other half named the query terms or described the menu category directly. Users who actively used the storage function, also used the specific terms "store" and/or "(in) treasure chest". This behaviour allows us to detect possible voice commands automatically. Different children also used synonyms for the same controls. For example, to flip through the search results, six children used relative descriptions like "continue" or "next page", whereas the others used an absolute description like "second page". Hence, the system also has to support alternative voice commands for each interaction.

The commands used during the search were very often ambiguous. For example, a child previously used the search bar or the navigation menu and then he or she used "space" for the next command. It was unclear, whether the pupil intended to search for it or wanted to select a corresponding menu category. For such commands a context, i.e., the previously used element, is important to carry out the commands without errors. The system has to take the context and the user interaction sequence into account to interpret the user correctly.

Nevertheless, some children's interaction strategies were not always possible in the original interaction graph of the *Knowledge Journey*. For example, participants wanted to start a new search, while being within the "treasure chest", skipping the command of closing it first. For some of the children, it was extremely difficult to name "clickable" elements that only contained pictures within web pages or on the SUI surface. For example, Figure 7.8 shows a website with a memory game that was opened by one of the pupils. It was problematic for this child to name a certain card and its position, in particular the cards in the center presented the greatest difficulty. While the card at the borders could be named like "upper left" or "second row right", the cards in the center, which require numbers for both rows and columns, were difficult to explain. Also the thumbnails for stored elements in the treasure chest (see Figure 7.4 at the bottom) were difficult to select. Children often referred to an object in a certain thumbnail to access a website. In future, this problem could be solved by labelling those elements with numbers or symbols. Another solution is to combine the voice-controlled search engine with touch input. 70% of the young partic-ipants explicitly told us that they would rather use touch to accomplish certain tasks directly on the user interface, but they would like to use voice control for keyword search as it is faster than using a keyboard.

Fig. 7.8: Screenshot of a webpage with a memory game: For children, it is difficult to name a certain card and its position.

This screenshot was taken from the naturkundemuseum-kassel.de. http://www.naturkundemuseum-kassel.de/kinderseite/basteln-spielen/merkspiel/merkspiel.html

Table 7.2 provides some examples of children's voice commands. In ad-dition, we noticed that the children in the user study did not use natural language search queries. This fact and the results for the search queries in the previous user study with *Knowledge Journey* support our assump-tion (see Section 5) that if asked to conduct an answer-oriented search for a pre-defined question setting, children simply can use the questions for their search without much abstraction. Given an exploratory search task without a pre-defined question, children use short queries.

Interaction	Voice Command
Search for	- I'm searching for Lord of the Rings movies - I would like to ahem ... search for ... YouTube - I would like to ahem ... I'm searching for a ... for ahem information about - put animals in above - hmm horses - the stars

Menu navigation	- I'd like er to go to the bag
	- at culture er at history I'd like ahem to the
	  steering wheel at the volcano
	- I would like ... (click) on st at in steering
	  wheel to ahem the calculation task
	- click nose below
	- steering wheel tree
	- once again to the tree
	- that where the man is running

Next page	- I would like to see the second page please - I would like to see the second page - page five - the next
Open a search result	- open the (web) page - I want that you open it - click on it - please enlarge - show me

Table 7.2: Examples for young user's voice commands [pub:10].

7.5 Summary and Discussion

The main research question in this chapter was

> **RQ5a**
>
> How can the user interface better support search to fulfill a child's information needs considering children in a concrete operational development stage (age 7-11)?

In order to answer this question, we derived seven conceptual challenges in the design of search user interfaces for children in the primary school age (concrete operational development stage according to Piaget [154]) such as emotional, language, cognitive, memory, interaction, relevance and diversity support. We also proposed possible solutions for the challenges. In order to demonstrate simple and intuitive solutions, a novel user interface, called *Knowledge Journey*, was designed. The user interface of Knowledge Journey is colourful and audio supported, and contains possibilities for both searching through text input and browsing in menu categories. The browsing menu supports children who have difficulties in query formulation. In addition, Knowledge Journey offers spelling suggestion for the language support. It also has a guidance figure for the emotional support and a result storage functionality to support children's cognitive recall (memory support). In order to provide the cognitive support, a treasure hunt metaphor is used in Knowledge Journey. Furthermore, the browsing menu only contains real-world categories and has a two-level hierarchical organised menu that children are comfortable to use. Simple point-and-click interactions, appropriate font size and appropriate size of clickable UI elements aim to support children on the interaction level.

The *Knowledge Journey* interface was prototypically implemented. A significant contribution of this work is a comparative user study we did to evaluate our search interface against a classic keyword-based SUI with a vertical result listing. To our knowledge we are the first to do a comparative user study of search UIs for children with a fixed backend. We used a latin square design and let each of the 28 participants compare between the two UIs. Many participants preferred Knowledge Journey UI over a Google-like UI. They liked the new features of Knowledge Journey, particularly the treasure chest.

We also conducted a user study in the form of a Wizard-of-Oz-Experiment to investigate the potential of voice control. Voice control can be a means of interaction support for children (see Section 7.1). Additionally, a user's voice can be used for emotion detection and knowing a user's current emotional state would allow the system to provide emotional support and react not only in cases of obvious failure (see Section 7.1). However, the results of this study indicate that a voice controlled search user interface might be difficult for children to operate and that children prefer touch over the voice control. Therefore, we decided to leave the voice control for further work.

The first user study (Section 7.3) also showed differences in children's preferences for the search user interface, e.g. in search result presentation. In order to tackle the challenge of diversity (see Section 7.1), we developed the idea of an adaptive system that meets the requirements of a particular young user. The work we did in this direction is described in Chapter 8.

Chapter 8

Addressing User Diversity

Current research on SUI design for children [e.g. 60, 90] targets children of a wide age range and the SUIs are optimised and adapted to general user group characteristics. However, in particular young users undergo relatively fast changes in cognitive, fine motor and other abilities [102]. Design requirements change rapidly as well and a flexible modification of the SUI is needed. Furthermore, the abilities of a particular child may be different from those of another child of the same age. This imposes a further requirement on the search user interface. The search user interface has to cover the needs of individual young users. We called this challenge the *diversity support* (see Section 7.1).

In order to tackle this issue, we suggest to provide users with an *evolving search user interface (ESUI)*. It dynamically adapts to individual user characteristics and allows for changes not only in properties of UI elements like colour, but also influences the choice of UI elements themselves and their positioning. Some UI elements are continuously adaptable (e.g. font size, button size, space required for UI elements), whereas others are only discretely adaptable (e.g. type of results visualisation). Not only SUI properties, but also the complexity of search results is continuously adaptable and can be used as a personalisation mechanism for users of all age groups. An ESUI enables personalisation and therefore increases the usability of a SUI. In specific, it follows general ergonomic principles in terms of the *ISO 9241-110* standard[1] like suitability for individualisation and conformity with user expectations. These user interface qualities tend to ensure satisfaction of a user interacting with it which positively correlates with effectiveness and efficiency.

In general, researchers agree that UIs for children should allow individual personalisation in areas such as colour and graphics [pub:13, 112].

---

[1] ISO 9241-110 describes ergonomic design principles that should be applied to the analysis, design and evaluation of interactive systems. These principles are suitability for the task, self-descriptiveness, conformity with user expectations, suitability for learning, controllability, error tolerance, suitability for individualisation.

Therefore, Azzopardi et al. [9] introduced the *MaSe* SUI prototype that provides a sandbox environment for high school students to create their own personalised search interface. It allows personalisation of colour scheme, the search engine's name, custom arrangement of search results using drag-and-drop, and the customisation of search services. Moreover, the number of results and the type of the results can be changed. In contrast to previous work, we suggest to go further and provide users with an evolving search user interface that adapts continuously and smoothly to an individual user's characteristics. This SUI should allow for changes both in properties of UI elements and in UI elements type. In contrast to the work of Azzopardi et al. [9], we have a strong focus on the frontend and children as a target group. We aim to customise UI elements of a SUI such as menu type, result visualisation, surrogate structure, font, audio, theme and more. This is the first step towards an ESUI. The content of this chapter was partially published in [pub:5, pub:11, pub:12].

8.1 Evolving Search User Interface

In this section we share our vision of an ESUI. In general, we suggest to use a mapping function between the user skill space and the UI elements and adapt the SUI using it, instead of building a SUI for a specific user group. Using a generic model of an adaptive system, as discussed in [184], we depict the model of an ESUI as following (see Fig. 8.1). We have a set of user characteristics (or skills) on one side. In the ideal case, the system detects the skills automatically, e.g. based on the user's interaction with the information retrieval system (user's queries, selected results, etc.). On the other side, there is a set of options to adapt the SUI, e.g. using different UI elements for querying or visualisation of results. In between, an adaptation component contains a set of logic rules to map the user' skills to the specific UI elements of the ESUI. We envision the ESUI as an adaptive system. According to Oppermann and Rasher [145, p. 173], "systems that adapt to the users automatically based on the system's assumptions about user needs are called *adaptive*." The adaptability can be also initiated by the user. "Systems that allow the user to change certain system parameters and adapt their behaviour accordingly are called *adaptable*" [145, p. 173].

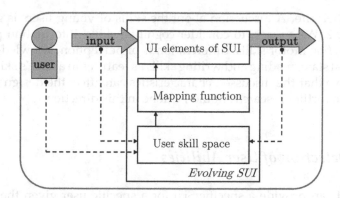

Fig. 8.1: Model of an ESUI. This model is based on the generic model of an adaptive system that is described in [184].

8.1.1 Mapping Function

A function between the user skill space and the options to adapt the UI elements of the SUI has to be found. We suggest using the knowledge about human development, e.g. from medical, cognitive, psychosocial science fields to specify the user skill space. The results of user studies about users' search behaviour and SUI design preferences can provide recommendations for UI elements. As far as the research provides information about the studied age group, we can use the age group as a connector between the skill space and the UI elements. Note that we use age groups in the sense of a more abstract category defining a set of specific capabilities while growing up. A lot of research is already done and can be used (see Chapter 3). In addition, if the set of adaptable UI elements is defined, we can evaluate the mapping function by letting users from different age groups put the UI elements of a SUI together.

8.1.2 Evolving Skills

In order to allow a SUI to evolve together with a user we first have to determine those characteristics that vary from user to user and change during their life. A discussion about the skills of young users is given in Section 2.2. We suggest to consider cognitive skills, information processing rates, fine motor skills, different kinds of perception, knowledge base, emotional state, reading and writing skills as features in a user's skill space. We believe that the discussed characteristics can affect the design of SUIs. However, further research should be done in this direction.

8.1.3 Detection of User Abilities

An ESUI can provide a specific SUI for a specific user given the knowledge of their specific abilities. A simple case is an adaptable SUI, where a user manually adjusts the search user interface to their personal needs and tasks. An adaptable SUI may also provide several standard settings for a specific user selection to explore the options (e.g. young user, adult user, elderly user). More interesting and challenging is the case of an adaptive SUI, where a system automatically detects the abilities of a user and provides them with an appropriate SUI. Concepts for an automatic detection of user's abilities have been studied in the past. We can use the age of a registered and logged-in user. However, the age provides only an approximation of a user's capabilities. For an individual user an appropriate mapping to the age group has to be found, e.g. using psychological tests in the form of games. Those games can be used to derive the quality of the user's fine-motor skills as well. Furthermore, we can use the user history from log files, in particular, issued queries (their topic and specific spelling errors) and accessed documents. However, research is required to determine how to adapt a SUI in a way users would accept the changes.

8.1.4 Design Concepts

When designing an ESUI, we first have to define the components of a SUI that should be adapted. An overview of different SUI elements is given in [81]. We consider three main components. The first component is the search *input*, i.e. UI elements which allow a user to transform their information need into a textual query. This component is traditionally represented by an input field and a search button. Other variants are a menu with different categories or voice input. The second component is the result *output* of an information retrieval (IR) system. The output consists of UI elements that provide an overview of retrieved search results. There can be different kinds of output, e.g. a vertical list of snippets (Fig. 8.2a), coverflow (Fig. 8.2b) or tiles (Fig. 8.2c). The third is the *management* component. Management covers UI elements that support users in information processing and retaining. Examples of management UI elements are bookmark management components or history mechanisms like breadcrumbs. Historically, UI elements for management are not part of a SUI. But our research (see Chapter 7) shows that young users are highly motivated to use such elements. Besides these main components, there also exist general properties of UI elements which affect all the three categories, e.g. font size or colour. We propose to adapt these three main components of a SUI and its general UI properties to the user's skills.

Ideally, an evolving search user interface should be continuously adaptable. Unfortunately, this cannot be done smoothly for all elements. Some UI elements are continuously adaptable, e.g. font size, button size, space required for UI elements, trade-off between the length of a snippet and thumbnail size, whereas others like type of result visualisation are only discretely adaptable. Not only SUI properties, but also the complexity of the retrieved content is continuously adaptable and can be used as a personalisation mechanism for users of all age groups.

In order to demonstrate the concept of an ESUI, we consider a young girl called Jenny who is developing from six to fourteen. This age range is broader than the age range we focus on in this thesis, but it allows us to demonstrate the idea of an ESUI more expressively. In the following, we show how input and output of a SUI can be adapted to changes of Jenny's abilities.

Use Case 1: Jenny is six years old. She started to learn reading, but she has difficulties with writing. Jenny's active vocabulary is limited to 5,000 words. She cannot yet think in abstract categories and is not able to process much information. Due to her limited writing abilities, Jenny is not able to use an input field and write a query. She is learning to read, so she can use a menu with different categories which are supported by images. In order to search for information Jenny can *draw* her query[2]. Jenny also cannot process much information at once. Therefore, the coverflow (Fig. 8.2b) result visualisation fits her abilities. Coverflow allows her to concentrate on one

---

[2] The query-by-drawing interface would require a good image recognition algorithm.

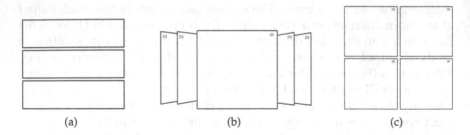

(a)   (b)   (c)

Fig. 8.2: Different kinds of result output of an information retrieval system: a) *Vertical list of snippets* offers a fast overview of several results at once. b) *Coverflow view of results* uses a familiar book metaphor, the central element is clearly separated from the rest. Coverflow offers an attractive animation during browsing. c) *Tiles of search results* offer a fast overview of several results at once. A user has small jumps when reading within results, however the ordering of results is not so clear compared to a list [pub:11, pub:12].

item at a time, thus, her cognitive load is reduced. Jenny can interact with it using simple point-and-click interactions. An integrated text-to-speech reader supports Jenny by reading the results to her.

Use Case 2: Jenny is nine years old. Jenny can read and write short stories with just a few spelling errors. Jenny has some difficulties with typing using a keyboard. She "hunts and pecks" on the keyboard for the correct keys. This increases the amount of spelling errors and also slows down the process. Jenny is frustrated because the system does not understand her well. Thus, a standard keyword input field does not fit Jenny's abilities well. Jenny still cannot think in abstract categories and process a lot of information. But her language skills improved and her vocabulary size has increased. Therefore, she can use *voice input* to search for information. A menu with different categories in addition to voice input can inspire Jenny to search for some new information. However, these categories should match her cognitive abilities. Jenny can already manage different interaction techniques and is able to process more information than the six-year-old Jenny. Therefore, a list of snippets (Fig. 8.2a) is an adequate output visualisation. It requires less cognitive recall than tiles, but allows to process more result items at a time than the coverflow does.

Use Case 3: Jenny is 14 years old. Jenny's writing skills are further developed with use of correct grammar, punctuation and spelling. She learns to think logically about abstract concepts. Her vocabulary size is about 20,000 words. She chats a lot with her friends which results in solid typing skills using a keyboard. Therefore, Jenny is able to use a keyword-oriented input search supported by spelling correction and suggestion mechanisms. A SUI can still support Jenny by finding the "right" keywords, for example using a *query cloud*[3]. The query cloud contains term suggestions subject to the current query. Related terms are shown near one another. It also allows a user's interaction with the cloud, i.e. a user can explore further related terms mousing over a term of the cloud. Jenny can already manage different interaction techniques and is able to process more information than the nine-year-old Jenny. Therefore, a vertical list visualisation or even tiles (Fig. 8.2c) would allow Jenny a good overview of results.

8.2 Adaptation of a Search User Interface towards User Needs

In this section, we present a prototype study of the first prototypical implementation of an ESUI[4]. We aim to develop an adaptable SUI to examine the user acceptance and different ways to adapt the UI elements of a SUI. Based on this work an adaptive SUI can be implemented in the future.

8.2.1 Design & Implementation

Our SUI is based on the SUI *Knowledge Journey (KJ)* described in Section 7.2. In addition to the original features of Knowledge Journey, the new SUI allows customisation towards the users' wishes. In order to achieve a coherent design between different variations of the ESUI, we suggest to fix the positions of different SUI parts. Fig. 8.3 depicts the general structure of the developed ESUI. It consists of five groups of elements: a help section, a storage for bookmarked results, a visualisation of results, elements

---

[3] Similar to the *quinturakids.com* search engine, accessed on 2013-05-02.

[4] This interface was prototypically implemented as a part of this thesis project in [stud:3]. Jana Vos assisted in a user study that was conducted in Section 8.3 and helped analyse the results.

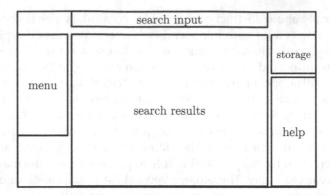

Fig. 8.3: General structure of the developed SUI with search elements, menu, help, storage for bookmarked pages and result visualisation (modified from [pub:12]).

for keyword search and a menu for navigation. The search input consists of elements for text search and a menu for navigation to provide different ways for children to formulate their information need. A menu supports children who have problems with query formulation.

In the following we elaborate on the ways to adapt different UI elements and their properties. We focus on children in the first instance and implement parameters that bring some advantages for children, for example, having a browsing menu, coverflow result visualisation, graphical separation of search results etc. A summary of adaptable elements, their properties and the options that we implemented is given in Table 8.1. In our implementation, we also offer some parameters that, based on the state of the art, are considered to be unsuitable for kids, e.g. having a small font size. This choice was made to show a wide range of options along with the desire to make the changes stand out when switching between different SUIs (this will be also discussed later in Section 8.3). Furthermore, it is hard to tell the set of options that would be the best for a particular age group due to the lack of comparative studies. Therefore, several options that might offer some advantages have been implemented for each element and will be discussed further.

Element	Parameter	Options
menu	type	no menu, classic, pie-menu
	categories	for children, for adults
	structure	number of categories, hierarchy depth
results	visualisation	list, tiles, coverflow
	number	on a page for coverflow
	separation	no separation, lines, boxes
	page view	preview on/off, same window, same tab, new window
surrogate	website picture	on/off
	thumbnail size	thumbnail vs. snippet size
	URL	on/off
	keyword highlighting	different colour, on/off
font	size	from 10 pt to 18 pt
	type	Comic Sans MS, Arial, Times New Roman, Impact
theme	type	no theme, different themes
avatar	type	no avatar, different avatars
audio	active	on/off
	voice gender	male, female, girl, boy
	number of repetitions	only the first time, twice, always

Table 8.1: Adaptable elements of the implemented ESUI, their parameters and options [pub:12].

8.2.2 Search Input

In order to support users who have difficulties in query formulation, a menu with many categories is offered. One can adapt the menu type, the number of categories and the structure.

Menu type: First of all, different kinds of menu can be used. We implemented two menu types, a *pie-menu* (Fig. 8.4a) and a *classic menu* (Fig. 8.4b). If desired by a user, the menu can be hidden from the SUI. A pie-menu can be operated with simple point-and-click interactions and presents a good overview of available categories. Each category is presented as an icon and a tooltip provides further information about the item. Initially, the top-level categories are shown. Corresponding subcategories are opened when a user clicks on a top-level category. As an alternative a classic menu

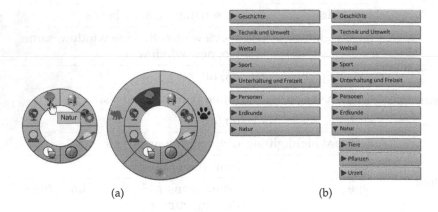

(a)   (b)

Fig. 8.4: Different kinds of menu: a) pie-menu: initial visualisation (left) and after selecting the "Nature" category (right); b) classic menu: initial visualisation (left) and after selecting the "Nature" category (right) [pub:12, stud:3].

was implemented. In our implemented version, this menu can be operated with simple point-and-click interactions as well. The top-level categories are presented as a list. Here, we use only text to provide information about categories. By clicking on a category, corresponding subcategories open. Users can open subcategories of multiple categories at once (which is not possible using a pie-menu). However, depending on the text type and size, the classic menu requires more space and even scrolling. This is not an issue with a pie-menu. Note that scrolling can be difficult for young users as their fine motor skills are still developing (see Section 2.2).

Menu topics and structure: Independent of the menu type, further menu properties can be adapted. These are the offered categories and the menu structure. The chosen categories should reflect the information needs of children. Researchers suggest that search interfaces should address both educational and entertainment needs of children [112]. We chose menu categories like entertainment, sports and hobbies, history, universe, geography, nature and people, as they meet the information needs of children as described by Livingstone [120]. As an alternative, we also implemented categories of the *Yahoo*[5] portal. These categories include shopping, cars, travel, lifestyle and other topics. The menu structure can be also adapted. According to Bar-Ilan and Belous [12], children (in fourth and fifth grade) are comfortable with up to eight top-level categories and can create hierarchical structures with a depth of up to five. In our implementation, the number of top-level categories can be between 6 and 10, the depth is variable between 1 and 4 in order to better fit into the pie-menu structure. Both parameters can be changed independently.

8.2.3 Result Output

Visualisation type: We implemented different kinds of output, i.e. a *vertical list* of surrogates (Fig. 8.2a), *coverflow* (Fig. 8.2b) and *tiles* (Fig. 8.2c). Other visualisation types also exist such as graph visualisation [80], but we considered graph visualisation to be too difficult for children due to their abstract nature. All the visualisation types have their advantages and disadvantages. A vertical list of surrogates offers a fast overview of several results at once. Tiles of search results offer a fast overview of several results at once too, but provide more results per page than a list. A user performs small jumps when reading within results. However the ordering of results is not as clear as it is for a list. Therefore, we explicitly support users by presenting the search result rank in the GUI for all result visualisations. Note that when using a vertical list, a user performs larger reading jumps within an item compared to a tile. Coverflow is a good choice for children. In Section 7.3 we showed that many children prefer having a Coverflow. Its central element is clearly separated from the rest and a user can concentrate

---

[5] http://www.yahoo.de, accessed on 2013-04-05

on one item at once, thus resulting in a smaller cognitive load. Coverflow offers an attractive animation while browsing through results.

Number of results: Children get frustrated if the search engine returns too many results [111]. Most children examine only the first three results (Chapter 5). Therefore, the number of results per page should be limited. We used a fixed number of results on one page to avoid scrolling: three results in the list, four in the tiles. The number of results in the coverflow is also continuously adaptable from three to nine.

Separation of results: The list result items and single tiles can be visualised differently in respect to the separation in the GUI. Children can be confused in case there is no clear separation of results items through UI elements (see Section 7.3). In that case multiple results are seen as one. We implemented three ways to adapt the separation: *no separation*, separation using *lines* or *boxes*. One can also adapt the space between the boxes. The more space between the boxes, the clearer the separation is. However, as the item size gets smaller, more precise movements are required to click an item. We consider separation using lines and boxes to be a better choice for children; however children's preferences should be evaluated.

Surrogate structure: By default, a surrogate consists of the results title and the textual summary. The text is left-aligned as recommended for children by Budiu and Nielsen [25]. Each surrogate also contains the search result rank to provide children with relevance judgement support. There are multiple ways to customise a result surrogate. In addition to the textual summary, a representative picture can be shown. Pictures provide a quick overview about the website content and support children with limited reading abilities. In our implementation, we provide a website thumbnail. The size of the picture is continuously adaptable. However, there exists a trade-off between the picture size and text size, if the size of a result UI element is fixed. Additional binary adaptable surrogate features are URL display and keyword highlighting. In our implementation, a colour can be selected to highlight keywords.

Results page view: There are several possibilities to view a result page. One can open a page in a *new window*, a *new tab* or the *same window*. Opening a page in a new window has the advantage that a user can open several results at once and, if needed, can compare them. A disadvantage is that this requires some cognitive work. Users have to keep track of windows and children especially can easily get lost. A better navigation between several opened webpages offers the view in a new tab. Again, users can benefit from several opened results and can visit some tabs later. However, it is difficult to orientate in tabs. It also inhibits the children's *backtracking* behaviour with the browsers back-button [17]. In contrast, opening the results in the same window overcomes these problems. It is better for children's orientation and backtracking can be largely avoided. However, only one result can be seen at once. Furthermore, a preview of the result page can be turned *on* or *off*. Preview is an intermediate stage where the page is enlarged, however users can interact within the page and stay in the SUI surface (Fig. 8.5).

Fig. 8.5: Interactive website preview at the center of the SUI screen (kidsweb.de is opened). Using the "arrows" button one can open the search result in the full mode, return to the results overview by clicking the "X" button or save the page in the bookmark storage using the "floppy disk" button [pub:12, stud:3].

8.2.4 General Properties

General properties have an influence on all SUI elements. These properties are *font type* and *size*, *theme* and *avatars*, as well as *audio support*. Font size, for example, influences the length of the text in the search result snippet in case the snippet has a fixed size.

Fonts: Font sizes larger or equal to 14 pt are most suitable for children [25]. In our implementation, the font size can be customised from *10 pt* to *18 pt*. Sans-serif fonts are suitable for children as they increase the text readability [25]. At the same time playful fonts make texts visually appealing for children [25]. Therefore, we used the fonts *Comic Sans MS* and *Arial*. In addition, the fonts *Times New Roman* and *Impact* can be chosen, but are considered to be not usable for children because of their bad readability. One can also assign different font and font sizes for search input, help section, menu and surrogate.

Theme & Avatars: Theme and avatars allow individual personalisation that is welcomed by children (see Section 7.3). Besides the *pirate* theme offered in Knowledge Journey (Section 7.2), we implemented the *space, animals* and *princess* themes in order to have more options for personalisation. They are familiar to children and have a connection to the physical world as recommended by Budiu and Nielsen [25]. In our opinion, pirates' treasure hunt and space travel fit into the search metaphor best, because information search can be seen as a journey to gather relevant results into a treasure chest or logbook and a steering wheel or coordinate panel provides a navigation functionality. The theme choice influences the colour scheme, background picture, background colour of search results, the set of corresponding avatars and the metaphor used for the storage. For each theme there is an option to select an avatar from a predefined set. Besides these themes, we also implemented a SUI option without any theme and avatars.

Audio: When hovering over a pie menu item, a voice explanation is played telling which category is selected. Voice explanation is also added to other UI elements. A voice support is important especially for young children, who need more time to read. One can turn the sound *on* or *off*, select the number of times to repeat the voice explanation, i.e. only the *first time, twice* or *always*. Users can also choose between a *male, female, girl* or *boy* voice. The latter was desired by children in our previous evaluation (see Section 7.3). The audio tooltip helps users who have difficulties to read or are not familiar with SUIs at all. Frequent naming of UI elements triggers behavioural learning and thus allows users to learn how to use the system faster.

8.2.5 Configuration and Further Details

A first step in developing an adaptable SUI is to examine user acceptance and different ways to adapt the SUI. In order to personalise the SUI, we implemented a configuration unit that allows users to manipulate the SUI directly. We ordered the adaptable elements according to their decreasing influence on the entire SUI from theme to audio (Fig. 8.6). Later this configuration unit can be hidden from users and used internally in the backend.

We aim to develop an application that is platform-independent. Therefore, we implemented our ESUI in HTML 5[6], Cascading Style Sheets (CSS)[7] 3 and JavaScript. We optimised our application for the *Google Chrome Browser*. Our application also works on touchscreen devices. For the backend we used the *Bing Search API*[8] with the safe search option turned on. For the audio-tooltip we used the text-to-speech functionality of an online voice generator called *Acapela Box*[9]. However, there are only female and male voices available. In order to create the voice of a child, we had to alter the audio files. An interaction example for our SUI is shown in Fig. 8.7. An online demonstration of the evolving search user interface is available at http://www.dke-research.de/KnowledgeJourney.html

8.3 Evaluation

We defined the set of adaptable UI elements and evaluate the mapping function between users with different abilities and those UI elements. For this, we let users from different age groups customise the UI elements of a SUI. In the following, we describe the design and results of this user study.

We conducted a user study not only with kids, but adults participated in the study as well. Adults were chosen as a reference group as their abilities are different (Section 2.2). This allows us to compare users' preferences in the visualisation of different UI elements of a SUI. In particular, our hypothesis was that *users from different age groups would prefer to use different*

---

[6] http://www.w3.org/TR/html-markup/spec.html, accessed on 2013-04-05

[7] http://www.w3.org/TR/css-2010/, accessed on 2013-04-05

[8] https://datamarket.azure.com/dataset/5BA839F1-12CE-4CCE-BF57-A49D98D29A44, accessed on 2013-06-12

[9] http://www.acapela-box.com/, accessed on 2013-06-12

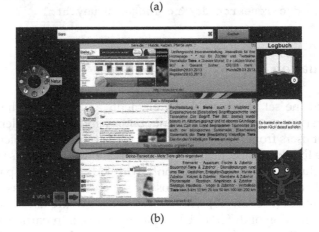

(a)

(b)

Fig. 8.6: Screenshot of the configuration unit (a) and the corresponding SUI (b). Space theme with alien avatar, list view, pie-menu, a complex menu structure with topics for children, result preview is turned on, page surrogate contains URL and a webpage preview, keyword highlighting in yellow, Arial fonts in 16 pt are selected [pub:12, stud:3].

(a) Initial view of a personalised SUI.

(b) The category "space" is selected from the menu. The category name is placed in the search box. In addition, a loading screen will appear until the search results can be shown.

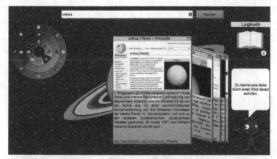

(c) SUI view after the results have been loaded. Users can browse within the coverflow and open a webpage by clicking on the item in focus.

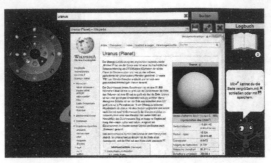

(d) SUI view after selecting a webpage if the preview option is active. One can open the page in full mode, return to coverflow or bookmark the page.

(e) Webpage (here de.wikipedia.org) is opened in the same window. One can close the view and return to either (d) or (c).

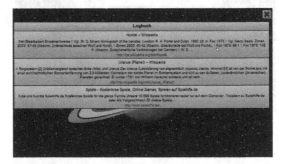

(f) Content of the bookmark storage with three stored search results. By clicking on an item, the webpage is opened.

Fig. 8.7: ESUI interaction example [pub:12, stud:3].

UI elements and different general UI properties. We intend to use our findings to offer default SUI settings. We concentrated on user satisfaction in our user study. We consider this factor to be a highly relevant usability factor for children as positive attitudes towards the system keeps children motivated. This is also consistent with other research, e.g. Mohd, Landoni, and Ruthven [132] suggest that *fun* should be measured when evaluating online systems designed for children. In order to conduct a user study with children, we collaborated with a primary school in Magdeburg, Germany[10]. Our evaluation was done using 17" displays which were kindly provided by the school director. Adults were recruited from an academic context and tested the SUI in a lab.

8.3.1 Study Design

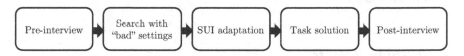

Fig. 8.8: General evaluation procedure [pub:12].

The general evaluation procedure is shown in Fig. 8.8. A pre-interview was conducted to obtain participants' demographic data and their Internet experience. Afterwards the general structure of the developed SUI was explained. Then each participant was asked to try the system out and to perform a free search. However, initially child-unfriendly settings were used in the SUI. There was no menu and no theme, Impact font of size 10 pt was selected, no picture was provided in the surrogate etc. We also used list result visualisation with no separation of items. A search result was opened in a new window. We chose these settings in order to increase participants' motivation to configure the SUI and also for changes to be more noticeable. During this stage, participants also become familiar with the system.

In the next step, all the configuration options were introduced. To provide a better overview for some options, like font type or result visualisa-

---

[10] All the relevant agreements from the parents had been obtained.

tion, we prepared a printed sheet where all the options for each UI element or property could be seen at once. This makes it easier for participants to be aware of all options. Using the configuration unit, each participant went through all adaptable elements, starting from those that had the strongest influence on the whole SUI like theme, then selecting the result set visualisation and customising a surrogate etc. At the end, the participant was able to select whether to turn on the voice and, if so, to customise voice gender and the number of times to repeat the voice explanation.

After a participant customised his or her own SUI to his or her preferences, a search task was given. This step was designed for subjects so they can use their own created SUI. Afterwards, they were given the possibility to change SUI settings. Our search task was gender independent, could be solved in a reasonable amount of time using a menu or a keyword search. We asked the participants to find out how many moons the planet Uranus has. In the last step, a post-interview was conducted to gather users opinion about the proposed ESUI. The questionnaire for the structured interview with children is provided in Appendix A.4. Each test session lasted about 30 minutes.

8.3.2 Study Results

The user study was conducted in February 2013 with children and in March 2013 with adults. 44 subjects participated in the study, 27 children and 17 adults. The children were between eight and ten years old (8.9 on average), 19 girls and 8 boys from third (18 subjects) and fourth (9 subjects) grade. The adults were between 22 and 53 years old (29.2 on average), five women and 12 men. Nine of them were students of computer science and four worked in the IT sector. One child claimed to have no Internet experience. The distribution according to the frequency of the Internet usage is following: several times a week (57%), once a week (8%), once a month (31%), once a year (4%). All the adults use the Internet more than once a week. 81% of the young participants and 100% of the adults use the Internet without supervision. Children use the Internet mostly to play online games and watch videos. 67% of the children use the Internet to search for information. 94% of the adults use the Internet to search for information and write emails. They also use the Internet for work (65%), to play games (41%) and meet with friends (47%). 78% of the pupils use the Google search engine on a regular basis. Some of them also named Wikipedia. 56% of the kids also know search engines for children, e.g. Blinde-Kuh.de. All the adults use Google. Only one adult also uses Bing. Tables B.11, B.12, B.13 and B.14 provide more detailed information about the participants.

8.3.3 Preferred UI Settings

In the following, we summarise the settings preferred by the participants. Both children and adults used the theme option (Fig. 8.9a). All the children selected a theme, almost 60% of them preferred the space theme[11]. Only 11% of the adults chose no theme, whereas the rest preferred the space or the pirate theme. These results are consistent with the fact that children like personalisation in design (Section 7.3, [112]). Surprisingly, the adults also liked to have a theme, but, they mentioned that they would rather have more modest adult themes. Only one adult subject indicated that he did not care about the "graphical gimmicks" as he uses the search engine just for search.

All the pupils and 82% of the adults wished to have a menu in addition to the text input (Fig. 8.9b). However, adults had a tendency towards the classic menu (65%) and children had a tendency towards the pie-menu (56%). 93% of the adult users chose adult topics for the menu. 92% of the children chose topics meant for them. However, many adults wished to select the menu topics by themselves. Both children and adults wanted to have as many menu categories as possible. Surprisingly, not only adults but children also wished to have a deep hierarchy. 74% of the pupils and 62% of the adults selected four hierarchy levels which was the maximum offered. Perhaps this was the result of the strong wish to have a lot of categories as the more levels the more subcategories appear.

The majority of the children preferred the coverflow result visualisation, whereas the adults had a weak tendency towards tiles (see Fig. 8.9c). These results can be explained by the fact that on average children can process less information than adults. Thus, it is easier for children to use coverflow. Many adults told us that they prefer tiles. Since many results can be compared at once, tiles offer a good overview of results. Note that

---

[11] This choice may have been biased by the search task about the moons of the planet Uranus that children were given. However, we think that the space theme is particularly interesting for children of this age.

in our implementation the tiles view provides more results per page than the list view. Further studies are required to compare the two views in case scrolling is allowed and there is no result limit per page. All the participants who chose a list view also chose a separation of results through boxes. 60% of the children and 60% of the adults who chose a coverflow selected the maximum possible number of results. Both children (95%) and adults (100%) selected to have a website preview as part of a surrogate. This option was very popular as it supports a user by immediately providing a visual description of a website. As for the picture size, there was a tendency to have more place for the picture than for the textual summary. Almost 50% of the users in both groups selected a keyword highlighting with colour. In general, the remaining 50% were satisfied with bold writing of keywords. Both children (78%) and adults (100%) chose to add the URL to a surrogate.

The children were not uniform about the way a search result should be opened (Fig. 8.9d). As discussed in Section 8.2, opening the results in the same window better fits children's abilities. However, only 37% of the children chose that option. 41% preferred to open results in a new tab and 22% in a new window. Many children were already familiar with tab functionality and therefore chose it. 82% of the adults preferred to open the results in a new tab because they use it regularly. All the eight-year old children chose either a new tab or the same window. Unfortunately, due to a technical error the settings for the website preview were not stored and cannot be reported.

There was a clear tendency regarding font and font size. Young participants chose Comic Sans MS (almost 56%) and Arial (19%). 11% of the children selected the Impact font. 76% of the adults preferred Arial, 12 % preferred Times New Roman and 12 % chose Comic Sans MS. 85% of the pupils selected a font size which is suitable for them (Fig. 8.9e), i.e. 12 pt (37%) or 14 pt (48%). Adults preferred font size of 10 or 12 pt. They said that they could read text in 10 pt. However, they chose 12 pt as there was enough place within the UI for larger texts. Both children and adults did not use the opportunity to adjust the text properties for individual components separately. Only one pupil chose different fonts for different UI elements.

A feature of our SUI was that a voice explanation was incorporated for each clickable UI element in order to support young users who can only read slowly. 67% of the children chose to have the audio option on (Fig. 8.9f), whereas only 6% of the adults found this option to be useful. Almost

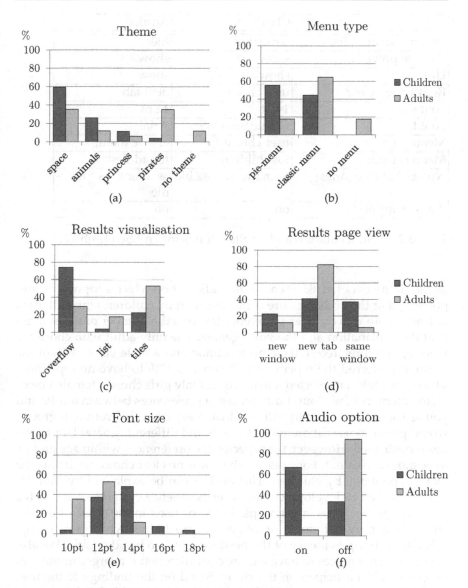

Fig. 8.9: Study results: children and adults preferences for type of theme; type of menu; type of visualisation; type of results opening; font size; audio option [pub:12].

	Children	Adults
Result visualisation	coverflow	tiles
Website preview	show	show
URL	show	show
Result page view	user choice	new tab
Font size	14 pt	12 pt
Font type	Comic Sans MS	Arial
Menu type	user choice	classic menu
Menu categories	for children	for adults
Number of categories	as many as possible	as many as possible
Audio support	on	off

Table 8.2: Default children and adults settings for an ESUI [pub:12].

all the eight-year olds (83%) chose the audio option which supports the hypothesis that the audio feature is most needed by children who still learn to read. There was no clear preference towards the number of times to repeat the explanation and the voice gender. The only adult who chose the voice option, prefered to have no repetition and a male voice. 39% of the children preferred the repetition to be on and 33% to have no repetition. 44% of the children selected a male voice. Only girls chose a female voice.

To summarise, we found differences in preferences between adults and young users. Thus, our hypothesis that users from different age groups would prefer to use different UI elements and different general UI properties is confirmed. However, we expected the preferences within age groups to be more consistent. For example there was no clear choice regarding the menu type made by children. This artifact can be explained by individual differences in development and user experience even if they are in the same age group. Thus, age groups should be used in the sense of a more abstract category defining a set of specific capabilities while growing up. It is also a strong evidence of the need for a SUI to be adaptable. We also expect the preferences to have a more clear direction if a larger number of people would participate in the study. Based on the findings of the user study initial settings for the ESUI can be determined. Table 8.2 shows these settings.

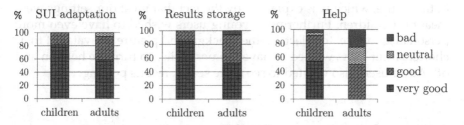

Fig. 8.10: User opinion about: a) the option to adapt the SUI; b) the option to store interesting pages; c) the help option [pub:12].

8.3.4 User satisfaction

In the post-interview we asked the participants how they liked to adapt the SUI. The results are shown in Fig. 8.10a. The SUI adaptation towards user wishes was very positively received by young participants. On a Likert scale from very good to very bad they chose good (19%) or very good (81%). The adults participants also liked it, 60% found it to be very good. In addition we asked for user feedback about "unusual" elements of our SUI like the storage functionality and the help element. The storage functionality was also very well received (Fig. 8.10b), 85% of the pupils found it to be very good and 15% good. They told us that with its help they can find their favourite pages very fast. In contrast, one adult found this feature to be unusual for a search engine and difficult for him to accept. This is a clear case of a user experience shaping user habits. The help SUI element was also better received by young users (Fig. 8.10c). This is consistent with previous research which states that in contrast to adults, less experienced young users (and thus those who especially require support) are willing to read instructions and thus would pay attention to help instructions [25]. 55% of the pupils found the help option to be very good, 38% good and 4% neutral. All the adults, except four participants, ignored the help. Children and adults who used the help wished it to be more informative, e.g. to provide query suggestions. Positive feedback is also reflected in the question about what search engine the participants would prefer to use. 60% of the pupils chose our SUI and 40% found our SUI to be as good as the one they normally use. In contrast, only 29% of the adult participants found our SUI to be better and 53% would prefer to use their usual search engine in the future, which was explained by the fact that most our settings were meant for children. Furthermore, young users wished to have even more personalisation, i.e. to select another background picture or avatar of their choice. Adult users wished to have the possibility to turn the help on and off. Adult users also wanted to see more search results per page.

8.4 Knowledge Journey Exhibit

In the following, we describe the *Knowledge Journey Exhibit (KJE)*[12] that implements the *Knowledge Journey* as an information terminal device and has an age-adaptable SUI. Furthermore, different to the desktop version, KJE is primary developed as a touch application, has an improved SUI and a new backend. KJE was exhibited at the "ScienceStation" exhibition[13] for children and adults that annually takes place at multiple train stations in Germany. This environment imposed additional requirements:

▶ The exhibit must be robust to be run at a train station in a stand-alone mode.
▶ The exhibit can be used without supervision.
▶ The exhibit can be used without an Internet connection.
▶ The search index is child-safe and child-appropriate.
▶ There is a good coverage of web documents.

The content of this section has been partially published in [pub:1].

8.4.1 Hardware

The exhibit was designed in form of a robust information terminal for interactive search that can be operated by a user. It has a 32" touch monitor, a metal keyboard and a trackball. A computer is placed within the box. The Mozilla Firefox browser is opened and the computer is set to run Firefox

---

[12] KJE was developed as a part of the project "A Companion-Technology for Cognitive Technical Systems" (SFB), http://www.sfb-trr-62.de/, accessed on 2014-07-03.

[13] http://www.digital-ist.de/veranstaltungen/science-station-2014.html, accessed on 2014-09-10.

in kiosk mode. For safety reasons, in order to avoid the risk of stumbling in a public place, we did not build a step construction. The height of the box is adjusted for both children and adults. The height of 130 cm is calculated as a mean between the height of an average child and an average adult in order to be appropriate for both user groups. Fig. 8.11 shows the Knowledge Journey Exhibit (in the middle) at Munich train station during the "ScienceStation" exhibition days.

Fig. 8.11: Knowledge Journey Exhibit at Munich train station. [Photo by Natalia Marutenkova.]

8.4.2 Frontend

The SUI of KJE was iteratively developed. Several user studies were conducted in our previous research. Here, we describe improvements of the SUI based on the results from the previous user study (Section 8.3). The previous version had a configuration window where a user was able to customise the SUI. However, we considered the configuration window to be too difficult for children to operate without supervision and in a public place. Therefore, a decision was made to replace the configuration window with a slider where each point on the slider corresponded to a SUI configuration for a specific age starting with a configuration for young children and ending with a setting for young adults. We used the age parameter to adapt the SUI. At the beginning a user is asked to input his or her age. Then, the user is forwarded to the corresponding SUI, where they can explore other settings for the SUI using the slider.

The settings for the slider were derived based on the results from the previous user study (see Section 8.3). The settings for young children are a pirate theme, coverflow result visualisation, large font size in Comic Sans MS. The settings for young adults are no theme, tiles result visualisation, smaller font size in Arial. The search results for adults contained twice as much text in summaries and smaller thumbnails. Each point of the slider changed one of the setting parameters, e.g. the font. We did not use audio-tooltip as it was considered to be too noisy at train stations.

Further SUI improvements of the Evolving Knowledge Journey were made. The user is now supported not only by spelling correction after the query is submitted, but also suggestions for the term the user is currently typing are made. The bookmarking functionality of the Evolving Knowledge Journey was improved. Users can bookmark the relevant search results using the storage functionality. We used a star symbol that was added to the result surrogate to indicate if the search result is already bookmarked. Users can click directly on the star symbol to bookmark or unbookmark the result (simple interaction) or they can place the search result into the storage using drag-and-drop (more complex interaction). They can review the stored results which are grouped by the issued query in order to provide more context information.

Furthermore, we used information about the web page complexity that was calculated using the Flesch-Reading-Ease (FRE) readability index for the German language [5]. The Flesch-Reading-Ease index uses the average sentence length (ASL) and the average number of syllables per word (ASW) as parameters to determine how easy the text is for understanding:

$$FRE_{german} = 180 - ASL - (58.5 \times ASW) \qquad (8.1)$$

Texts are considered to be more complex if they contain long sentences and long words. The values for the Flesch-Reading-Ease vary from 0 to 100. Texts with Flesch-Reading-Ease below 30 are hard to understand and are meant for academics. Texts with Flesch-Reading-Ease above 90 are easy to understand and are appropriate for an 11-year-old pupil.

We applied a traffic light metaphor and visualised each search result that is easy to understand in a green frame, while a search result that is hard to understand is visualised in a red frame, with varying levels of colour in between. The traffic light metaphor was also applied to the slider. An interaction example for the SUI is shown in Fig. 8.12.

8.4.3 Backend

In the previous prototype version (Section 8.3) we used the Bing Search API in order to retrieve search results for a user query. However, the Bing Search API requires Internet access and the returned results were not of a good quality for children. Some of the results are still not child-safe even with the safe search option turned on. Moreover, the first results usually belong to Wikipedia and web shops pages and are not child-appropriate. For example, Wikipedia pages are complex and not easy to understand. Therefore, we decided to create our own search index. First, we tried to obtain the seeds automatically using the *DMOZ's kids&teens directory*[14], but the quality of the gathered web pages was too low and we chose to create the seeds manually. A seed set of 81 web portals was manually derived and a focused crawler was implemented that crawled and indexed web pages that belonged to those domains. The included portals were mainly special web portals for children. However, we also selected some portals that were at least child-safe and informative such as zoo portals or the pages of the federal ministry of education and research. The portals were crawled with consideration of the *robots.txt* protocol[15].

As one of the requirements was to be able to use the exhibit without the Internet, we faced the challenge of showing the result pages in an offline mode. Therefore, we decided to create high-quality, full screen images of the web pages being indexed using the *Tika*[16] library. Users get an image of the web page after clicking at a search result. It is not possible to navigate

---

[14] http://www.dmoz.org/Kids_and_Teens/International/Deutsch/

[15] http://www.robotstxt.org/

[16] http://tika.apache.org/

(a) The user is asked to provide information about their age.

(b) An example query for Pinguine (German for penguins) and the corresponding results are shown [pub:1].

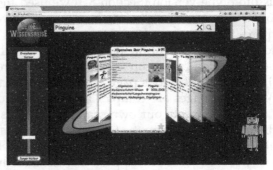

(c) Search result (here medienwerkstatt-online.de) is opened in the same window.

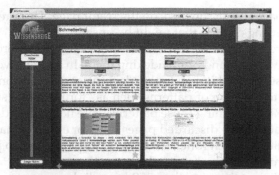

(d) The user has adapted the SUI to a more adult setting using the slider. Two of the shown search results marked with a yellow star are bookmarked.

(e) The left search result has a red frame; this indicates the complexity of the result web page.

(f) Bookmark storage is opened. Stored pages are grouped by the search query.

Fig. 8.12: Interaction example of Knowledge Journey Exhibit.

to other web pages using the links on the result page. This prevents young users from viewing content that might be unsafe.

Furthermore, we used a heuristic during the crawl in order to detect non-informative pages and omit indexing them. In specific, we created two lists, a blacklist and a whitelist. In the blacklist, restrictions on the crawled URLs were listed in form of patterns such as "forum" and "suche=". Web pages with URLs containing those patterns were not included in the index. Using these patterns we discarded pages that, for example, have been generated by a built-in search function of the corresponding web portal. Those web pages contained only the search query.

Pages which contain more than 150 hyperlinks were also not indexed, except for those pages that were classified as good overview pages. Pages that mostly contain hyperlinks are not useful in our offline mode. The user in this mode cannot follow the links and can only view the result pages. The limit of 150 was selected after manually reviewing the pages. Good overview pages were pages that contained information however also had a navigation list (e.g. from A to Z) to other articles. For them a whitelist was used. Pages in the whitelist had strings like "encyclopedia" or "wiki" in the URLs. Those pages have been crawled even if they had more than 150 hyperlinks.

Based on the main text extracted with the Tika library, the Flesch-Reading-Ease index was calculated and stored in the index. In a few cases, due to some HTML parsing errors, the Flesch-Reading-Ease index was out of range. We normalised it, setting values larger than 100 equal to 100 and values smaller than 0.1 equal to 0.1. The latter was used for the ranking to make the multiplier factor larger than 0 (see Eq. 8.2). In the post-processing step duplicates (pages that have the same main text) were removed. The obtained index contains approximately 67,000 pages.

The relevance score of a web page was calculated as a product of the Lucene[17] score, the Flesch-Reading-Ease index and the boost score for high-quality web pages[18] as shown in Eq. 8.2. Using the Flesch-Reading-Ease index, documents that are easier to understand are placed slightly upwards in the ranking. In this version of the Knowledge Journey Exhibit we focused on the adaptivity of the SUI. In addition to the SUI, it is also possible to change the ranking function depending on the targeted user

---

[17] http://lucene.apache.org/

[18] Web pages from the *kindernetz.de*, *medienwerkstatt-online.de* and *palkan.de* were considered to be a high-quality pages and got a boost score of 1.5. The selection of the high-quality web pages was performed manually.

group. For example, the ranking function for young adults can rank complex results higher in the list using the following scoring function. This is an interesting direction for future work.

$$Score_{final} = Score_{lucene} \times boost \times FlashIndex/100 \qquad (8.2)$$

For the query suggestion feature, we used a freely available dictionary of 1.6 million German words. The dictionary was indexed with Lucene. Ten suggestions for the term the user is currently typing are made based on the Levenshtein distance to the indexed dictionary term. After the user has submitted the query, a suggestion "did you mean" is assembled from the top suggestions for each search term. A demonstration video of the Knowledge Journey Exhibit is available at http://www.dke-research.de/KnowledgeJourneyExhibit.html.

8.5 Summary and Discussion

RQ5b

How can the user interface better support search to fulfill a child's information needs? Designing an IR system that grows with children.

In order to answer the research question, we presented in this chapter our concept of an evolving search user interface. An ESUI enables a flexible adaptation of the SUI to address changing user characteristics in order to tackle the issue of diversity support described in Section 7.1. We elaborated which SUI elements can be adapted and how. We suggested to personalise three groups of SUI elements, i.e. search input (menu properties), result output (surrogate properties, results visualisation) and general UI properties (theme, font, audio). We implemented an adaptable SUI with a focus on children (Section 8.2) and carried out a user study with children and adults (Section 8.3).

Our user study had a novel design, i.e. participants built their own SUI and customised its pieces. This can be seen as a novel approach to conduct evaluations of user interfaces with children. As children have problems with abstract thinking, it is difficult for them to provide good feedback about a UI based on mockups which are usually used in user studies with adults. In our user study children were able to give active feedback through direct manipulation of a SUI. They could build a SUI by customising its parts to their preferences, and therefore were able to experience the impact of their selection.

The goal of the user study was to find a mapping between users of different age groups and SUI elements. We confirmed our hypothesis that children and adults would prefer different settings. For example, pupils chose a coverflow results view, whereas adults preferred to use a tiles view. We also received a very positive user feedback about the possibility to adapt the SUI. All the young participants rated our SUI to be at least as good as the one they normally use. However, this user study has some limitations. The testing period with customised settings was relatively short. Users had a large novelty effect and especially children, who are novice users, are not well adept at choosing settings that support their productive use of systems. Therefore, it is possible that after a longer period of SUI usage, users would reconsider and choose some other parameters for the SUI. Thus, a longitudinal study in the future would provide more reliable results. We also only evaluated children of third and fourth grade and adults. In order to develop an ESUI, user studies with users of gradually different ages should be conducted.

Based on the ESUI and the results of the user study, the Knowledge Journey Exhibit was developed (Section 8.4). It enables a flexible adaptation of the search user interface to address changing requirements of users at different age groups. The interface is operated using touch interactions as they are considered to be more natural for children than using a mouse. Users search within a safe environment. For this purpose a search index was created using a focused crawler. KJE is independent from other services (e.g. Bing API). Several adjustments were made to make the system age-adaptable and robust. The next step is to make the system adaptive. An adaptive system will require a backend algorithm to detect user's age, e.g. based on the issued queries (see Section 8.1.3).

Chapter 9

Supporting Visual Searchers in Processing Search Results

In this chapter, we explore alternative ways to visualise search results for children. We propose a novel search result visualisation using characters. The main idea is to represent each web document as a cartoon style character where a character visually provides clues about the webpage's content. The goal we want to achieve with this approach is twofold: We aim at supporting children in processing the search results and provide appropriate relevance cues (*relevance judgement support*, cf. Section 7.1). Furthermore, we want to provide children with *language support* (cf. Section 7.1). Visual clues in search results can support children who have difficulties processing textual information. They are also important because children prefer visual clues when processing the search results (see Chapter 6).

This chapter is structured as follows. Related work is described in Section 9.1. The character concept is described in Section 9.2. Following the user-centered development approach, we conducted a preliminary user study to determine how children would represent a webpage as a sketch based on a given template of a character (Section 9.3). Using the study results the first prototype of a search engine was developed (Section 9.4). We evaluated the search interface on a touchpad and a touch table in a second user study and analysed user's satisfaction and preferences (Section 9.5). The content of this chapter has been published in [pub:4].

9.1 Related Work

In the following, we provide more details about the aspects that are in focus of our research, i.e. the presentation of search results and the usage of avatars.

9.1.1 Presentation of Search Results

An important part of a SUI is the visualisation of search results. Common presentation forms of search results that are currently in use are described by Hearst [81]. Usually search results are displayed as a vertical list of information summarising the retrieved documents. An item in the result list consists of the web document's title, source (URL) along with a brief summary of a relevant portion of the document. This collection of information is also called a document *surrogate* [81, Chapter 5]. The surrogate's content aims to provide relevance clues, i.e. help the searcher to judge the relevance of the document before seeing it. Relevance is a measure of how closely a given web document matches a user's information need. This judgment is done by the user and depends on different factors, e.g. his domain-knowledge, the context of the search, previously seen results. Given a query, so called query-oriented summaries are provided, which contain text references to query terms. Furthermore, query terms are highlighted to make them more visually salient, which enables a faster information access.

A summarisation of preattentive techniques for visualisation of information relevance is given by Deller et al. [42]. Preattentive techniques allow a user to unconsciously accumulate information before actively focusing on an information entity. They do not require much effort or attention of a user. Features such as the search result's position, orientation, colour and intensity, size, animation, and stereoscopic depth have been discussed in terms of their effectiveness, comprehensibility, and visual interference and evaluated with adults. Based on the previous research, e.g. [112], animation, colour and size are promising features for children. However, the usage of these features as relevance clues should be evaluated in future user studies.

Most search engines for children use a vertical list visualisation of search results similar to common search engines. However, the surrogates of some search engines for children also contain a webpage picture. Furthermore, surrogates in search engines for children may also contain information about rank, category of the result, the target age group or reading level (e.g. see Fig. 9.1).

Previous SUIs for primary school children use three basic forms of search result visualisation, i.e. a vertical list visualisation of search results

---

[3] http://blinde-kuh.de, accessed on 2013-11-01.

Fig. 9.1: First search result of the German search engine Blinde-Kuh[3]. The surrogate contains meta information about web documents, e.g. the target age group in categories "S", "M", "L", "XL" for children from six to thirteen [pub:4].

(e.g. *Emma Search* [60]), coverflow (e.g. *Knowledge Journey* [pub:13], *ImagePile* [3]) or tiles (e.g. *International Children's Digital Library* [84]). They also use a "standard" surrogate visualisation as a block that contains a webpage picture or thumbnail, title and textual summary. To our knowledge, there was no research on how children would represent a webpage as a surrogate, what information they would consider to be important and how they would visualise it. This research is important to support children during relevance estimation. Therefore, in this work, we investigate an alternative visualisation of search results for children with characters following a user-centered development approach.

9.1.2 *Usage of Avatars*

The idea to use characters for search result visualisation is related to the usage of avatars in user interfaces. Boberg, Piippo, and Ollila [19] define avatar as the embodiment of the user in a digital environment. For example, the avatar idea was employed in music information research. Haro et al. [78] suggested to use a musical avatar to visualise a user's musical preferences. Musical preferences of a given user are mapped to the visual domain. Specifically, music genre, mood and other features are mapped to avatars head, eyes, mouth, hair, hat and instrument. Moreover, avatars have been used in SUIs for children in a role of a guidance figure that provides additional support for children, e.g. by spell checking [60, pub:13]. Children like to have a guidance figure (Section 7.2), thus, an avatar creates an emotional bond with an SUI which increases children's willingness to accept its help during the search. Here, we propose to visualise search results as characters, where a character visually provides clues about the webpage's content. Characters in this work are not the same as avatars because they do not define the users but the search results.

Our character approach is also related to the graphical method to represent multidimensional data with faces [31]. Chernoff [31] proposed to visualise each data point in the data set as a computer-drawn cartoon face. Different parts of the face, such as nose, eyes, mouth, correspond to the parameter values of the data point by their shape, size, placement and orientation. This graphical approach makes it easier for people to process the data.

9.2 Character Concept

In the following, we elaborate on the character concept. We describe the character idea, its advantages for children and possible implementation.

9.2.1 Idea and Advantages

Appropriate metaphor: The idea to represent a webpage as a person or character[2] is motivated by the fact that children often ask adults about information they would like to know. Vygotsky [192] describes this process in his social development theory. He argues that a child learns many important things through social interaction with a skillful tutor and social factors play a role in a child's cognitive development. A skillful tutor can be a parent, a relative, a person in the child's environment or another child, e.g. a schoolmate. The theory of Vygotsky applies to pre-school and school age children [192]. Information exchange between people can serve as a metaphor for searching for information on the Internet. Each webpage is a person that can explain some facts to a child.

Visual clues: Images better match the cognitive skills of children than written words [75]. Therefore, we suggest to visualise each search result as a character, where a character visually provides clues about the webpage's content.

Motivation factor: Furthermore, search result visualisation with characters is playful and will bring children likely more joy than just textual labeling of search results. Therefore, this approach is a means of emotional support for children as positive disposition towards the system keeps them motivated.

9.2.2 Template Structure

We considered the following criteria for a character design to be important: simple and concise layout, adding features through layers is easy, cute and fun design.

Simple and concise layout: Characters can serve as a unique representation of a web document, i.e. each character is unique. However, this method is not feasible due to the huge size of the Internet. Another solution is to use a template of a character and map different webpage features to the template parts. In this way, a compromise between a characters' indi-

---

[2] The character approach and the SUI with characters were developed as a part of this thesis project in [stud:2]. Rene Müller assisted in two user studies described in the current chapter and helped to analyse the results.

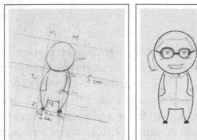

Fig. 9.2: Character development: design, rough drawing, fine drawing, vector graphics [pub:4, stud:2].

viduality and its adaptability for all pages can be found. By analysing popular applications for children, a compromise solution was found. Nintendo has Wii avatars also called Mii[3] which are characterised by a template with a few degrees of freedom. All avatars have a simple 3D template which is enriched with features that make the figure customisable without large deviation from the basic template. Generated avatars look similar, however small face adjustments make them unique.

Adding features through layers is easy: A character template can be designed in different ways. The challenge in this work was to design a child-friendly character which is also adaptable. Therefore, we chose a comic look for the characters, similar to the look of musical avatars in [78]. Characteristics of comic characters are easier to recognise because they are added through layers [130]. Comic characters are a popular medium and well known to children. They have a simple look and bring both fun and game feeling, which is not achievable with realistic characters. Furthermore, we decided to create a 2D template of a character. A 2D template is simpler than a 3D one and allows the creation of a character with less computational effort.

Cute and fun design: In order to achieve a cute and fun design, we decided to use anime styles, specifically a Chibi [22] like character: Chibis' head size is large. It is equal to the size of the body. This makes the character look cute because of the resemblance with babies. The final process of character development is shown in Fig. 9.2.

---

[3] http://www.miicharacters.com/, accessed on 2013-11-01.

9.2.3 Visualised Features

The type of features that should be visualised with the character's help presents an open question. We propose to divide features into two categories: *explicit* and *implicit*. Explicit features come directly from the webpage's elements such as text, images, background colour etc. Implicit features, on the other hand, have to be extracted from the webpage first, using diverse algorithms. Examples of implicit features are the webpage's topic, the age of the webpage (time of the last modification) or the webpage's complexity in terms of text size or reading level. The number of features that should be visualised by a character presents an open question as well. The more features a character reflects, the harder it is to learn and recognise the coded information. Children in primary school age are in the concrete operational stage of their development (see Section 2.2). They can classify physical objects according to several features and order them along a single dimension such as e.g. size [146]. Children are also able to coordinate at most two dimensions of an object simultaneously [146]. Therefore, we suggest that the number of coded features for children of this age is limited to two.

9.3 Webpage Mapping by Children

We conducted a first user study in order to investigate how children would represent webpages by a sketch based on a given colouring template of a character (see Fig. 9.3). Children's interest in painting was used as a motivation factor to participate in the study. Painting is known as an effective tool in the user interface development with children [44, 139, 193].

9.3.1 Tasks

We had two tasks. For the first task, children had to assign one or several colours to a topic. This information could later be used to decide on a colour coding of the webpage topics. We selected topics to support both educational and entertainment needs of children, as recommend in [112].

Fig. 9.3: Evaluation with children. Children painted webpages based on a given colouring template of a character.

Specifically, we chose topics like games, sports, hobbies, leisure, news, science, nature, travel (geography) to also meet the information needs of children [120]. For the second task, children painted a sketch of a character in order for it to represent a specific webpage. For this, we selected web documents for children from different topics described above. Character templates and web documents were printed in A4 format. After studying the webpage, children drew a character that they would associate with the page. Children could paint as many webpages as they liked. Web documents were selected randomly for each child. We did not provide information about the webpages' topics to the participants. After each painting was finished, we asked the children to explain what they had drawn and why using a follow-up interview.

9.3.2 Results

The study was conducted in June 2013 during Magdeburg University Science Day where the public is invited to visit exhibits provided by the university researchers. This event always attracts much attention of parents with children. The children were approached and asked if they wish to participate in the study. Their parents signed the consent form and were free to visit other exhibits in the meantime. We used a large table for participants to paint. Children worked individually on their study assignments and were supervised by study conductors. Children used colouring markers and pencils for painting (see Fig. 9.4).

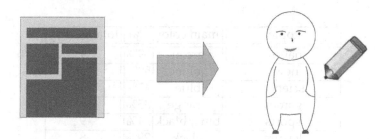

Fig. 9.4: Mapping a webpage to a given colouring template of a character [stud:2].

18 children participated in the user study, eleven boys and seven girls between six and thirteen (see Table 9.1). The first task was solved by 17 of 18 children. A six year old child could not solve the task because he did not understand the connection between a topic and a colour. This conforms with human development theory of Piaget [154] that states that younger children have difficulties with abstract thinking.

Age	6	7	8	9	10	11	12	13	#	$\varnothing age$
Girls	0	1	1	2	0	1	2	0	7	9.71
Boys	1	0	2	1	2	3	0	2	11	10
Overall	1	1	3	3	2	4	2	2	18	9.89

Table 9.1: Demographic data of participants [pub:4].

The results of the first task show that the children could easily assign colours to half of the topics. These topics are nature, news, games and science (see Table 9.2). The children probably had differing associations with other topics and therefore the variety of colours is larger. In order to determine a colour for topics with less agreement among the participants, we used topic colours that were chosen by a high percentage of participants (green, blue, orange). We assigned topics to one of the three groups (each group had a topic with a dominant colour assignment) and sorted them by the degree of membership to the education and entertainment topics. The dominant colours were interpolated on the remaining topics using a colour gradient. The final colour assignment is shown in Fig. 9.5.

topic	main color	%	total variety
nature	green	59%	4
news	blue	59%	6
science	blue	47%	6
games	orange	35%	7
sports	blue/black	24%	9
leisure	black	29%	8
hobbies	yellow	29%	10
travel (geography)	blue	17%	9

Table 9.2: Colour distribution: 59% of the children assigned a green colour to the nature topic, the remaining participants suggested three other colours. For the sports topic there were two dominant colours that received an equal number of user's votes [pub:4].

For the second task, the participants were asked to paint a webpage using a character template. Four participants (among them also older ones) did not understand the task. One participant (thirteen years old) understood the task, had however no ideas on what to draw. Furthermore, some older children did not know how to implement their ideas in pictures. In that case, children were given other webpages to work with. Fig. 9.6 depicts the most interesting paintings and the corresponding (German) webpages. In the following, we briefly summarise the explanations of the children regarding their paintings:

Example 1 (Fig. 9.6a) Webpage about German family in Spain: The colours of the character's t-shirt represent Germany and Spain. The blue head represents water (an island was mentioned in the text). A green colour was used because the text mentioned nature. The sun was painted on the pants because the webpage is about Spain. Gray colour was used because of the

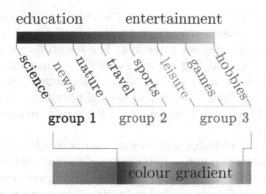

education   entertainment

science news nature travel sports leisure games hobbies

group 1   group 2   group 3

colour gradient

Fig. 9.5: Design of colour distribution for topics [pub:4, stud:2]. Colour gradient between blue (group 1), green (group 2) and orange (group 3) colours is used to interpolate the dominant colours on the remaining topics.

mountains. "They are hiking in the mountains," the boy said (mountains were mentioned in the text).

Example 2 (Fig. 9.6b) Webpage about sightseeing in Paris: The character has both "boy and girl" hair. The exclamation marks represent "information, a lot of text." The text header "Paris" was used because Paris is mentioned in the webpage's text. A world atlas was painted on the head because Paris is "famous, known everywhere." "Blue (colour of the t-shirt) stands for lots of information." "Yellow (colour of the pants) because one becomes smarter." The boy also painted a brain to show that the reader gets "smarter and cheerful."

Example 3 (Fig. 9.6c) Webpage about scavenger hunt (The website has a textual description of the game and a picture of a hand reaching for tree branches.): The character is a girl "just because." The characters' clothing also has no special meaning. The girl painted trees and nature because the game described in the text is outside. She painted different paths and markings because the webpage's title is scavenger hunt.

Example 4 (Fig. 9.6d) Webpage about spring season (The website has a text about spring and two images of a snowdrop flower and a pussy-willow): The girl painted four seasons as the character's background. The character is a girl because of "personal" reasons.

Example 5 (Fig. 9.6e) Webpage about sightseeing in Paris: The character has a skin colour and hair "like a normal person." The character wears a blue jacket and jeans like "normal people". The character is "going to Paris." It has a baguette because a baguette is "typical for France." It also has a bag because one needs a bag for travelling. The french flag is painted on the bag. (Baguette, bag and flag are not explicitly mentioned in the text and are not present on the webpage's images.) The character imagines what he is going to visit in Paris. That is why thought bubbles are painted where each Paris sight is shown. (The images of the sights are similar to the ones on the webpage.)

Example 6 (Fig. 9.6f) Webpage about mathematics, milliliter to liter conversion: A thought bubble was painted on the character's forehead "so that children know they have to count". T-shirt has a text "milliliters conversion" taken from the webpage. The character has "normal" hair and pants.

Overall, children depicted explicit features of webpages such as text and images and implicit features such as objects or colours which to them represent the topic. Interestingly, many children tried to humanise the character by drawing hair or complexion. A summary of depicted features and techniques applied by children is shown in Table 9.3.

22% of the children embedded objects which were directly mentioned in the text or were a part of a webpages' image. For example, a squirrel was added to the character's surrounding because the web document contained text about squirrels. 17% of the children also incorporated text from web documents in their drawings (e.g. Fig. 9.6b,f).

44% of the children used colours and 33% depicted objects associated with words in the text or the webpage's images. For example, a character's head was painted in blue because the text contained information about water, and a sun was painted because the webpage was about Spain (Fig. 9.6a).

28% of the children drew outside the character. 17% of the children painted the character's surrounding to show the context (e.g. Fig. 9.6c,d). However, the characters itself do not provide any information about the webpages. The information about the webpage was drawn around the character. 11% of the children attached objects and features to the character, e.g. a lightsaber to depict a webpage about computer games. One child embedded the character in a scenario: Fig. 9.6e shows that the character is set in the context of Paris and travel. Therefore, Paris related objects such as baguette, and travel related objects such as a hat and a bag were painted. Thought bubbles were used to show that the character is going to visit different sights in Paris, a bubble for each sight, because the webpage was about traveling to Paris.

(a) boy, 9   (b) boy, 10   (c) girl, 12

(d) girl, 9   (e) girl, 11   (f) boy, 11

Fig. 9.6: Preliminary study: most interesting children's paintings and corresponding (German) webpages for children: story about German family in Spain (helles-koepfchen.de), sightseeing in Paris (boeser-wolf.schule.de), scavenger hunt (labbe.de), spring season (medienwerkstatt-online.de), sightseeing in Paris (boeser-wolf.schule.de), math (kidstation.de) [pub:4].

One child (6%) employed many techniques. He depicted meta information about the webpage in his drawing using symbols (e.g. to express information complexity in Fig. 9.6b). The child also used colours in his other drawings, e.g. to describe emotions about the content. He used orange for fun to signal that the web document is about games and blue for cold to signal that the webpage is about winter song lyrics.

feature category	webpage feature	technique	N	%	age
explicit	objects described in text/image	drawings	4	22%	7,8,13
	text	incorporation	3	17%	10,11
implicit	associations with word or image context	usage of colours	8	44%	6,8,9,10,13
		drawing of objects	6	33%	6,8,9,10,11
		objects/features are attached	2	11%	8,10
		painting of character's surrounding	3	17%	8,9,12
		character embedded in a scenario	1	6%	11
	meta-information	usage of symbols	1	6%	10
	emotions	usage of colours	1	6%	10

Table 9.3: Depicted features and techniques applied by the children (n=18) during the study, participants' number and age [pub:4].

9.4 Search Result Visualisation with Characters

Most of the children that participated in the study were able to depict a webpage using a character. This encouraged us to continue along this design path and to make some decisions about the SUI design based on the study results. For the first prototype, we concentrated on the design of the characters and the SUI layout. For the character's design we used the ideas from the children's paintings such as a thought bubble, the inclusion of a background, the use of colour, the characters' humanisation with hair and complexion, and the collapsing of character accessories into the subject categories.

We also considered webpage features that children paid attention to in the study. However, a too large number of coded features is considered to be difficult for children to comprehend [146], we decided for a character to depict two webpage features: One feature used by the majority of children in the user study was the association with words or images. For association we used topics. Topics are a level of abstraction, e.g. the set "bag, flag of Germany, flag of England, airplane, bus, train" can be summarised as the travel topic. The number of topics is significantly smaller than the possible number of low-level subjects. Therefore, it is easier and faster for children to learn the meaning of each topic representation.

We used a dual coding approach to depict topics. The topic information is visualised using the colours which were determined in the first user study. Characters representing different topics have a specific clothing colour. We also used the idea from the user study about painting a character's surrounding to show the context. Characters representing different topics have a specific background (e.g. Fig. 9.7). For example, a character that belongs to the "Nature" topic has a landscape with trees around it (as seen in children's paintings Fig. 9.3c,d). Thus, topic information is dually coded with colours and background images.

Another feature was a representative picture from the webpage. For this, we used the children's idea about comic elements such as thought bubbles. Each character has a thought bubble with further explicit informa-

Fig. 9.7: "Nature" topic design: character's surrounding to show the context; a pair of characters that represent two different webpages that are distinguished using different hair and complexion; and a final character design [pub:4, stud:2].

tion about the webpage's content such as a representative picture from the webpage. In order to distinguish between different characters which belong to the same topic, character elements such as hair, glasses, hat, shoes, eyes and lips shapes are used. Thus, a particular webpage has a distinctive combination of those elements.

The SUI itself has an input field for textual queries. Under the input field a category bar is placed. The category bar consists of eight topics which are visualised as boxes. Boxes transmit both background and colour information at the same time. This makes it easy to associate each search result with the corresponding topic. The category bar also provides information about which topic the search results belong to. In case a topic is not presented among the results, the box is faded.

Fig. 9.8: First users have to choose between the Alice and Tim layout of the SUI [stud:2].

We designed two versions of search result visualisation using characters (see Fig. 9.8). The first one, called Alice (Fig. 9.9), is an analogue of cover-flow. Coverflow was found to be the best choice for younger children (see Chapter 7 and Chapter 8). The selected element is clearly separated from the rest and a user can concentrate on one item at a time, thus resulting in a smaller cognitive load. The second version, called Tim (Fig. 9.10), is an

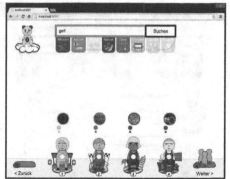

(a) Search for (German) "golf", first four results are shown.

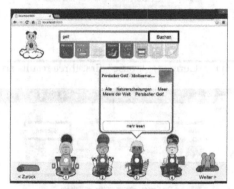

(b) Third result was clicked.

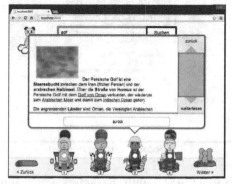

(c) Third result is opened.

Fig. 9.9: Screenshot of the SUI with characters: horizontal result arrangement ("Alice") [pub:4, stud:2].

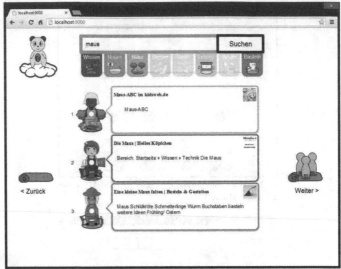

(a) Search for (German) "mouse", first three results are shown.

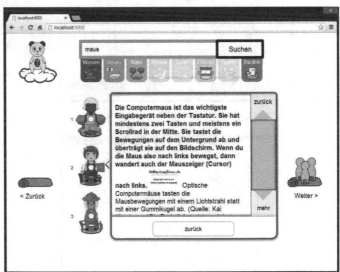

(b) Second result is opened.

Fig. 9.10: Screenshot of the SUI with characters: vertical result arrangement ("Tim") [pub:4, stud:2].

analogue of the list result visualisation and is meant for older children. A vertical list of surrogates offers a fast overview of several results at once. By clicking on the snippet the result webpage is opened in the same window (Fig. 9.10b). The same window was chosen to better support the children's navigation in the search engine and to prevent backtracking.

For the backend we used Lucene to create a search index. Our index contained 311 web documents[4] selected from webpages for children to assure a high quality of search results. In comparison, in earlier studies we used 60 web documents for children (Section 7.3) or the Bing Search API with general web documents (Section 8.3). Each document was manually assigned to one of the eight topics. We also used the Readability.com[5] API to process web documents in order to show them in a clean and readable view (common format, no advertisement) which makes it easier for children to read. Our application works on touchscreen devices. We think that touch interaction is more natural for children than the usage of mouse. Touchscreen devices also become a part of our everyday life in the form of smartphones.

9.5 User Study

The goal of this user study was to evaluate usability aspects of the SUI with characters such as learnability, satisfaction, children's layout and search engine preferences. We also wanted to gather users' feedback about the SUI.

9.5.1 Study Design

Our user study was designed as follows: we used a pre-interview to gather children's demographic information, their Internet and touch device experience. Then a lab experiment was performed using two versions of the SUI with characters, Alice and Tim. In order to reduce the bias due to the order in which the participants are using the UI, we applied a latin square design.

---

[4] A subset of these documents (25 documents) was used in the drawing study.
[5] http://readability.com/, accessed on 2013-11-01.

Thus, half of the participants were asked to use Alice interface first and then to use Tim, whereas the other half did this in reverse sequence. Using each interface, children performed a task-oriented search, i.e. focussed on the completion of a particular task. In addition, we took notes about participants' unexpected behaviour. After that, children were interviewed about UI features they liked most or disliked and what could be done to improve the SUI. Finally, we asked the participants what user search interface they preferred. The supervisors encouraged the participants to share their opinion to help the scientists build better search engines for children. The questionnaire for the structured interview with children is provided in Appendix A.5.

We used search tasks during the lab experiment as we believe a search task helps the participants to better explore the SUI in comparison to try-out sessions without a particular task. The search tasks were administered verbally. Children were asked to enter a pre-defined query for each task. The search tasks were designed to show the benefits of the visualisation of topic information with characters:

▶ *Task 1:* Find out the location of the Persian Gulf (German "Persischer Golf") using the search query "golf".

▶ *Task 2:* Find out the names of three species of mice using the search query "mouse".

The predefined queries were ambiguous. For example, in task 1, there were results about golf as a game and golf as a bay. Knowing the result topic, the participants should be able to determine the relevance of a search result in a more efficient way. After a child entered a query, he or she was also asked to assign each of the first three search results to one of the eight topics.

Two touch devices were used in the user study, an Apple iPad and a 30-inch touchscreen tabletop Microsoft Surface 1.0. Each participant performed a lab experiment individually, either using the touchpad or the touch table. Children were randomly assigned to one of the devices. For efficiency reasons we conducted experiments on both devices in parallel with a supervisor each. The session lasted on average 30 minutes.

Participants: The study was conducted in July 2013 during children's university days. 22 children participated in the user study, twelve boys and ten girls between six and twelve (see Table 9.4).

In our study, 51% of six and seven year old children seldom use the Internet or did not use it at all, whereas 88% of older children use the Internet

Age	6	7	8	9	10	11	12	#	$\varnothing age$
Girls	0	2	2	1	2	4	1	12	9.58
Boys	2	3	2	1	0	2	0	10	8
Overall	2	5	4	2	2	6	1	22	8.86

Table 9.4: Demographic data of participants [pub:4].

at least once a week. 68% of the children use the Internet without supervision. The distribution is uniform over the various age groups. Children use the Internet mostly to play online games (68%) and search for information mainly regarding homework (36%). In order to search for information, 68% of the children use Google.de, 23% use the search engine for children Blinde-Kuh.de. Less than 10% of the children also mentioned the search engines for children FragFinn.de and Helles-Koepfchen.de. Participants were familiar with touch devices: 68% of the children had used a touch device before, among them 50% of the six and seven year old children. Information about the participants is summarised in Section B.5.

9.5.2 Study Results

Learnability: The children were asked to assign each of the first three search results to one of the eight topics. In total, there were six search results with different topics given two interface versions and tasks. The largest recognition rate was 90%, i.e. 90% of the children correctly recognised that a search result belonged to the sports or travel topic. The leisure topic had the smallest recognition rate, it was recognised by 50% of the children. We observed, however, a positive learning effect: Using the second interface, three characters from the other three topics were correctly identified by all 22 subjects and the maximum error rate was only 25%. We noticed that the characters helped the children to be more efficient. Especially in the first task, they skipped the first characters with the wrong topic and directly selected the right result. However, more accurate data should be collected in the future.

User satisfaction: 76% of the children assessed our SUI with characters as easy to use. The rest of the participants (six and seven year old) gave a

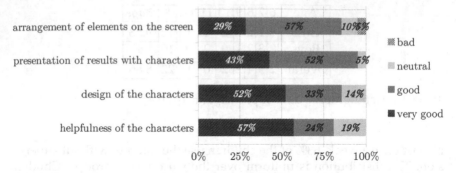

Fig. 9.11: Assessment of different UI aspects.

negative assessment because they had difficulties with reading texts and had to read too much. Younger children had difficulties with reading and supervisors had to help them by reading the texts for them. Therefore, a text-to-speech function should be provided for those children. One twelve year old child wished that the results were sorted by the topic. He told us that he had attention difficulties (ADHS).

More than 80% of the children rated the usability of different UI elements as at least good (see Fig. 9.11). We used a five-point Likert scale from very good to very bad. Each scale was visualised with smileys. This "Smileyometer" [161] was shown to the participants. The children assessed the arrangement of the elements on the screen as very good (29%) and good (57%). The Alice layout was criticised because too much free space was not used. The children assessed the presentation of results with characters as very good (43%) and good (52%). The children assessed the design of the characters as very good (52%) and good (33%). However, the participants opinion was divided. Whereas the younger children found the figures rather "funny" and "nice", the older participants would have preferred "more professional" figures and assessed the used ones as "odd". The children assessed the characters as being very helpful (57%) and helpful (24%) in topic recognition.

Search engine preferences: The new SUI received a positive response: 50% of the six and seven year old, 67% of the eight and nine year old, and 11% of the children between ten and twelve found it to better than the ones they used before. The rest of the participants between six and nine were unsure or found both to be equally good. Only the children between ten and twelve appeared to be more biased towards the conventional search engine Google (44%). However, the only explanation we received after asking for the preference reasons was "because Goolge is cool."

We also experienced that children have associated the search user interface with the used device or the search task difficulty, indicating the lack of abstraction. For the usability questions, supervisors had to emphasise the fact that children were asked about the SUI and not the devices or the search task.

Layout preferences: Comparing the two layouts (Fig. 9.9 and Fig. 9.10) the children preferred the Tim (52%) over the Alice (24%) layout, the rest of the children could not decide. The results are summarised in Fig. 9.12. Against our assumption, even younger children (six and seven year old) had a preference towards the Tim (33%) over the Alice (17%). However, 50% of the children were uncertain. The children did not like that in Alice they had to do one extra click to get to the webpage content. They preferred to see the textual summary right away and to be able to view several results at once as in the Tim layout. "One sees a bit of text right away and can have a look (at the web page) straight away." Children who chose the Alice liked the layout simplicity and visual attractiveness. Alice is "lovely", "easier", "does not have as much text (as Tim)".

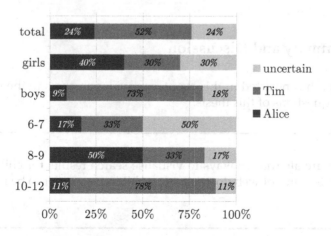

Fig. 9.12: Layout preferences grouped by gender and age: Alice versus Tim search result arrangement [pub:4].

Touch devices: Participants who used the Apple iPad rated search tasks to be more difficult than the ones who used the Microsoft Surface, especially for the second search task (iPad, 25% and Surface, 70% of the children found the task to be easy). For the second search task, one had to do more navigation effort and go to the next result pages in contrast to the first task, where the answer could already be found on the first result page. The screen size of the iPad is smaller than the one of the Microsoft Surface and it is harder to read the coded topic information. 86% of the children found the browsing of the search results to be easy. Only some participants who used the iPad found it to be hard (however without explanation). We suppose that the smaller screen size of the iPad could have a negative impact on the result browsing. 81% of the participants found touch interaction to be easy. Children who found touch interaction to be difficult were between six and eight, they told us however they have already used touch devices before.

User Feedback: The children especially liked that the UI is touch-based. They also liked the thought bubble with pictures and the characters. Search engine "with characters is made more for children". One child wished the results to be grouped and ordered by categories or that one could filter the results belonging to one category using the category bar. One child emphasised the appropriate size of the input field.

9.6 Summary and Discussion

The research conducted in this chapter provides answers to the following research questions of this thesis:

> **RQ6a**
>
> What are alternative ways to visualise search results for children? What features of web documents do children consider to be important?

We can positively answer the question about the possibility of alternative ways to visualise search results for children. In this thesis, an alternative visualisation approach using characters was introduced. A web document is represented as a character, where the features of a web document are mapped to different parts of a character. The user studies that were conducted in this research show the potential of search result visualisation with characters. We were able to determine the children's view on web pages, what features of a web page are important for children and how they would visualise them. For this, we asked them to paint a sketch of a character in order for it to represent a specific webpage and analysed the paintings. The results of this user study indicate that the children consider features such as objects described in text and images, text, associations with words in text or image content, meta information and emotions to be important.

RQ6b

What are alternative ways to visualise search results for children? How do children visualise a web document as a search result?

They use colours, symbols and depicted objects, e.g. attached to the character. This takes us a step further in the direction to support children in relevance estimation (see Section 7.1). The usage of visual clues in result surrogates that are conformant with the children's view on web documents help children in judging the relevance of a document (relevance judgement support). It also supports children who have difficulties processing textual information (language support).

The results of the second study indicate that the SUI we developed is mostly preferred by eight and nine year old children. We determined the advantages and disadvantages of two possible layouts for search results with characters, and a stronger preference towards the Tim layout. However, in order to support diversity both layouts can be offered to users to choose from. This work also has some limitations. We used a wide age range of children in our studies. However, it helped us to determine the specific age of a target group that would use our SUI (eight and nine year old children). We also left out the evaluation of the effectiveness of our SUI. We saw some indicators of higher effectiveness (children skipped irrelevant results without opening the web pages). However, a comparative user study to investigate children's performance using a SUI with characters and one without should be conducted.

Overall, the result visualisation with characters presents many opportunities for information retrieval: Besides search result visualisation, a character can be used in a query by example scenario [29, 77], where the character represents an abstract search query. One can use a library for character's clothing, objects etc. for the user to chose from. A user creates a character using the library to provide an example for similar webpages he or she would like to find. Each feature of the created character serves as an abstract representation of a hypernym term for the query. Furthermore, a character can be used for personalised ranking. A user creates his own profile using a character (as an avatar) which reflects the users' interests.

The character concept offers many opportunities for further development: One can increase the number of web document features that are visualised with the help of a character using the findings of our first user study. For example, one could add meta information such as text complexity, e.g. determined based on the readability level [64, 152] or text coherence [117] and visualise it using exclamation marks. It is also possible to extract emotions of the web document with sentiment analysis algorithms [11, 118] and visualise emotions using colours. Another idea for the future work is for the character to literally represent the kind of person the child would like to get an answer from. Thus, characters can be divided into parental figures, friends or teachers, where, for example, friends are web documents that contain information written in a child's language.

Part IV
Conclusion and Outlook

Chapter 10

Conclusion

In this thesis, criteria and guidelines on how to design search user interfaces for children have been proposed and discussed. They contribute in different ways to the achievement of the overall main goal: the development of interactive systems for information search for children as a targeted user group with special focus on the user interface. The work is summarised in Section 10.1. Section 10.2 points out the main contributions of this thesis. But while arguably significant steps have been taken, the problem is still only partially solved. Section 10.3 discusses limitations of the proposed approaches and points out directions of future research.

10.1 Summary

Part I served as a foundation for the work of this thesis: A general introduction of the Information Retrieval (IR) research field was given in Chapter 2. In particular, the basics of IR were explained. The specifics of IR for children were elaborated using theories from the humanities. This chapter also covered the main methods and types of user studies, and the specifics of user studies with children. Chapter 3 provided a systematic overview of the state of the art in information retrieval for children. The survey summarised the findings of previous user studies about children's information search behaviour. It also provided an overview of existing algorithms, search user interfaces and web search engines that were developed for children as a target group.

In Part II, open issues about children's information seeking behaviour have been identified. In Chapter 4, a methodology to estimate the usability of existing search engines for young users was developed. Using this methodology, a case study with English and German web search engines was conducted. The results indicate that current search engines do not always match children's cognitive and fine motor skills. In Chapter 5, a large-scale analysis of children's queries and searching interactions was conducted based on the log data from three major German search engines for children. The findings indicate that children experience difficulties while searching. Short search queries of children indicate that young users may have difficulties with query formulation. Short search sessions of children can be a sign of children becoming frustrated and giving up faster than adults in the case that they do not find the desirable search results. In order to study the differences in children's and adults' perception and performance of targeted search engines, an eyetracking user study was conducted and described in Chapter 6. The results show differences in the perception of SERPs and the search performance between the two user groups. For example, the results of this study indicate that user interface elements such as thumbnails and embedded media attract children much more than adults and affect their reading flow.

Part III tackled the challenges in design of search user interface for children. In Chapter 7 conceptual challenges were derived based on our findings in Part II, findings from previous research and the human science theories. These challenges are emotional, language, cognitive, memory, interaction, relevance judgement and diversity support. In particular, Chapter 7 proposes various possible solutions for challenges in the design of search user interfaces for children. In order to demonstrate these solutions, a search user interface for children called *Knowledge Journey* was designed, prototypically implemented and evaluated in a user study. While some of the solutions were simple, the solutions for emotional, diversity and relevance judgement support required novel approaches and further research. A voice-controlled search was identified as a means of emotion detection. Therefore, a pilot study in form of a *Wizard-of-Oz-Experiment* was conducted in order to investigate the potentials of a voice-controlled version of *Knowledge Journey*. However, the results of the study indicate that children have difficulties with voice-control and would rather prefer input by touch.

In Chapter 8, an evolving search user interface was proposed in order to tackle the issue of user diversity. Conceptually, this is an adaptive system that enables a flexible adaptation of the SUI to address changing user characteristics. In this thesis, we concentrated on the frontend of the search engine and developed a prototype that can be customised to the user's needs (Section 8.2). This interface was prototypically implemented as a part of a supervised master thesis [stud:3]. A user study was conducted in order to study the feasibility of the solution and to find out the default ESUI settings for children and adults. Based on the Evolving Knowledge Journey and the results of the user study, the *Knowledge Journey Exhibit* (KJE) was developed as a robust information terminal for an exhibition that takes place annually at multiple train stations in Germany. KJE is a system that takes user's age as a parameter for adaptation (Section 8.4).

In Chapter 9 a novel approach for search result visualisation with cartoon style characters was elaborated. This approach was developed by supervised master thesis [stud:2]. The main idea is to represent each web document as a character where a character visually provides clues about the webpage's content. Characters were co-designed with children. In a user study with children, we found out what features of web documents children consider to be important and how they would visualise the documents as characters. A follow-up user study investigated usability aspects of the SUI with characters and children's layout preferences. The results of Chapter 9 take us a step further in the direction to support children in relevance estimation. The usage of visual clues in result surrogates that correspond with children's view on web documents, help children judging the relevance of a document.

10.2 Contributions

In the following, the *major* contributions of this thesis are summarised:

▶ **Characteristics of information retrieval for children (cf. *RQ*1):** Based on the theories of human development (Section 2.2), characteristics of information retrieval for children in comparison to adults have been derived (Section 2.4). The connection between cognitive science and information retrieval is important in order to design appropriate IR systems for children.

▶ **A systematic overview of the state of the art in information retrieval for children (cf. *RQ*2, *RQ*4):** The overview given in Chapter 3 is the first attempt to summarise the field. Both findings from user studies about information-seeking behaviour of children and existing algorithms and user interface concepts are discussed. We classified the algorithms and user interface concepts according to the architecture of an IR system and elaborated which components of an IR system can be adapted to the targeted user group children. This work can serve as a basis how to build IR systems for children and guide developers of IR systems for children.

▶ **Assessment of existing search engines for young users (cf. *RQ3*):** Pioneering work was undertaken in order to develop a methodology for the usability assessment of web search engines for children (Chapter 4). Although this methodology is most likely only a starting point, it can be useful for usability engineers to estimate whether current search engines are appropriate for the motor and cognitive skills of children. Using the developed methodology, a case study with twelve search engines was conducted. We hope that the results will increase the awareness among search engine developers and that they will pay more attention to the usability aspects.

▶ **Differences in children's and adults' web information search behaviour (cf. *RQ4*):** In order to better understand the differences in children and adults' web information search behaviour, two user studies were conducted, using logfile analysis (Chapter 5) and an eye-tracker study (Chapter 6). A large-scale logfile study of search behaviour was conducted on targeted web search engines for children. This research is unique. To our knowledge, this is the first large-scale logfile study on children's web search engines. We analysed a high amount of user data over a longer period of time that describe the children's search behaviour in a natural, uncontrolled environment. The author is not aware about other large-scale log studies on targeted web search engines for children. A comparative study about children and adults' performance on and perception of targeted web search engines with eye-tracking is also unique. To our knowledge, this is the first comparative study between children and adults, during both informational and navigational search, on both standard and children's search engine.

▶ **Analysis of conceptual challenges in the design of SUI for children (cf. *RQ5*):** We derived criteria and guidelines on how to design search user interfaces for children (Section 7.1). In particular, we analysed the global objectives (we called challenges) in the design of SUIs for children. The seven conceptual challenges such as emotional, language, cognitive, memory, interaction, relevance judgement and diversity support were elaborated and possible solutions have been discussed. This classification is the first of its kind.

▶ **New approach to address the changing characteristics of the users (cf. *RQ5*):** In order to address changing characteristics of users who are growing up, an *evolving search user interface* that provides means of adaptation was proposed (Chapter 8). It adapts to individual user characteristics and allows for changes not only in properties of UI elements like colour, but also influences the choice of UI elements themselves and their positioning.

▶ **New approach to visualise search results for children (cf. *RQ6*):** A novel type of search result visualisation with cartoon style characters for children was proposed in Chapter 9. The idea is to represent each web document as a character where a character visually provides clues about the webpage's content. This approach aims to support children in processing the search results and provide appropriate relevance cues in order to improve children's reading flow. It takes children's preference for visual information into account. This new concept with characters has many opportunities for information retrieval, for example characters can be used in a query by example scenario.

▶ **Two prototype applications as a demonstrator of the proposed solutions for the conceptual challenges (cf. *RQ5*, *RQ6*):** The first prototype, called *Knowledge Journey*, was developed in three stages and was extensively tested: The first prototype version was developed in order to demonstrate some of the possible solutions for the derived conceptual challenges. This prototype version is presented in Chapter 7. A significant contribution is also a comparative user study that was undertaken to evaluate the search interface against a classic keyword-based SUI with a vertical result listing. While some of the solutions were simple, the solutions for emotional, diversity and relevance judgement support required novel approaches and further research. A voice-controlled search was identified as a means of emotion detection. The potential of voice-controlled searching was investigated in a small user study conducted in form of a *Wizard-of-Oz-Experiment* presented in Section 7.4. Based on the first version of *Knowledge Journey* and the results of previous studies an *evolving search user interface* was prototypically implemented (Chapter 8). A user study both with children and adults was conducted in order to investigate the feasibility of this solution, find the differences between the user groups and derive appropriate default settings for the ESUI. Based on the results of this study, we developed the third prototype version of *Knowledge Journey*. Several adjustments were made to make the system age-adaptable and robust.

The second prototype was developed to demonstrate our approach to visualise search results with characters (Chapter 9). The big contribution here was a user-centered design. We investigated the children's view on web documents, what document features children would consider to be relevant and what visualisation techniques they would apply in order to visualise a document surrogate in form of a character. The search user interface with characters was prototypically implemented and evaluated in a further user study with children.

Based on the previous discussion, it can be concluded that all research questions defined in Section 1.1 have been addressed appropriately with this thesis. The overall research goal, which was to develop interactive systems for information search for children as a targeted user group with special focus on the user interface, has been achieved with this thesis.

10.3 Directions for Future Research

This thesis builds the foundation for interesting research in the future. Several open questions and challenges remain which have not been addressed in this thesis and would nicely continue this work. In the following, limitations and extensions to the work presented in this thesis are briefly discussed:

▶ **Adaptive ESUI:** In Chapter 8, the vision of an evolving search user interface was presented. An evolving search user interface should adapt itself to the specific characteristics of an individual user. In this thesis, we concentra'ed on the frontend of the search engine and developed two prototypes, one which can be customised to the user's needs (Section 8.2) and one that takes user's age as a parameter for adaptation (Section 8.4). However, in order to have an adaptive system, backend algorithms to detect a user's abilities are required. In this thesis, we only elaborated the possible approaches in Section 8.1.3. Moreover, in this work, age was used in order to approximate user's skill space. However, the age is only a fuzzy indicator of what the user's skills are. The design of a mapping function between the user skill space and the options to adapt the UI elements of the SUI is a great challenge for future work. In order to develop an ESUI, user studies with users of gradually different skills should be conducted.

▶ **More features in a SUI with characters:** In Chapter 9, a SUI with characters was developed following a user-centered design. We suggested that the number of coded features for children of primary school age should be limited to two, because children of this age are able to coordinate at most two dimensions of an object simultaneously [146]. Therefore, in our implementation we had a limited number of document features that were depicted by a character such as category and a representative picture. However, a larger amount of features would bring more advantages for a user because it offers more relevance cues. So the open question is whether children can recognise and work with multiple features depicted by a character and where the limit is.

▶ **More detailed evaluation:** In this thesis, we followed a formative evaluation process in order to early detect possible usability problems. A summative usability evaluation would nicely continue this work. The search result visualisation with characters can be integrated into the evolving search user interface and this system can be evaluated in a final user study. This user study should cover two issues: It is important to study the user's usage of the SUI over a longer period of time than a half an hour session because novelty effects could influence the evaluation results. A longitudinal study can provide more reliable results. For this, the SUI can be installed in schools or made available online. Users' interactions with the system can be logged and analysed. For example, the log data can show which UI elements are actually used by users and in what context. This online study would require a functioning infrastructure for the search engine. For example, for a search engine that is supposed to be used over a period of time, it is essential to update the search index. The crawler has to run and dynamically update the search index because some previously indexed web pages might have changed their content or gone offline. Furthermore, it requires quite some time to build an infrastructure in a school or for the search engine to be noticed online by its potential users. The logfile study alone does not provide information about the usability aspects of a system such as efficiency and effectiveness. Therefore, in addition to the logfile study, a comparative user study should be conducted, similar to user studies in Chapter 6 and Section 7.3, that covers all the usability aspects.

Chapter 11

Open Research Issues

This chapter provides a brief overview of more general open research issues in the field of information retrieval for children. We discuss directions concerning search histories for children, ranking algorithms, collaborative IR systems for children and cognitive models for IR system evaluation.

11.1 Search History for Young Users

In Section 7.1 we outlined that children can benefit from new approaches in *personal information management*. According to information processing theory [102], the information processing of children differs from that of adults in terms of how they apply information and what memory limits they have, i.e. children can represent and process less information. Information retrieval processes may cause children's memory to overload. This explains children's "looping" behaviour during the information seeking process. Children click, repeat searches and revisit the same result web page more often than adults do [pub:15, 17]. Children also heavily and more often than adults use the back-button of the web browser [17]. The back-button is a very simple tool for web history [107]. Thus, there is empirical evidence that children do require search history and different history mechanisms incorporated in information retrieval systems for children are of importance. These mechanisms can mitigate memory overload. Besides the memory support, mechanisms of history tracking are important for children as part of an educational process. Children can learn to plan their searches and better understand the workings of a search system by revisioning their own search history. If the "looping" behaviour of children is intentional and a part of a learning process, then a search history would also support children and make revisiting relevant information easier.

The general idea of a search history is to record information-seeking steps of a user, i.e. his or her queries, search results and relevant contextual information [107]. This history provides the user with several benefits. Besides memory support, it also helps to re-find, manage and use information, and it even gives the possibility to exchange information and the search process with other users in case of collaborative search [107]. The idea to support the users' search process by means of a search history is not new. In web search, the back/forward buttons, history lists, and bookmarks in the browser are usually used as history tools where the last two require more mental effort [107]. The back-button is easy to use and thus suits the abilities of children, but only allows to navigate back to a short list of previously visited pages. In addition, there is no overview of the visited pages. A browser's built-in history provides a longer list of visited pages that can be revisited, however it does not contain explicit information about the users' search queries and corresponding (visited) results. A long list of URLs without any contextual information is also hard to process, which makes it hard to use for young users. In order to use bookmarks the user has to annotate a web page as a favourite. Furthermore, he or she can also organize the link bookmarks into folders. The management of bookmarks is still problematic [107]. The usage of bookmarks without a folder structure is difficult. In addition, bookmarks do not provide the time information. Several systems were proposed to support the search history in a more advanced way, e.g. the search history interface proposed by Kaasten and Greenberg [100], the *Ariadne* system [191] and the *DLITE* system [35]. To our best knowledge there exist no search history interfaces that are designed for children. The design of search history interfaces for children is an open issue and an interesting research direction.

11.2 Child-focused Ranking

To our knowledge there exist only one ranking algorithm for children, *AgeRank* [74], that we described in Section 3.2. However, this algorithm was developed and evaluated without children. An open issue is the design of algorithms that would support the children's view on the document relevance. In order to develop a child-focused ranking function, children can be given a search task and asked to provide relevance feedback [165, 168] for documents. Based on the relevance feedback, one can determine what document features should be incorporated in the ranking function and how. It is also possible to learn the ranking function using machine learning techniques [2, 119, 160]. However, it will also require an appropriate amount of children's search data.

Furthermore, children search the Web for information about basic facts and explanations. They have universal questions about the physical world [173]. The results of our logfile study [pub:15] indicate that the information need in terms of the *Broder taxonomy* [24] of children differs from that of adults. The children's queries have a more informational intention. The purpose of *informational queries* is to find information about a topic assumed to be available on the web, in order to read about it. Meanwhile, the adults most frequent queries are *navigational* or *transactional*, with the immediate intent to reach a particular website that the user has in mind, or even further carry out some transactions, e.g. purchasing a product. Children also use the search engines for homework, i.e. queries like "egypt" could reflect the curriculum of their schools. Our hypothesis is that children would prefer web sites which have explanatory information rather than a website where the facts are explained shortly, assuming that the reader already has the basic knowledge to understand it.

In order to support children's informational queries, one can use the *Hyperlink-Induced Topic Search* (HITS) algorithm (see Section 2.1.2) which distinguishes between two types of web pages: hubs and authorities. The idea is that there are authoritative sources of of topic-specific information and pages that contain a collection of links to good authorities pages about some topic e.g. a scientist with an interest in the topic has spent time putting links together. Usually the ranking score of a page accounts for both the authority score and the hub score. We suggest that children specific ranking should consider pages with a high authority score as more relevant. However, this ranking approach should be examined in the future.

11.3 Collaborative IR for Children

Collaborative search is a set of search activities that make use of social interactions with others before, during and/or after the search. These interactions may be explicit or implicit, co-located or remote, synchronous or asynchronous [63, 69]. During collaborative search all participants have the same searching goal and actively conduct a specific search together in order to achieve this goal [70]. In case of an implicit collaboration, the retrieval system supports users by taking the historical search data of other users into consideration and adapting the search result lists for a current user based on it [177, 178]. Users who collaborate explicitly share the same information need and conduct a search activity together to achieve this goal. An IR system that supports an explicit search can influence the search process via the search user interface or may also affect the search results using algorithms that consider each user's search activity [69].

We believe that children can also benefit from existing algorithms for implicit collaboration and that those algorithms can be applied without modification. However, an explicit collaborative search offers new directions especially for children and should be studied more in the future. The explicit collaborative search was mostly studied with adults. For example, the influence of different group size and location of members on the quality of search results was investigated [70]. Soulier, Shah, and Tamine [180] suggested an algorithm to mine users' roles in a synchronous collaborative search session. Researchers have shown benefits of collaboration, for example in the number of unique relevant documents that can be retrieved in a group in comparison to an individual searcher [155, 172]. Early studies with children have been also reported, e.g. Large, Beheshti, and Rahman [113] studied collaborative search behaviour in same-sex groups of boys and girls. However, only co-located, synchronous collaboration was studied with children. Other types of collaborative search with children, e.g. remote collaboration, present an open research direction. An open issue is also the design of SUIs for children that support collaboration. Children can benefit from explicit collaboration with peers because it can be more fun to search in groups. From a pedagogical perspective, child-parent or pupil-teacher pairs in a collaborative search can be a good learning environment for children in order to gain the necessary skills in information enquiry.

11.4 Cognitive Modeling of Information Search

Evaluation usually accompanies the whole development process of interactive systems (formative evaluation, Section 2.3). An iterative testing of user interfaces in user studies is an effective, but also a costly and time-intensive method to develop an appropriate final user interface. A complementary method is the application of cognitive models that make quantitative predictions about the search behaviour of users for a given search user interface and a search task [188]. This allows an automatic evaluation of the search interfaces at each stage of the design process without the involvement of a real end-user. Model-based software can take the cognitive, visual, fine motor abilities and emotional states of a user into account and simulate the user's behaviour during a web search. Cognitive models are successfully used for evaluation of interactive user interfaces [96]. However, previously developed models of information search mimic the interactions of an adult user. For example, Sutcliffe and Ennis [187] elaborated a cognitive model of users' information searching behaviour. It consists of individual activities during information searching and strategies that lead to physical or cognitive user actions. The model can be applied as a formal basis in a cognitive walkthrough evaluation [116]. Teo, John, and Blackmon [189] developed a model of goal-directed user exploration that predicts novice exploration behaviour on different user-interface layouts. To our knowledge there is no model of information searching that takes children's cognitive, visual, fine motor abilities, emotional states and knowledge into account. Research would benefit from such models, as evaluation with children is even more difficult to organise than with adults (see Section 2.3).

Part V
APPENDIX

Appendix A

User Study Documents

Various documents were designed for each user study. In order to conduct the user study at an elementary school, the parental consent was required (see Section 2.3.3). Therefore, the parents were informed with a letter about the planned user study. They signed a consent form to approve the child's participation in the study. Furthermore, a questionnaire was designed as a basis for the *structured interview* that was conducted in the user study. This appendix contains the questionnaires for the user studies described in this thesis:

▶ eye-tracking user study, Appendix A.1;
▶ usability evaluation of the Knowledge Journey, Appendix A.2;
▶ voice-controlled search, Appendix A.3;
▶ evaluation of the evolving search user interface, Appendix A.4;
▶ search result visualisation with characters, Appendix A.5.

A.1 Eye-tracking User Study

The eye-tracking study is described in Section 6. For the eye-tracking study, we collaborated with a primary school in Biederitz, Germany. We also obtained approval of the state administration office for education and culture in Sachsen-Anhalt, Germany. The following documents were used in the user study: There were two questionnaires, one for children and one for adults. Their main difference is the style of the salutation. In addition, children were asked about the school grade they attend, whereas adults we asked about their job. Formal style was used with adults and informal style with children. Here, the questionnaire for children is provided.

Leitfaden der Usability-Studie

Evaluation: Standard-Websuchmaschine (Google) vs. Kinder-Websuchmaschine (Blinde-Kuh)

Die vergleichende Nutzerstudie zur *„Analyse des Suchverhaltens von jungen Nutzern mit Hilfe von Eyetracking"* besteht aus drei Teilen: Einer Befragung vor der Suche, der Verwendung der Suchmaschinen und einer Befragung nach der Suche.

Testperson-Nr.	
Ort	
Datum	
Uhrzeit	

Vorbefragung: Kinder

Inhalt:

Erhebung demographischer Daten

Erhebung von Daten bzgl. der Nutzung des Internets

1. Geschlecht:

Weiblich ▢

Männlich ▢

2. Wie alt bist du?

_____ Jahre

3. In welche Schulklasse gehst du?

_____ Klasse

4. Warst du schon einmal im Internet?

Ja ▢

Nein ▢

5. Wie oft benutzt du das Internet?

1 Mal pro Jahr ▢

1 Mal pro Monat ▢

1 Mal pro Woche ▢

2 – 4 Mal pro Woche ▢

Täglich ▢

6. Sitzt du in der Regel allein, wenn du ins Internet gehst?

Ja ▢

Nein ▢ , und zwar mit _____

7. Was machst du im Internet?

Spielen ☐

Chatten ☐

Mit Freunden treffen ☐

Informationen suchen ☐

Anderes ☐

8. Welche Suchmaschine(n) benutzt du gewöhnlich?

Google ☐

Helles Köpfchen ☐

Blinde Kuh ☐

Frag Finn ☐

Andere ☐ , und zwar _____

9. Warum benutzt du gerade diese Suchmaschine(n)?

Ich benutze diese Suchmaschine(n), weil _____

_____

_____

Leitfaden der Usability-Studie

Evaluation: Standard-Websuchmaschine (Google) vs. Kinder-Websuchmaschine
(Blinde Kuh)

Die vergleichende Nutzerstudie zur *„Analyse des Suchverhaltens von jungen Nutzern mit Hilfe von Eyetracking"* besteht aus drei Teilen: Einer Befragung vor der Suche, der Verwendung der Suchmaschinen und einer Befragung nach der Suche.

Testperson-Nr.	
Testkonfiguration	
Ort	
Datum	
Uhrzeit	

Nachbefragung

Verwendete Suchmaschine:

    Google   ▢

    Blinde Kuh   ▢

Such-Modell einer Sitzung:

    1 einstufige, informationsorientierte Suchaufgabe

    1 einstufige, navigationsorientierte Suchaufgabe

    Vorgegebene Suchanfrage mit vorgegebenen SERPs

    Unterschiedlicher Suchaufwand

Suchaufgabe:

_____

Initiale Suchanfrage:

_____

Anfragetyp:

_____

1. Wie angemessen war die vorgegebene Suchanfrage für dich?

2. Wie schwierig war die Suche für dich?

3. Hast du das passende Suchergebnis gefunden?

Ja   ▢   die Antwort ist _____

Nein   ▢

Mit Unterstützung   ▢

4. Wie hat dir die Suchmaschine gefallen (bzgl. Gestaltung der SERPs)?

4.1 Was hat dir am meisten gefallen?

_____

_____

4.2. Was hat dir _nicht_ gefallen?

_____

_____

5. Welche Suchmaschine findest du besser?

Google

Blinde Kuh

A.2 Usability Evaluation of Knowledge Journey

The user study about the usability of the Knowledge Journey is described in Section 7. This user study was conducted during Magdeburg University Science day in 2012. In the following, the questionnaire used in the user study is provided.

Nummer: 1   Setting: 1   22.05.2012

Evaluation einer speziell für Kinder entwickelten Web-Suchmaschine

Nutzerstudie zum *Design eines ergonomischen User-Interfaces für Kinder* besteht aus 3 Teilen:
Interview vor der Suche, Verwendung der Suchmaschinen und Interview nach der Suche. Die
Ergebnisse der Studie werden **anonymisiert** ausgewertet und gespeichert.

Alter:	_____ Jahre	Schulklasse _____ Klasse	
Geschlecht:	weiblich ☐	männlich ☐	
Händigkeit:	Linkshänder ☐	Rechtshänder ☐	

Pre-Interview

1. Hast du schon einmal einen Computer verwendet?   ja ☐   nein ☐

2. Wie oft benutzt du einen Computer?

       1x pro Jahr ☐   1x pro Monat ☐   1x pro Woche ☐   2-4 x pro Woche ☐   täglich ☐

3. Hast du einen eigenen Computer?   ja ☐   nein ☐

4. Welches ist dein bevorzugtes Zeigegerät?   Touchscreen ☐   Touchpad/Mauspad ☐   Maus ☐

5. Warst du schon einmal im Internet?   ja ☐   nein ☐

6. Wie oft benutzt du das Internet?

       1x pro Jahr ☐   1x pro Monat ☐   1x pro Woche ☐   2-4 x pro Woche ☐   täglich ☐

7. Sitzt du in der Regel alleine wenn du ins Internet gehst?   ja ☐   nein,☐ und zwar mit _____

8. Was machst du im Internet?
   Spielen   ☐   Chatten/Nachrichten schreiben   ☐
   Mit Freunden treffen   ☐   Suche nach Informationen   ☐
   Anderes _____

9. Welche Suchmaschine benutzt du gewöhnlich?
   Google   ☐   Helles Köpfchen   ☐
   Blinde Kuh   ☐   Frag Finn   ☐
   Andere _____

10. Was würdest du an den Suchmaschinen ändern? _____

_____

_____

1

Nummer: 1   Setting: 1   22.05.2012

Post-Interview: Google

Suchaufgabe: verwende die Suchmachine und finde raus
"Wo kann es am heißesten werden: auf der Erde in Wüsten oder auf dem Planet Venus?"

1. Hast du das passende Suchergebnis gefunden?   ja ☐ die Antwort ist_____

                                          nein ☐

2. Hattest du Probleme bei der Lösung der Aufgaben?   ja ☐   nein ☐
     Falls ja, wo traten die Probleme auf?   _____

_____

3. Was hat dir an der Suchmaschine am meisten gefallen? _____

_____

4. Was fandest du doof?_____

_____

5. Würdest du die Suchmaschine erneut verwenden?   ja ☐   vielleicht ☐   nein ☐

6. Würdest du diese Suchmaschine deinen Freunden empfehlen?   ja ☐   vielleicht ☐   nein ☐

7. Was würdest du an der Suchmaschine verändern? _____

_____

_____

_____

_____

2

Nummer: 1   Setting: 1   22.05.2012

Post-Interview: Wissensreise

Suchaufgabe: verwende die Suchmaschine und finde raus
"Wo kann es am kältesten werden: auf der Erde im Nordpol oder auf dem Planet Jupiter?"

1. Hast du das passende Suchergebnis gefunden?   ja □   die Antwort ist_____

                                                  nein □

2. Hattest du Probleme bei der Lösung der Aufgaben?   ja □   nein □
   Falls ja, wo traten die Probleme auf?   _____

_____

3. Was hat dir an der Suchmaschine am meisten gefallen? _____

_____

4. Was fandest du doof?_____

_____

5. Würdest du die Suchmaschine erneut verwenden?   ja □   vielleicht □   nein □

6. Würdest du diese Suchmaschine deinen Freunden empfehlen? ja □   vielleicht □   nein □

7. Was würdest du an der Suchmaschine verändern?
   Thema(Piraten-/Schiffreise)_____

   Menü   _____

   Kategorien   _____

   Ergebnissasgabe   _____

   Farben/Bilder   _____

   Hilfefigur   _____

   Sprachausgabe   _____

   Schatzkiste   _____

   _____

   _____

   _____

Nummer: 1   Setting: 1   22.05.2012

Vergleich

1. Welche Suchmaschine findest du besser?   Wissensreise □   Google □

Vielen Dank für deine Teilnahme!!!

A.3 Voice-Controlled Search User Interfaces

The user study about the voice-controlled search user interfaces is described in Section 7.4. The study was conducted at the trilingual international elementary school in Magdeburg, Germany. Parents signed a consent form to approve the child's participation in the study. In the following, the questionnaire for children is provided.

Nummer: _____   19.12.2012

Nutzerstudie zur Sprachsteuerung von Suchmaschinen

Eine Nutzerstudie zur Sprachsteuerung bei Suchmaschinen junger Nutzer, bestehend aus vier Teilen:
1. Interview vor Durchführung einer Suche, 2. Einführung in die Bedienung der Suchmaschine, 3.
Verwendung der Suchmaschine, 4. Interview nach einer Suche.

Die Ergebnisse der Studie werden **anonymisiert** ausgewertet und gespeichert und nur für
Forschungszwecke verwendet, i.B. nicht für gewerbliche Zwecke.

> Alter: _____ Jahre   Klassenstufe: _____ Klasse
>
> Geschlecht: weiblich ☐   männlich   ☐

Pre-Interview

1. Wie oft benutzt du einen Computer?

   nie ☐   1x pro Jahr ☐   1x pro Monat ☐   1x pro Woche ☐   2-4 x pro Woche ☐   täglich ☐

2. Fällt dir die Bedienung des Computers mit einer Maus leicht?   ja ☐ nein ☐ keine Ahnung ☐

3. Fällt dir das Schreiben mit der Tastatur leicht?   ja ☐ nein ☐ keine Ahnung ☐

4. Wenn du schon mit Touchgeräten gearbeitet hast, wie leicht fiel dir damit die Bedienung?

                      leicht ☐   mittel ☐   schwer ☐

5. Hast du schon mal mit dem Computerprogramm oder einem bestimmten Gerät gesprochen, um es zu
steuern?   ja ☐   nein ☐

6. Wie oft benutzt du das Internet?

   nie ☐   1x pro Jahr ☐   1x pro Monat ☐   1x pro Woche ☐   2-4 x pro Woche ☐   täglich ☐

7. Sitzt du in der Regel alleine vor dem Computer, wenn du ins Internet gehst?   ja ☐   nein,☐ und zwar
mit _____

8. Was machst du im Internet?
   Spielen   ☐   Chatten/Nachrichten schreiben   ☐
   Mit Freunden treffen   ☐   Suchen / Googlen   ☐
   Anderes _____

9. Welche Suchmaschine benutzt du gewöhnlich?
   Google   ☐   Helles Köpfchen   ☐
   Blinde Kuh   ☐   Frag Finn   ☐
   Andere: _____

1

Nummer: 19.12.2012

Wizard of Oz: Wissensreise

Tutorial.

Verwende die Suchmaschine und sammle alle Webseiten zur Planung einer Weihnachtsfeier.

Post-Interview: Wissensreise

10. Haben dir die Möglichkeiten der Sprachsteuerung Spass gemacht?

    ja ☐, weil _____

    nein ☐, weil _____

11. War die Sprachsteuerung für dich ungewohnt?   ja ☐   nein ☐

12. Was findest du besser?:
    Sprachsteuerung   ☐   Tastatur   ☐
    Maus   ☐   Touch   ☐

    Anderes: _____

2

Nummer: 19.12.2012

Vielen Dank für deine Teilnahme!!!

Notizen

_____

_____

_____

_____

_____

_____

_____

_____

_____

_____

_____

_____

_____

_____

_____

_____

_____

_____

_____

3

A.4 Evolving Search User Interface

The user study about the usability of the ESUI is described in Section 8.3. For the user study, we collaborated with a bilingual primary school in Magdeburg, Germany. The following evaluation documents were used in the user study. There were two questionnaires, one for children and one for adults. Their main difference is the style of the salutation. In addition, children were asked about the school grade they attend, whereas adults we asked about their job. Formal style was used with adults and informal style with children. Here, the questionnaire for children is provided.

Proband: 26.02.2013

Usability-Studie zu adaptierbaren Suchmaschinen für junge Nutzer

Die Nutzerstudie besteht aus vier Teilen: 1. Fragebogen vor Verwendung der Suchmaschine, 2. Einführung in die Bedienung der Suchmaschine, 3. Anpassung und Verwendung der Suchmaschine und 4. Fragebogen nach Verwendung der Suchmaschine.

Die Ergebnisse der Studie werden **anonymisiert** ausgewertet, gespeichert und nur für Forschungszwecke verwendet, im Besonderen nicht für gewerbliche Zwecke.

Bitte kreuze die am ehesten zutreffende Antwort an: ☒ ja ☐ nein

Kreuze bitte bei der Skala das am ehesten zutreffende Gesicht an:

| sehr gut | gut | neutral | schlecht | sehr schlecht |

Alter: _____ Jahre   Schulklasse: _____ Klasse

Geschlecht: ☐ weiblich ☐ männlich

Vorkenntnisse

1. Wie oft benutzt du das Internet?

☐ 1x pro Jahr ☐ 1x pro Monat ☐ 1x pro Woche ☐ mehrmals pro Woche ☐ nie

2. Sitzt du in der Regel alleine vor dem Computer, wenn du das Internet benutzt?

☐ ja ☐ nein, und zwar mit _____

3. Was machst du im Internet?

☐ Spielen ☐ Nachrichten/E-Mails schreiben
☐ Mit Freunden treffen ☐ Informationen suchen
☐ Arbeiten
☐ Anderes: _____

4. Welche Suchmaschine benutzt du für gewöhnlich?

☐ Google.de ☐ Helles-Koepfchen.de
☐ Blinde-Kuh.de ☐ fragFinn.de
☐ Yahoo.de ☐ bing.de
☐ Andere: _____

Aufgaben unter Benutzung der Suchmaschine

a) Bitte führe eine beliebige Suche mit der Suchmaschine durch. Zum Beispiel nach deinem Lieblingstier, deinem Lieblingsspiel oder der Homepage deiner Schule.

b) Passe die Suchmaschine nach deinen Vorlieben an.

c) Löse bitte folgende Aufgabe: „Wie viele Monde hat der Planet Uranus?"

d) Bitte speichere deine Einstellungen mit dem „Speichern"-Button.

Proband: 26.02.2013

Getestete Suchmaschine

5. Hast du ein passendes Suchergebnis gefunden?

☐ ja   ☐ nein   ☐ bin mir unsicher

6. Möchtest du gerne ein anderes Hintergrund-Thema einstellen können?

☐ ja, und zwar _____   ☐ nein

7. Wie hat es dir gefallen, die Suchmaschine so einzustellen, wie du es gerne hättest?

sehr gut   gut   neutral   schlecht   sehr schlecht

Begründung/Kommentar: _____

_____

8. Wie haben dir die Bilder und Farben gefallen?

sehr gut   gut   neutral   schlecht   sehr schlecht

Begründung/Kommentar: _____

_____

9. Wie haben dir die angebotenen Internetseiten und deren Beschreibungen gefallen?

sehr gut   gut   neutral   schlecht   sehr schlecht

Begründung/Kommentar: _____

_____

10. Wie haben dir die Kategorien des Menüs gefallen?

sehr gut   gut   neutral   schlecht   sehr schlecht

Begründung/Kommentar: _____

_____

11. Wie hat dir die Audio-Ausgabe gefallen?

      sehr gut   gut   neutral   schlecht   sehr schlecht

Begründung/Kommentar: _____

_____

12. Wie hat dir die von der Suchmaschine angebotene Hilfe gefallen?

      sehr gut   gut   neutral   schlecht   sehr schlecht

Begründung/Kommentar: _____

_____

13. Wie hat dir die Möglichkeit zum Speichern von Seiten gefallen?

      sehr gut   gut   neutral   schlecht   sehr schlecht

Begründung/Kommentar: _____

_____

14. Findest du die getestete Suchmaschine besser als die Suchmaschine, die du sonst benutzt?

   ☐ ja   ☐ nein   ☐ beide gleich gut

15. Was würdest du noch gerne an der Suchmaschine ändern können?

   ☐ Farben   ☐ Anordnung der Elemente

   ☐ eigenes Hintergrundbild   ☐ eigener Avatar

   ☐ Hilfe an- und ausschalten

   ☐ Anderes: _____

Proband:

Sonstige Anmerkungen:

Danke für deine Unterstützung!

A.5 Search Result Visualisation with Characters

Two user studies are described in Section 9. The first user study was conducted in order to investigate how children would represent webpages by a sketch based on a given colouring template of a character. The study took place in June 2013 during Magdeburg University Science day where the public is free to visit exhibits provided by the university researchers. The second user study about the usability of search result visualisation with characters was conducted during children's university days in July 2013. In the following, the two questionnaires developed for the mentioned user studies are provided.

Informationen zur Person

Probanden-Nr: ____

Alter: _____

Schulklasse: _____

Geschlecht: ☐ Weiblich   ☐ Männlich

Aufgabe 1)

Male zu den Wörtern eine Farbe, die dazu passt.

Tiere & Natur	Wissen	Kreativität	Unterhaltung
Katze	Mathe	Malen	Kino
Bäume	Geschichte	Basteln	Musik

Sport	Nachrichten	Reisen	Spiele
Fußball	Wetter	England	Computerspiele
Laufen	Neues vom Tag	Amerika	Kartenspiele

Aufgabe 2)

Schau dir die Webseite an und male eine Figur, die dazu passt.

Webseite

Probanden-Nr: _____   Webseiten-Nr: _____

_____

_____

_____

_____

_____

_____

_____

_____

_____

_____

_____

Probanden-Nr: _____   Webseiten-Nr: _____

_____

_____

_____

_____

_____

_____

_____

_____

_____

_____

_____

_____

Usability-Studie

Die Nutzerstudie besteht aus vier Teile: 1. Fragebogen vor Verwendung der Suchmaschine, 2. Einführung in die Bedienung der Suchmaschine, 3. Verwendung der Suchmaschine und 4. Fragebogen nach Verwendung der Suchmaschine.

Die Ergebnisse der Studie werden **anonymisiert** ausgewertet, gespeichert und nur für Forschungszwecke verwendet, im Besonderen nicht für gewerbliche Zwecke.

Bitte kreuze die am ehesten zutreffende Antwort an: ☒ ja ☐ nein

Kreuze bitte bei der Skala das am ehesten zutreffende Gesicht an:

gut   schlecht

Allgemein

Alter: _____ Jahre

Schulklasse: _____ Klasse

Geschlecht: ☐ weiblich ☐ männlich

Vorkenntnissen

1. Wie oft benutzt du das Internet?

☐ 1x pro Jahr   ☐ 1x pro Monat   ☐ 1x pro Woche   ☐ mehrmals pro Woche   ☐ nie

2. Sitzt du in der Regel alleine vor dem Computer, wenn du das Internet benutzt?

☐ Ja   ☐ Nein, und zwar mit _____

3. Was machst du im Internet?

   ☐ Spielen   ☐ Chatten/Nachrichten schreiben
   ☐ Mit Freunden treffen   ☐ Informationen suchen
   ☐ Anderes:

_____

4. Welche Suchmaschine benutzt du für gewöhnlich?

   ☐ Google.de   ☐ Helles-Koepfchen.de
   ☐ Blinde-Kuh.de   ☐ fragFinn.de
   ☐ Yahoo.de   ☐ bing.de

   ☐ Andere: _____

5. Hast du schon mit Touch-Geräten gearbeitet, also indem man den Computer durch Berührung des Bildschirms steuert?

   ☐ Ja   ☐ Nein

Proband: IPad – Version 1   17.07.2013

Einführung

Um was geht es?

Google - http://www.google.de   Webseite - http://de.wikipedia.org/wiki/Affen

Es geht um das Suchen im Internet. Wir möchten gern das Suchen verbessern und du kannst uns helfen. Man kann im Internet nach Wörtern suchen und findet dann eine Webseite die Information enthält nach dem man gesucht hat.

Was wird gemacht?

Du sollst zwei Aufgaben mit unserer Suchmaschine lösen. Danach wollen wir wissen, ob dir das Suchen gefallen hat.

Beschreibung der Geräte

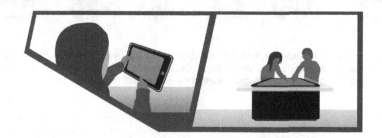

Die Geräte kann man berühren. Wenn du also etwas auswählen willst, kannst du es einfach mit deinen Finger berühren und sehen, was der Computer macht.

Proband: IPad – Version 1 17.07.2013

Die Suchmaschine

Die Eingabe:

Hier kannst du deinen Suchbegriff eingeben. Wenn die Suche losgehen soll, berühre einfach das Wort „Suchen". Die Bereiche mit bunten Farben sind die Themen, die man finden kann.

Die Ergebnisse:

Wenn die Suche beendet ist, siehst du die Ergebnisse unten auf einer Fläche stehen. Du kannst sie berühren um mehr zu erfahren. Berühre das Bild mit dem Wort „Weiter" um mehr Figuren zu sehen. Mit „Zurück" kannst du wieder alte Figuren sehen.

Proband: IPad – Version 1   17.07.2013

Aufgaben

1. Aufgabe:

Schritt 1:   Wähle Tim aus, indem du ihn berührst.

Schritt 2:   Suche nach "Maus" und schreibe zu den ersten drei Ergebnissen das
                Thema auf, welche die Figur darstellt.

                Ergebnis 1: _____

                Ergebnis 2: _____

                Ergebnis 3: _____

                Folgende Themen stehen zur Auswahl:

                Wissen, Neues, Natur, Reisen, Sport, Freizeit, Spiele oder Basteln

Schritt 3:   Finde mittels der Suche drei Mäusearten aus dem Tierreich heraus.

_____

_____

_____

War die Aufgabe schwer?

☐ Ja   ☐ Nein

Wenn ja, warum?

_____

_____

_____

2. Aufgabe:

Schritt 1:   Wähle Alice aus, indem du sie berührst.

Schritt 2:   Suche nach „Golf" und schreibe zu den ersten drei Ergebnissen das Thema auf, welche die Figur darstellt.

Ergebnis 1: _____

Ergebnis 2: _____

Ergebnis 3: _____

Folgende Themen stehen zur Auswahl:

Wissen, Neues, Natur, Reisen, Sport, Freizeit, Spiele oder Basteln

Schritt 3:   Finde mittels der Suche heraus, wo sich der Persische Golf befindet.

_____

_____

_____

War die Aufgabe schwer?

☐ Ja   ☐ Nein

Wenn ja, warum?

_____

_____

_____

Proband: IPad – Version 1 17.07.2013

Auswertung

6. War es leicht die Suchmaschine zu bedienen?

☐ Ja   ☐ Nein   ☐ Bin mir unsicher

7. Welche Suche findest du besser, die von Alice oder die von Tim?

Alice   Tim

☐ Alice   ☐ Tim   ☐ Bin mir unsicher

Begründung/Kommentar: _____

_____

8. Findest du die getestete Suchmaschine besser als die Suchmaschine, die du sonst benutzt?

☐ Ja   ☐ Nein   ☐ Beide gleich gut

Begründung/Kommentar: _____

_____

9. Wie findest du die Anordnung der Elemente auf dem Bildschirm?

sehr gut   sehr schlecht

Begründung/Kommentar: _____

_____

10. Wie hat dir die Darstellung der Ergebnisse gefallen?

sehr gut   sehr schlecht

Begründung/Kommentar: _____

_____

11. Wie gut haben dir die Figuren gefallen?

sehr gut   sehr schlecht

Begründung/Kommentar: _____

_____

12. Konntest du die Ergebnisse leicht durchsuchen?

☐ Ja   ☐ Nein   ☐ Bin mir unsicher

Begründung/Kommentar: _____

_____

Proband: IPad – Version 1 17.07.2013

13. Wie gut haben dir die Figuren geholfen, die Themen herauszufinden?

sehr gut   sehr schlecht

Begründung/Kommentar: _____

_____

14. Ist dir die Bedienung per Touch/Berührung schwer gefallen?

☐ Ja ☐ Nein ☐ Bin mir unsicher

Begründung/Kommentar: _____

_____

15. Was hat dir gefallen?

_____

_____

_____

16. Was hat dir nicht gefallen?

_____

_____

_____

17. Hast du eine Idee um das Suchen besser zu machen?

_____

_____

_____

Danke für deine Unterstützung!

Sonstige Anmerkungen:

_____

_____

_____

_____

_____

_____

Proband: IPad – Version 1   17.07.2013

Notizen

_____

_____

_____

Aufgabe1: Dem Kind wurde nach 4 Minuten geholfen ☐
       Anzahl von Hilfen:

_____

_____

_____

_____

_____

_____

Aufgabe 2: Dem Kind wurde nach 4 Minuten geholfen ☐
       Anzahl von Hilfen:

_____

_____

_____

_____

_____

_____

_____

_____

_____

Appendix B

Characteristics of Participants

This appendix describes the participants of the user studies described in this thesis. This data includes demographic information of the participants, their frequency of Internet usage and support during Internet usage.

B.1 Eye-tracking User Study

Age	8	9	10	11	#	$\varnothing age$
Girls	1	2	1	1	5	9.2
Boys	0	7	2	0	9	9.4
Overall	1	9	3	1	14	9.3

Table B.1: Eye-tracking user study: demographic data of children.

Age	22	23	24	25	26	28	31	33	37	59	#	$\varnothing age$
Female	0	1	1	0	1	1	0	1	0	0	5	26.8
Male	1	1	0	1	2	1	1	2	1	1	11	31.2
Overall	1	2	1	1	3	2	1	3	1	1	16	29.8

Table B.2: Eye-tracking user study: demographic data of adults.

Frequency	Children #	Adults #
Once a year or less	1	0
Once a month	4	0
Once per week	6	0
More than once a week	3	17

Table B.3: Eye-tracking user study: frequency of Internet usage.

Support	Children #	Adults #
Without supervision	9	17
With supervision	5	0

Table B.4: Eye-tracking user study: supervision during Internet usage.

B.2 Usability Evaluation of Knowledge Journey

Age	7	8	9	10	11	12	#	$\varnothing age$
Girls	2	0	3	6	3	0	14	9.6
Boys	0	3	5	2	3	1	14	9.6
Overall	2	3	8	8	6	1	28	9.6

Table B.5: Usability evaluation of Knowledge Journey: demographic data of participants.

Frequency	Children #
Once a year or less	0
Once a month	5
Once per week	9
More than once a week	14

Table B.6: Usability evaluation of Knowledge Journey: frequency of Internet usage.

Support	Children #
Without supervision	18
With supervision	10

Table B.7: Usability evaluation of Knowledge Journey: supervision during Internet usage.

B.3 Voice-Controlled Search User Interfaces

Age	8	9	10	#	$\varnothing age$
Girls	4	2	1	7	8.6
Boys	0	2	1	3	9.3
Overall	4	4	2	10	8.8

Table B.8: Voice-control study: demographic data of participants.

Frequency	Children #
Once a year or less	1
Once a month	4
Once per week	1
More than once a week	4

Table B.9: Voice-control study: frequency of Internet usage.

Support	Children #
Without supervision	4
With supervision	6

Table B.10: Voice-control study: supervision during Internet usage.

B.4 Evolving Search User Interface

Age	8	9	10	#	$\varnothing age$
Girls	6	12	1	19	8.7
Boys	0	5	3	8	9.4
Overall	6	17	4	27	8.9

Table B.11: ESUI study: demographic data of children.

Age	22	23	24	26	28	30	33	49	53	#	$\varnothing age$
Female	0	2	1	1	0	0	0	1	0	5	29.0
Male	1	0	3	2	2	1	2	0	1	12	29.3
Overall	1	3	4	3	2	2	2	1	1	17	29.2

Table B.12: ESUI study: demographic data of adults.

Frequency	Children #	Adults #
Once a year or less	2	0
Once a month	8	0
Once per week	2	0
More than once a week	15	17

Table B.13: ESUI study: frequency of Internet usage.

Support	Children #	Adults #
Without supervision	22	17
With supervision	5	0

Table B.14: ESUI study: supervision during computer usage.

B.5 Search Result Visualisation with Characters

Age	6	7	8	9	10	11	12	13	#	$\varnothing age$
Girls	0	1	1	2	0	1	2	0	7	9.7
Boys	1	0	2	1	2	3	0	2	11	10
Overall	1	1	3	3	2	4	2	2	18	9.9

Table B.15: Drawing study: demographic data of participants.

Age	6	7	8	9	10	11	12	#	$\varnothing age$
Girls	0	2	2	1	2	4	1	12	9.6
Boys	2	3	2	1	0	2	0	10	8
Overall	2	5	4	2	2	6	1	22	8.9

Table B.16: Usability study: demographic data of participants.

Frequency	Children #
Once a year or less	4
Once a month	3
Once per week	5
More than once a week	10

Table B.17: Usability study: frequency of Internet usage.

Support	Children #
Without supervision	15
With supervision	7

Table B.18: Usability study: supervision during Internet usage.

References

[1] A. Abran, A. Khelifi, W. Suryn, and A. Seffah. "Usability meanings and interpretations in ISO standards". In: *Software Quality Journal* 11:4 (2003), pages 325–338.

[2] E. Agichtein, E. Brill, and S. Dumais. "Improving web search ranking by incorporating user behavior information". In: *Proceedings of the 29th annual international ACM SIGIR conference on Research and development in information retrieval*. ACM. 2006, pages 19–26.

[3] S. Akkersdijk, M. Brandon, H. Jochmann-Mannak, D. Hiemstra, and T. Huibers. *ImagePile: an Alternative for Vertical Results Lists of IR-Systems*. Technical report ISSN 1381-3625. TR-CTIT-11-11, University of Twente, 2011.

[4] G. Almpanidis, C. Kotropoulos, and I. Pitas. "Combining text and link analysis for focused crawling- An application for vertical search engines". In: *Information Systems* 32:6 (2007), pages 886–908.

[5] T. Amstad. "Wie verständlich sind unsere Zeitungen?" PhD thesis. Universität Zürich, 1978.

[6] I. Arapakis, K. Athanasakos, and J. M. Jose. "A comparison of general vs personalised affective models for the prediction of topical relevance". In: *Proceedings of the 33rd international ACM SIGIR conference on Research and development in Information Retrieval*. ACM. 2010, pages 371–378.

[7] A. Aula, P. Majaranta, and K.-J. Räihä. "Eye-tracking reveals the personal styles for search result evaluation". In: *Human-Computer Interaction-INTERACT 2005*. Springer, 2005, pages 1058–1061.

[8] L. Azzopardi, M. Bevc, A. Gardner, D. Maxwell, and A. Razzouk. "PageFetch 2: gamification the sequel". In: *Proceedings of the First International Workshop on Gamification for Information Retrieval*. ACM. 2014, pages 38–41.

[9] L. Azzopardi, D. Dowie, K. A. Marshall, and R. Glassey. "MaSe: create your own mash-up search interface". In: *Proceedings of the*

35th international ACM SIGIR conference on Research and development in information retrieval. ACM. 2012, pages 1008–1008.

[10] R. Baeza-Yates and B. Ribeiro-Neto. *Modern information retrieval: The Concepts and Technology behind Search*. Addison-Wesley New York, 2011.

[11] M. Baldoni, C. Baroglio, V. Patti, and P. Rena. "From tags to emotions: Ontology-driven sentiment analysis in the social semantic web". In: *Intelligenza Artificiale* 6:1 (2012), pages 41–54.

[12] J. Bar-Ilan and Y. Belous. "Children as architects of Web directories: An exploratory study". In: *Journal of the American Society for Information Science and Technology* 58:6 (2007), pages 895–907.

[13] M. J. Bates. "The design of browsing and berrypicking techniques for the online search interface". In: *Online Information Review* 13:5 (1989), pages 407–424.

[14] P. Behrens and T. Rathgeb. *KIM-Studie 2010. Kinder + Medien. Computer + Internet. Basisuntersuchung zum Medienumgang 6- bis 13-Jähriger in Deutschland*. Technical report. Stuttgart: Medienpädagogischer Forschungsverbund Südwest, 2010.

[15] P. Behrens and T. Rathgeb. *KIM-Studie 2012. Kinder + Medien. Computer + Internet. Basisuntersuchung zum Medienumgang 6- bis 13-Jähriger in Deutschland*. Technical report. Stuttgart: Medienpädagogischer Forschungsverbund Südwest, 2012.

[16] D. Bilal. "Children's use of the Yahooligans! Web search engine: II. Cognitive and physical behaviors on research tasks". In: *Journal of the American Society for Information Science and Technology* 52:2 (2001), pages 118–136.

[17] D. Bilal and J. Kirby. "Differences and similarities in information seeking: children and adults as Web users". In: *Information Processing & Management* 38:5 (2002), pages 649–670.

[18] D. Bilal. "Children's use of the Yahooligans! Web search engine: I. Cognitive, physical, and affective behaviors on fact-based search tasks". In: *Journal of the American society for information science* 51:7 (2000), pages 646–665.

[19] M. Boberg, P. Piippo, and E. Ollila. "Designing Avatars". In: *Proceedings of the 3rd International Conference on Digital Interactive Media in Entertainment and Arts*. DIMEA '08. ACM, 2008, pages 232–239.

[20] C. L. Borgman, S. G. Hirsh, V. A. Walter, and A. L. Gallagher. "Children's searching behavior on browsing and keyword on-

line catalogs: the Science Library Catalog project". In: *Journal of the American Society for Information Science* 46:9 (1995), pages 663–684.

[21] C. L. Borgman. "Why are online catalogs still hard to use?" In: *Journal of the American Society for Information Science* 47:7 (1996), pages 493–503.

[22] R. E. Brenner. *Understanding Manga and Anime*. Greenwood Publishing Group, 2007.

[23] S. Brin and L. Page. "The anatomy of a large-scale hypertextual Web search engine". In: *Computer networks and ISDN systems* 30:1 (1998), pages 107–117.

[24] A. Broder. "A taxonomy of web search". In: *ACM Sigir forum*. Volume 36. 2. ACM. 2002, pages 3–10.

[25] R. Budiu and J. Nielsen. *Usability of Websites for Children: Design Guidelines for Targeting Users Aged 3–12 Years, 2nd edition*. Nielsen Norman Group Report, 2010.

[26] G. Buscher, S. T. Dumais, and E. Cutrell. "The good, the bad, and the random: an eye-tracking study of ad quality in web search". In: *Proceedings of the 33rd International ACM SIGIR conference on Research and development in information retrieval*. ACM. 2010, pages 42–49.

[27] S. Card, T. Moran, and A. Newell. "The model human processor-An engineering model of human performance". In: *Handbook of perception and human performance*. 2 (1986).

[28] G. Ceschi and K. Scherer. "Children's ability to control the facial expression of laughter and smiling: Knowledge and behaviour". In: *Cognition & Emotion* 17:3 (2003), pages 385–411.

[29] N.-S. Chang and K.-S. Fu. "Query-by-pictorial-example". In: *Software Engineering, IEEE Transactions on* 6 (1980), pages 519–524.

[30] M. Chau, X. Fang, and O. R. Liu Sheng. "Analysis of the query logs of a web site search engine". In: *Journal of the American Society for Information Science and Technology* 56:13 (2005), pages 1363–1376.

[31] H. Chernoff. "The use of faces to represent points in k-dimensional space graphically". In: *Journal of the American Statistical Association* 68:342 (1973), pages 361–368.

[32] E. F. Codd. "A relational model of data for large shared data banks". In: *Communications of the ACM* 13:6 (1970), pages 377–387.

[33] A. Cooper. "A survey of query log privacy-enhancing techniques from a policy perspective". In: *ACM Transactions on the Web (TWEB)* 2:4 (2008), page 19.

[34] L. Cooper. "Developmentally appropriate digital environments for young children". In: *Library trends* 54:2 (2006), pages 286–302.

[35] S. Cousins, A. Paepcke, T. Winograd, E. Bier, and K. Pier. "The digital library integrated task environment (DLITE)". In: *Proceedings of the second ACM international conference on Digital libraries*. ACM. 1997, pages 142–151.

[36] N. Cowan, N. M. Fristoe, E. M. Elliott, R. P. Brunner, and J. S. Saults. "Scope of attention, control of attention, and intelligence in children and adults". In: *Memory & Cognition* 34:8 (2006), pages 1754–1768.

[37] S. Cucerzan and E. Brill. "Spelling correction as an iterative process that exploits the collective knowledge of web users". In: *Proceedings of EMNLP*. Volume 4. 2004, pages 293–300.

[38] K. Curran and J. Mc Glinchey. "Vertical Search Engines". In: *ITB Journal* 16:3 (2007), pages 22–26.

[39] E. Cutrell and Z. Guan. "What are you looking for?: an eye-tracking study of information usage in web search". In: *Proceedings of the SIGCHI Conference on Human Factors in Computing Systems*. CHI '07. San Jose, California, USA: ACM, 2007, pages 407–416.

[40] J. De Belder, K. Deschacht, and M.-F. Moens. "Lexical simplification". In: *Proceedings of itec2010: 1st international conference on interdisciplinary research on technology, education and communication*. 2010.

[41] J. De Belder and M.-F. Moens. "Text simplification for children". In: *Proceedings of the SIGIR workshop on accessible search systems*. 2010, pages 19–26.

[42] M. Deller, A. Ebert, M. Bender, S. Agne, and H. Barthel. "Preattentive visualization of information relevance". In: *Proceedings of the international workshop on Human-centered multimedia*. ACM. 2007, pages 47–56.

[43] S. Deterding, D. Dixon, R. Khaled, and L. Nacke. "From game design elements to gamefulness: defining gamification". In: *Pro-*

ceedings of the 15th International Academic MindTrek Conference: Envisioning Future Media Environments. ACM. 2011, pages 9–15.

[44] J. Dinet and M. Kitajima. ""Draw me the Web": impact of mental model of the web on information search performance of young users". In: *23rd French Speaking Conference on Human-Computer Interaction*. 2011.

[45] J. Dinet, J. M. C. Bastien, and M. Kitajima. "What, where and how are young people looking for in a search engine results page?: impact of typographical cues and prior domain knowledge". In: *Conference Internationale Francophone sur l'Interaction Homme-Machine, IHM '10*. Luxembourg, Luxembourg: ACM, 2010, pages 105–112.

[46] A. Donker and P. Reitsma. "Drag-and-drop errors in young children's use of the mouse". In: *Interacting with computers* 19:2 (2007), pages 257–266.

[47] A. Druin, E. Foss, L. Hatley, E. Golub, M. Guha, J. Fails, and H. B. Hutchinson. "How children search the internet with keyword interfaces". In: *Proceedings of the 8th International conference on Interaction Design and Children*. ACM. 2009, pages 89–96.

[48] A. Druin et al. *The design of children's technology*. Morgan Kaufmann Publishers San Francisco, 1999.

[49] A. Druin, E. Foss, H. B. Hutchinson, E. Golub, and L. Hatley. "Children's roles using keyword search interfaces at home". In: *Proceedings of the SIGCHI Conference on Human Factors in Computing Systems*. ACM. 2010, pages 413–422.

[50] S. Duarte Torres, D. Hiemstra, and P. Serdyukov. "An analysis of queries intended to search information for children". In: *Proceeding of the third symposium on Information interaction in context*. ACM. 2010, pages 235–244.

[51] S. Duarte Torres, D. Hiemstra, and P. Serdyukov. "Query log analysis in the context of information retrieval for children". In: *Proceedings of the 33rd international ACM SIGIR conference on Research and development in information retrieval*. ACM. 2010, pages 847–848.

[52] S. Duarte Torres and I. Weber. "What and how children search on the web". In: *Proceedings of the 20th ACM international conference on Information and knowledge management*. ACM. 2011, pages 393–402.

[53] S. Duarte Torres. "Information Retrieval for Children: Search Behavior and Solutions". PhD thesis. Centre for Telematics and Information Technology, University of Twente, 2014.

[54] S. Duarte Torres, D. Hiemstra, and T. Huibers. "Vertical selection in the information domain of children". In: *Proceedings of the 13th ACM/IEEE-CS joint conference on Digital libraries*. ACM. 2013, pages 57–66.

[55] S. Duarte Torres, D. Hiemstra, I. Weber, and P. Serdyukov. "Query recommendation for children". In: *Proceedings of the 21st ACM international conference on Information and knowledge management*. ACM. 2012, pages 2010–2014.

[56] A. Duchowski. *Eye tracking methodology: Theory and practice*. Springer-Verlag New York Inc, 2007.

[57] C. Eickhoff and A. P. de Vries. "Identifying Suitable YouTube Videos for Children". In: *3rd Networked and Electronic Media Summit (NEM)*. 2010.

[58] C. Eickhoff, P. Serdyukov, and A. P. de Vries. "Web page classification on child suitability". In: *Proceedings of the 19th ACM international conference on Information and knowledge management*. ACM. 2010, pages 1425–1428.

[59] C. Eickhoff, P. Dekker, and A. P. de Vries. "Supporting children's web search in school environments". In: *Proceedings of the 4th Information Interaction in Context Symposium*. ACM. 2012, pages 129–137.

[60] C. Eickhoff, L. Azzopardi, D. Hiemstra, F. De Jong, A. P. de Vries, D. Dowie, S. Duarte, R. Glassey, K. Gyllstrom, F. Kruisinga, et al. "Emse: Initial evaluation of a child-friendly medical search system". In: *Proceedings of the 4th Information Interaction in Context Symposium*. ACM. 2012, pages 282–285.

[61] D. Elliot, L. Azzopardi, R. Glassey, and T. Polajnar. "Filtering and Finding for Children". In: *Proceedings of the ACM SIGIR conference on Research and Development in Information Retrieval, Geneva, Switzerland*. 2010.

[62] E. Erikson. "Children and society". In: *New York: Narton* (1963).

[63] B. M. Evans and E. H. Chi. "Towards a model of understanding social search". In: *Proceedings of the 2008 ACM conference on Computer supported cooperative work*. ACM. 2008, pages 485–494.

[64] L. Feng, M. Jansche, M. Huenerfauth, and N. Elhadad. "A comparison of features for automatic readability assessment". In:

Proceedings of the 23rd International Conference on Computational Linguistics: Posters. Association for Computational Linguistics. 2010, pages 276–284.

[65] A. Fisher and V. Sloutsky. "When induction meets memory: Evidence for gradual transition from similarity-based to category-based induction". In: *Child development* 76:3 (2005), pages 583–597.

[66] E. Gabrilovich et al. "Classifying Search Queries Using the Web as a Source of Knowledge". In: *ACM Trans. on the Web* 3:2 (2009), pages 1–28.

[67] E. Garfield. "The permuterm subject index: An autobiographical review". In: *Journal of the American Society for Information Science* 27:5 (1976), pages 288–291.

[68] R. Glassey, D. Elliott, T. Polajnar, and L. Azzopardi. "Interaction-based information filtering for children". In: *Proceeding of the third symposium on Information interaction in context*. ACM. 2010, pages 329–334.

[69] G. Golovchinsky, J. Pickens, and M. Back. "A taxonomy of collaboration in online information seeking". In: *JCDL 2008 Workshop on Collaborative Exploratory Search*. 2008.

[70] T. Gossen, K. Bade, and A. Nürnberger. "A Comparative Study of Collaborative and Individual Web Search for a Social Planning Task". In: *Proceedings of the LWA 2011 Workshop*. 2011.

[71] L. Granka, M. Feusner, and L. Lorigo. "Eye Monitoring in Online Search". In: *Passive Eye Monitoring*. Edited by R. I. Hammoud. Signals and Communication Technology. Springer Berlin Heidelberg, 2008, pages 347–372.

[72] L. Granka, T. Joachims, and G. Gay. "Eye-tracking analysis of user behavior in WWW search". In: *Proceedings of the 27th international ACM SIGIR conference on Research and development in information retrieval*. SIGIR '04. Sheffield, United Kingdom: ACM, 2004, pages 478–479.

[73] K. Gyllstrom and M.-F. Moens. "A picture is worth a thousand search results: finding child-oriented multimedia results with collAge". In: *Proceeding of the 33rd international ACM SIGIR conference on Research and development in information retrieval*. ACM. 2010, pages 731–732.

[74] K. Gyllstrom and M.-F. Moens. "Wisdom of the Ages: Toward Delivering the Children's Web with the Link-based AgeRank

Algorithm". In: *Proceedings of the International conference in Information and Knowledge Management (CIKM)*. 2010.

[75] D. Hackfort. *Studientext Entwicklungspsychologie 1: Theoretisches Bezugssystem, Funktionsbereiche, Interventionsmöglichkeiten*. Vandenhoeck & Ruprecht, 2003, pages 71–98.

[76] L. Hanna, K. Risden, and K. Alexander. "Guidelines for usability testing with children". In: *interactions* 4:5 (1997), pages 9–14.

[77] H. Harb and L. Chen. "A query by example music retrieval algorithm". In: *Proceedings of the 4th European Workshop on Image Analysis for Multimedia Interactive Services (WIAMIS03)*. 2003, pages 122–128.

[78] M. Haro, A. Xambó, F. Fuhrmann, D. Bogdanov, E. Gómez, and P. Herrera. "The Musical Avatar: a visualization of musical preferences by means of audio content description". In: *Proceedings of the 5th Audio Mostly Conference: A Conference on Interaction with Sound*. ACM, 2010.

[79] H. R. Hartson, T. S. Andre, and R. C. Williges. "Criteria for evaluating usability evaluation methods". In: *International journal of human-computer interaction* 13:4 (2001), pages 373–410.

[80] S. Haun, T. Gossen, A. Nürnberger, T. Kötter, K. Thiel, and M. R. Berthold. "On the integration of graph exploration and data analysis: the creative exploration toolkit". In: *Bisociative Knowledge Discovery*. Springer, 2012, pages 301–312.

[81] M. Hearst. *Search user interfaces*. Cambridge University Press, 2009.

[82] J. P. Hourcade, B. B. Bederson, A. Druin, and F. Guimbretière. "Differences in pointing task performance between preschool children and adults using mice". In: *ACM Transactions on Computer-Human Interaction (TOCHI)* 11:4 (2004), pages 357–386.

[83] H. B. Hutchinson, B. B. Bederson, and A. Druin. *Interface design for children's searching and browsing*. Technical report. University of Maryland, HCIL, 2005.

[84] H. B. Hutchinson, B. B. Bederson, and A. Druin. "The evolution of the international children's digital library searching and browsing interface". In: *Proceedings of the 2006 conference on Interaction design and children*. IDC '06. Tampere, Finland: ACM, 2006, pages 105–112.

[85] H. B. Hutchinson, A. Druin, B. B. Bederson, K. Reuter, A. Rose, and A. C. Weeks. "How do I find blue books about dogs? The er-

rors and frustrations of young digital library users". In: *Proceedings of the 11th International Conference on Human-Computer Interaction (HCII 2005) (CD-ROM). Mahwah, NJ: Lawrence Erlbaum Associates. 2005.*

[86]   *ISO 9241-11:1998. Ergonomic requirements for office work with visual display terminals (VDTs).* 1998.

[87]   *ISO 9241-210:2010. Ergonomics of human system interaction – Part 210: Human-centred design for interactive systems.* 2010.

[88]   B. Jansen et al. "Defining a session on Web search engines". In: *Journal of the American Society for Information Science and Technology* 58:6 (2007), pages 862–871.

[89]   B. Jansen. "Search log analysis: What it is, what's been done, how to do it". In: *Library & information science research* 28:3 (2006), pages 407–432.

[90]   M. Jansen, W. Bos, P. van der Vet, T. Huibers, and D. Hiemstra. "TeddIR: tangible information retrieval for children". In: *Proceedings of the 9th International conference on Interaction Design and Children.* ACM. 2010, pages 282–285.

[91]   T. Joachims, L. Granka, B. Pan, H. Hembrooke, and G. Gay. "Accurately interpreting clickthrough data as implicit feedback". In: *Proceedings of the 28th International ACM SIGIR conference on Research and development in information retrieval.* ACM. 2005, pages 154–161.

[92]   H. Jochmann-Mannak, T. Huibers, L. Lentz, and T. Sanders. "Children searching information on the Internet: Performance on children's interfaces compared to Google". In: *Towards Accessible Search Systems - Workshop of the 33rd Annual International ACM SIGIR conference on Research and Development in Information Retrieval, Geneva, Switzerland.* Geneva, Switzerland: ACM, July 2010, pages 27–35.

[93]   H. Jochmann-Mannak, L. Lentz, T. Huibers, and T. Sanders. "How Interface Design and Search Strategy Influence Children's Search Performance and Evaluation". In: *Evaluating Websites and Web Services: Interdisciplinary Perspectives on User Satisfaction.* Hershey, PA, USA: IGI Global, 2014, pages 241–287.

[94]   H. Jochmann-Mannak. "Websites for children: Search strategies and inter face design. Three studies on children's search performance and evaluation". PhD thesis. Centre for Telematics and Information Technology, University of Twente, 2014.

[95] H. Jochmann-Mannak, L. Lentz, T. Huibers, and T. Sanders. "Three Types of Children's Informational Web Sites: An Inventory of Design Conventions". In: *Technical communication* 59:4 (2012), pages 302–323.

[96] B. E. John and D. E. Kieras. "Using GOMS for user interface design and evaluation: Which technique?" In: *ACM Transactions on Computer-Human Interaction (TOCHI)* 3:4 (1996), pages 287–319.

[97] S. Jones, S. J. Cunningham, R. McNab, and S. Boddie. "A transaction log analysis of a digital library". In: *International Journal on Digital Libraries* 3:2 (2000), pages 152–169.

[98] M. A. Just and P. A. Carpenter. "A theory of reading: From eye fixations to comprehension". In: *Psychological review* 87 (1980), pages 329–354.

[99] M. A. Just and P. A. Carpenter. "Eye fixations and cognitive processes". In: *Cognitive Psychology* 8:4 (1976), pages 441–480.

[100] S. Kaasten and S. Greenberg. "Integrating back, history and bookmarks in web browsers". In: *CHI'01 extended abstracts on Human factors in computing systems*. ACM. 2001, pages 379–380.

[101] R. Kail. "Developmental change in speed of processing during childhood and adolescence." In: *Psychological bulletin* 109:3 (1991), page 490.

[102] R. Kail. *Children and their development*. Prentice Hall Upper Saddle River, NJ, 2001.

[103] M. Kalsbeek, J. Wit, D. Trieschnigg, P. Vet, T. Huibers, and D. Hiemstra. *Automatic Reformulation of Children's Search Queries*. Technical report. 2010.

[104] Y. Kammerer and M. Bohnacker. "Children's web search with Google: the effectiveness of natural language queries". In: *Proceedings of the 11th International Conference on Interaction Design and Children*. IDC '12. Bremen, Germany: ACM, 2012, pages 184–187.

[105] J. M. Kleinberg. "Authoritative sources in a hyperlinked environment". In: *Journal of the ACM (JACM)* 46:5 (1999), pages 604–632.

[106] K. Klöckner, N. Wirschum, and A. Jameson. "Depth-and breadth-first processing of search result lists". In: *CHI'04 extended abstracts on Human factors in computing systems*. ACM. 2004, pages 1539–1539.

[107] A. Komlodi, G. Marchionini, and D. Soergel. "Search history support for finding and using information: User interface design recommendations from a user study". In: *Information Processing & Management* 43:1 (2007), pages 10–29.

[108] G. Krell, M. Glodek, A. Panning, I. Siegert, B. Michaelis, A. Wendemuth, and F. Schwenker. "Fusion of Fragmentary Classifier Decisions for Affective State Recognition". In: *Multimodal Pattern Recognition of Social Signals in Human-Computer-Interaction*. Springer, 2013, pages 116–130.

[109] C. Kuhlthau. "Meeting the Information Needs of Children and Young Adults: Basing Library Media Programs on Developmental States." In: *Journal of Youth Services in Libraries* 2:1 (1988), pages 51–57.

[110] N. Lanquetin. *Evaluation & Use of Metaphor in Advanced Interface Design*. Technical report. University of Abertay Dundee, School of Computing & Creative Technologies, 2007.

[111] A. Large and J. Beheshti. "The Web as a classroom resource: Reactions from the users". In: *Journal of the American Society for Information Science* 51:12 (2000), pages 1069–1080.

[112] A. Large, J. Beheshti, and T. Rahman. "Design criteria for children's Web portals: The users speak out". In: *Journal of the American Society for Information Science and Technology* 53:2 (2002), pages 79–94.

[113] A. Large, J. Beheshti, and T. Rahman. "Gender differences in collaborative Web searching behavior: an elementary school study". In: *Information Processing and Management* 38:3 (2002), pages 427–443.

[114] A. W. Lazonder, H. J. Biemans, and I. G. Wopereis. "Differences between novice and experienced users in searching information on the World Wide Web". In: *Journal of the American Society for Information Science* 51:6 (2000), pages 576–581.

[115] D. Lewandowski. *Web Information Retrieval: Technologien zur Informationssuche im Internet*. Frankfurt am Main: DGI, 2005.

[116] C. Lewis and C. Wharton. "Cognitive walkthroughs". In: *Handbook of human-computer interaction* 2 (1997), pages 717–732.

[117] Z. Lin, H. T. Ng, and M.-Y. Kan. "Automatically evaluating text coherence using discourse relations". In: *Proceedings of the 49th Annual Meeting of the Association for Computational Linguistics:*

Human Language Technologies-Volume 1. Association for Computational Linguistics. 2011, pages 997–1006.

[118] B. Liu and L. Zhang. "A survey of opinion mining and sentiment analysis". In: *Mining Text Data*. Springer, 2012, pages 415–463.

[119] T.-Y. Liu. "Learning to rank for information retrieval". In: *Foundations and Trends in Information Retrieval* 3:3 (2009), pages 225–331.

[120] S. Livingstone. "Children's use of the internet: Reflections on the emerging research agenda". In: *New media & society* 5:2 (2003), page 147.

[121] L. Lorigo, M. Haridasan, H. Brynjarsdóttir, L. Xia, T. Joachims, G. Gay, L. Granka, F. Pellacini, and B. Pan. "Eye tracking and online search: Lessons learned and challenges ahead". In: *Journal of the American Society for Information Science and Technology* 59:7 (2008), pages 1041–1052.

[122] L. Lorigo, B. Pan, H. Hembrooke, T. Joachims, L. Granka, and G. Gay. "The influence of task and gender on search and evaluation behavior using Google". In: *Information Processing & Management* 42:4 (2006), pages 1123–1131.

[123] M. Lupu, K. Mayer, J. Tait, and A. Trippe. *Current Challenges in Patent Information Retrieval*. Springer, 2011.

[124] E. Maccoby and C. Jacklin. *The psychology of sex differences*. Stanford University Press, 1976.

[125] C. D. Manning, P. Raghavan, and H. Schütze. *Introduction to information retrieval*. Cambridge University Press, 2008.

[126] C. D. Manning and H. Schütze. *Foundations of statistical natural language processing*. MIT press, 1999.

[127] G. Marchionini. "Information-seeking strategies of novices using a full-text electronic encyclopedia". In: *Journal of the American Society for Information Science* 40:1 (1989), pages 54–66.

[128] G. Marchionini. "Exploratory search: from finding to understanding". In: *Communications of the ACM* 49:4 (2006), pages 41–46.

[129] P. Markopoulos, J. C. Read, S. MacFarlane, and J. Hoysniemi. *Evaluating children's interactive products: principles and practices for interaction designers*. Morgan Kaufmann, 2008.

[130] S. McCloud. *Understanding Comics: The Invisible Art*. Kitchen Sink Press, 1993.

[131] D. Meyer, J. Keith-Smith, S. Kornblum, R. Abrams, and C. Wright. "Speed-accuracy tradeoffs in aimed movements: Toward a theory of rapid voluntary action." In: *Attention and Performance XIII* (1990).

[132] Y. Y. Mohd, M. Landoni, and I. Ruthven. "Assessing fun: young children as evaluators of interactive systems". In: *Proceedings of the Workshop on Accessible Search Systems held at the 33st Annual International ACM SIGIR conference on Research and Development in Information Retrieval, New York, USA.* 2010.

[133] M. Morris and E. Horvitz. "SearchTogether: an interface for collaborative web search". In: *Proceedings of the 20th annual ACM symposium on User interface software and technology. Newport, Rhode Island, USA.* 2007, pages 3–12.

[134] Y. Moshfeghi. "Role of emotion in information retrieval". PhD thesis. University of Glasgow, School of Computing Science, 2012.

[135] Y. Moshfeghi, B. Piwowarski, and J. M. Jose. "Handling data sparsity in collaborative filtering using emotion and semantic based features". In: *Proceedings of the 34th international ACM SIGIR conference on Research and development in Information Retrieval.* ACM. 2011, pages 625–634.

[136] S. Naidu. "Evaluating the usability of educational websites for children". In: *Usability News* 7:2 (2005).

[137] G. Navarro and R. Baeza-Yates. "A practical q-gram index for text retrieval allowing errors". In: *CLEI Electronic Journal* 1:2 (1998), page 1.

[138] V. Nesset. "An exploratory study into the information-seeking behaviour of grade-three students". In: *Canadian Society for Information Science and Technology* (2005).

[139] E. Nicol and E. Hornecker. "Using children's drawings to elicit feedback on interactive museum prototypes". In: *Proceedings of the 11th International Conference on Interaction Design and Children.* 2012.

[140] J. Nielsen. "Children's Websites: Usability Issues in Designing for Kids". In: *Jakob Nielsen's Alertbox* (2010).

[141] J. Nielsen and K. Pernice. *Eyetracking Web usability.* 2010.

[142] J. Nielsen. *Usability engineering.* Elsevier, 1994.

[143] J. Nielsen and R. Molich. "Heuristic evaluation of user inter-
       faces". In: *Proceedings of the SIGCHI conference on Human factors
       in computing systems*. ACM. 1990, pages 249–256.

[144] T. Ohl and W. Cates. "Applying metaphorical interface design
       principles to the World Wide Web". In: *Educational Technology* 37
       (1997), pages 25–38.

[145] R. Oppermann and R. Rasher. "Adaptability and adaptivity in
       learning systems". In: *Knowledge transfer* 2 (1997), pages 173–179.

[146] J. Ormrod and K. Davis. *Human learning*. Merrill, 1999.

[147] L. Page, S. Brin, R. Motwani, and T. Winograd. *The PageRank cita-
       tion ranking: Bringing order to the web*. Technical report. Stanford
       InfoLab, 1999.

[148] A. Paivio. *Mental representations: A dual coding approach*. 9. Ox-
       ford University Press, 1990.

[149] D. D. Palmer. "Text Pre-processing". In: *Handbook of Natural Lan-
       guage Processing, Second Edition*. Edited by N. Indurkhya and
       F. J. Damerau. ISBN 978-1420085921. Boca Raton, FL: CRC Press,
       Taylor and Francis Group, 2010.

[150] B. Pan, H. Hembrooke, T. Joachims, L. Lorigo, G. Gay, and L.
       Granka. "In Google we trust: Users' decisions on rank, position,
       and relevance". In: *Journal of Computer-Mediated Communication*
       12:3 (2007), pages 801–823.

[151] A. M. Pejtersen. *The BOOK House: Modeling user needs and search
       strategies as a basis for system design*. Roskilde, RisØ National Lab-
       oratory. (RisØ report M-2794). Nov. 1989.

[152] S. E. Petersen and M. Ostendorf. "A machine learning approach
       to reading level assessment". In: *Computer speech & language* 23:1
       (2009), pages 89–106.

[153] N. Phan, P. Bailey, and R. Wilkinson. "Understanding the rela-
       tionship of information need specificity to search query length".
       In: *Proceedings of the 30th annual international ACM SIGIR con-
       ference on Research and development in information retrieval*. ACM.
       2007, pages 709–710.

[154] J. Piaget and B. Inhelder. *The psychology of the child*. Basic Books,
       1969.

[155] J. Pickens, G. Golovchinsky, C. Shah, P. Qvarfordt, and M. Back.
       "Algorithmic mediation for collaborative exploratory search".
       In: *Proceedings of the 31st annual international ACM SIGIR con-*

ference on Research and development in information retrieval. ACM. 2008, pages 315–322.

[156] K. Poikolainen and P. Kärkkäinen. "Diary gives more accurate information about alcohol consumption than questionnaire". In: *Drug and alcohol dependence* 11:2 (1983), pages 209–216.

[157] T. Polajnar, R. Glassey, K. Gyllstrom, and L. Azzopardi. "Enabling Picture-based Querying and Learning with the JuSe Interface". In: *Proceedings of the 2nd Child Computer Interaction: Workshop on UI Technologies and Educational Pedagogy at CHI*. 2011.

[158] M. F. Porter. "An algorithm for suffix stripping". In: *Program: electronic library and information systems* 14:3 (1980), pages 130–137.

[159] J. Purvis and L. Azzopardi. "A preliminary study using page-fetch to examine the searching ability of children and adults". In: *Proceedings of the 4th Information Interaction in Context Symposium*. ACM. 2012, pages 262–265.

[160] F. Radlinski and T. Joachims. "Query chains: learning to rank from implicit feedback". In: *Proceedings of the eleventh ACM SIGKDD international conference on Knowledge discovery in data mining*. ACM. 2005, pages 239–248.

[161] J. C. Read, S. J. MacFarlane, and C. Casey. "Endurability, engagement and expectations: Measuring children's fun". In: *Interaction Design and Children*. Volume 2. Shaker Publishing Eindhoven. 2002, pages 1–23.

[162] T. C. Reeves, X. Apedoe, and Y. H. Woo. *Evaluating digital libraries: a user-friendly guide*. National Science Digital Library Boulder, 2005.

[163] R. S. Rele and A. T. Duchowski. "Using Eye Tracking to Evaluate Alternative Search Results Interfaces". In: *Proceedings of the Human Factors and Ergonomics Society Annual Meeting* 49:15 (2005), pages 1459–1463.

[164] C. J. van Rijsbergen. *Information Retrieval*. Butterworths, London Boston Sydney Durban Wellington Toronto, 1979.

[165] J. J. Rocchio. "Relevance feedback in information retrieval". In: (1971).

[166] M. Roy and M. Chi. "Gender differences in patterns of searching the web". In: *Journal of Educational Computing Research* 29:3 (2003), pages 335–348.

[167] G. Salton. *Automatic Information Organization and Retrieval*. Mc-Graw Hill Text, 1968.

[168] G. Salton and C. Buckley. "Improving retrieval performance by relevance feedback". In: *Readings in information retrieval* 24:5 (1997).

[169] G. Salton, A. Wong, and C.-S. Yang. "A vector space model for automatic indexing". In: *Communications of the ACM* 18:11 (1975), pages 613–620.

[170] G. Salton and C.-S. Yang. "On the specification of term values in automatic indexing". In: *Journal of documentation* 29:4 (1973), pages 351–372.

[171] W. Schneider and M. Pressley. *Memory development between two and twenty*. Lawrence Erlbaum, 1997.

[172] C. Shah and R. González-Ibáñez. "Evaluating the synergic effect of collaboration in information seeking". In: *Proceedings of the 34th international ACM SIGIR conference on Research and development in Information Retrieval*. ACM. 2011, pages 913–922.

[173] A. Shenton and P. Dixon. "Just what do they want? What do they need? A study of the informational needs of children". In: *Children and Libraries* 1:2 (2003), pages 36–42.

[174] F. Sluis and E. van den Broek. "Using complexity measures in information retrieval". In: *Proceeding of the third symposium on Information interaction in context*. ACM. 2010, pages 383–388.

[175] F. Sluis and B. Dijk. "A closer look at children's information retrieval usage: Towards child-centered relevance". In: *Workshop of the 33rd Annual International ACM SIGIR conference on Research and Development in Information Retrieval* (2010), pages 3–10.

[176] F. Sluis, B. van Dijk, and E. van den Broek. "Aiming for user experience in information retrieval: towards user-centered relevance (UCR)". In: *Proceeding of the 33rd international ACM SIGIR conference on Research and development in information retrieval*. ACM. 2010, pages 924–924.

[177] B. Smyth, E. Balfe, J. Freyne, P. Briggs, M. Coyle, and O. Boydell. "Exploiting query repetition and regularity in an adaptive community-based web search engine". In: *User Modeling and User-Adapted Interaction* 14:5 (2004), pages 383–423.

[178] B. Smyth, M. Coyle, and P. Briggs. "The altruistic searcher". In: *Computational Science and Engineering, 2009. CSE'09. International Conference on*. Volume 4. IEEE. 2009, pages 360–367.

[179] P. Solomon. "Children's information retrieval behavior: A case analysis of an OPAC". In: *Journal of the American Society for Information Science* 44:5 (1993), pages 245–264.

[180] L. Soulier, C. Shah, and L. Tamine. "User-driven System-mediated Collaborative Information Retrieval". In: *Proceedings of the 37th International ACM SIGIR Conference on Research and Development in Information Retrieval*. SIGIR '14. Gold Coast, Queensland, Australia: ACM, 2014, pages 485–494.

[181] D. Spencer. *Card sorting: Designing usable categories*. Rosenfeld Media, 2009.

[182] A. Spink and B. J. Jansen. "A study of web search trends". In: *Webology* 1:2 (2004), page 4.

[183] A. Spink and B. J. Jansen. *Web Search: Public Searching of the Web: Public Searching on the Web*. Volume 6. Springer, 2006.

[184] S. Stober and A. Nürnberger. "Adaptive music retrieval–a state of the art". In: *Multimedia Tools and Applications* (2012), pages 1–28.

[185] E. Strommen. "Children's use of mouse-based interfaces to control virtual travel". In: *Proceedings of the SIGCHI conference on Human factors in computing systems: celebrating interdependence*. CHI '94. Boston, Massachusetts, United States: ACM, 1994, pages 405–410.

[186] A. Stuart. *When Should Kids Learn to Read, Write, and Do Math?* WebMD. Online at http://children.webmd.com/features/when-should-kids-learn-read-write-math, accessed 2012-07-18. 2007.

[187] A. Sutcliffe and M. Ennis. "Towards a cognitive theory of information retrieval". In: *Interacting with computers* 10:3 (1998), pages 321–351.

[188] L. Teo. "Modeling goal-directed user exploration in human-computer interaction". PhD thesis. Carnegie Mellon University, 2011.

[189] L.-H. Teo, B. John, and M. Blackmon. "CogTool-Explorer: a model of goal-directed user exploration that considers information layout". In: *Proceedings of the SIGCHI Conference on Human Factors in Computing Systems*. ACM. 2012, pages 2479–2488.

[190] A. Tombros and M. Sanderson. "Advantages of query biased summaries in information retrieval". In: *Proceedings of the 21st*

annual international *ACM SIGIR conference on Research and development in information retrieval*. ACM. 1998, pages 2–10.

[191]   M. Twidale and D. Nichols. "Designing interfaces to support collaboration in information retrieval". In: *Interacting with computers* 10:2 (1998), pages 177–193.

[192]   L. S. Vygotsky. *Mind in Society*. Harvard University Press, 1978.

[193]   D. Xu, J. C. Read, G. Sim, and B. McManus. "Experience it, draw it, rate it: capture children's experiences with their drawings". In: *Proceedings of the 8th International Conference on Interaction Design and Children*. 2009.

[194]   S. Yildirim, S. Narayanan, and A. Potamianos. "Detecting emotional state of a child in a conversational computer game". In: *Computer Speech & Language* 25:1 (2011), pages 29–44.

[195]   J. Zobel and A. Moffat. "Inverted files for text search engines". In: *ACM computing surveys (CSUR)* 38:2 (2006), page 6.

List of Publications

Some ideas and figures have appeared previously in the following publications (in chronological order):

[pub:1] T. Gossen, M. Kotzyba, and A. Nürnberger. "Knowledge Journey Exhibit: Towards Age-Adaptive Search User Interfaces". In: *Advances in Information Retrieval, 37th European Conference on IR Research, ECIR 2015*. Edited by A. Hanbury, G. Kazai, A. Rauber, and N. Fuhr. Springer International Publishing, 2015, pages 781–784.

[pub:2] T. Gossen, J. Höbel, and A. Nürnberger. "A Comparative Study about Children's and Adults' Perception of Targeted Web Search Engines". In: *Proceedings of the SIGCHI Conference on Human Factors in Computing Systems, CHI '14*. ACM. 2014, pages 1821–1824.

[pub:3] T. Gossen, J. Höbel, and A. Nürnberger. "Usability and Perception of Young Users and Adults on Targeted Web Search Engines". In: *Proceedings of the 5th Information Interaction in Context Symposium, IIIX '14*. ACM. 2014, pages 18–27.

[pub:4] T. Gossen, R. Müller, S. Stober, and A. Nürnberger. "Search Result Visualization with Characters for Children". In: *Proceedings of the 2014 conference on Interaction design and children, IDC'14*. 2014, pages 125–134.

[pub:5] T. Gossen, M. Nitsche, and A. Nürnberger. "My First Search User Interface". In: *Advances in Information Retrieval, 36th European Conference on IR Research, ECIR 2014*. Edited by M. de Rijke, T. Kenter, A. P. de Vries, C. Zhai, F. de Jong, K. Radinsky, and K. Hofmann. Lecture Notes in Computer Science. Springer International Publishing, 2014, pages 746–749.

[pub:6] T. Gossen, J. Hempel, and A. Nürnberger. "Find it if you can: usability case study of search engines for young users". In: *Personal and Ubiquitous Computing* 17:8 (2013), pages 1593–1603.

[pub:7] T. Gossen and A. Nürnberger. "Specifics of Information Retrieval for Young Users: A Survey". In: *Information Processing & Management* 49:4 (2013), pages 739–756.

[pub:8]   T. Gossen. "Towards Appropriate Search User Interfaces for Children". In: *Magdeburger-Informatik-Tage 2. Doktorandentagung 2013 (MIT 2013)*. 2013, pages 7–14.

[pub:9]   T. Gossen, M. Kotzyba, S. Stober, and A. Nürnberger. "Sprachgesteuerte Benutzerschnittstellen zur Suche für junge Nutzer". In: *Proceedings of 43. Jahrestagung der Gesellschaft für Informatik*. 2013.

[pub:10] T. Gossen, M. Kotzyba, S. Stober, and A. Nürnberger. "Voice-Controlled Search User Interfaces for Young Users". In: *7th annual Symposium on Human-Computer Interaction and Information Retrieval*. 2013.

[pub:11] T. Gossen, M. Nitsche, and A. Nürnberger. "Evolving search user interfaces". In: *Proceedings of the Workshop on euroHCIR at SIGIR Conference*. 2013, pages 31–34.

[pub:12] T. Gossen, M. Nitsche, J. Vos, and A. Nürnberger. "Adaptation of a Search User Interface towards User Needs: A Prototype Study with Children & Adults". In: *Proceedings of the Symposium on Human-Computer Interaction and Information Retrieval*. ACM. 2013.

[pub:13] T. Gossen, M. Nitsche, and A. Nürnberger. "Knowledge Journey: A Web Search Interface for Young Users". In: *Proceedings of the Sixth Symposium on Human-Computer Interaction and Information Retrieval (HCIR 2012)*. ACM. 2012.

[pub:14] T. Gossen, M. Nitsche, and A. Nürnberger. "Search User Interface Design for Children: Challenges and Solutions". In: *Proceedings of euroHCIR 2012 Workshop*. 2012.

[pub:15] T. Gossen, T. Low, and A. Nürnberger. "What are the real differences of children's and adults' web search?" In: *Proceedings of the 34th international ACM SIGIR conference on Research and development in Information*. ACM. 2011, pages 1115–1116.

Furthermore, the following master's theses of students that I had the pleasure to supervise contributed to this work:

[stud:1] I. Bosse. "Design eines ergonomischen User-Interfaces für Kinder im Stadium des konkret-operationalen Denkens". Master's thesis. Otto von Guericke University, 2012.

[stud:2] R. Müller. "Suchmaschinen Interface für Kinder: Ein spielorientierter Ansatz mit Charakteren". Master's thesis. Otto von Guericke University, 2013.

[stud:3]   J. Vos. "Anpassung der Nutzungsschnittstelle einer Suchmaschine an die Wünsche des Nutzers – Eine prototypische Studie". Master's thesis. Otto von Guericke University, 2013.

Credit is given in the footnotes of respective chapters.

Printed in the United States
By Bookmasters